NO MATTER HOW I LOOK AT IT, IT'S YOU GU[...] POPULAR! ❶

Translation/Adaptation: Krista Shipley, Karie Shipley
Lettering: Lys Blakeslee

This book is a work of fiction. Names, characters, places, and incidents are the product of the author's imagination or are used fictitiously. Any resemblance to actual events, locales, or persons, living or dead, is coincidental.

WATASHI GA MOTENAI NOWA DOU KANGAETEMO OMAERA GA WARUI! Volume 1 © 2012 Nico Tanigawa / SQUARE ENIX CO., LTD. All rights reserved. First published in Japan in 2012 by SQUARE ENIX CO., LTD. English translation rights arranged with SQUARE ENIX CO., LTD. and Hachette Book Group through Tuttle-Mori Agency, Inc.

Translation © 2013 by SQUARE ENIX CO., LTD.

Yen Press
Hachette Book Group
237 Park Avenue, New York, NY 10017

www.HachetteBookGroup.com
www.YenPress.com

Yen Press is an imprint of Hachette Book Group, Inc. The Yen Press name and logo are trademarks of Hachette Book Group, Inc.

First Yen Press Edition: October 2013

ISBN: 978-0-316-24316-2

10 9 8 7 6 5 4 3

BVG

Printed in the United States of America

TRANSLATION NOTES 2

PAGE 47
Seicr•ss is a reference to the game *Seicross*, released by Nichibutsu for arcades, the Famicom console in Japan, and the NES system in the United States.

PAGE 54
A•B is another reference to the mega-popular girl group AKB48.

PAGE 54
In a **king game**, people draw sticks or straws, and the winner becomes "king." The king has the right to order each player to do one thing apiece, and the others must comply. Can get racy in a mixed group.

PAGE 55
Book-Of is a reference to the popular Japanese chain Book-Off, which sells used books, DVDs, CDs, and games.

PAGE 56
"Watching the house" is a common excuse used by unemployed shut-ins (*hikikomori/NEET*), who suggest that they are providing a service by looking after the house rather than just hiding themselves away.

PAGE 57
Usonma-kun is a reference to the manga *Ushijima-kun the Loan Shark*. *Uso* is the Japanese word for "lie."

PAGE 69
Mini Step is a reference to the Japanese convenience store chain Mini Stop.

PAGE 69
The **magazines** on the rack are references to the Japanese manga anthology magazines *Evening*, *Big Comic Spirits*, and *Shounen Sunday*, which are aimed at boys and young men. The magazine Tomoko is reading is a reference to *Weekly Manga Goraku*, which is aimed at middle-aged men.

PAGE 87
The **magazine with the UNITED CLOSE satin pouches** refers to the actual company UNITED ARROWS and the magazine *In Red*. This seems to be modeled on their October 2011 issue.

PAGE 89
Tomoko is being handed an **amidakuji** sheet, a kind of ladder lottery where people write their names at the top and then the lines are followed through a complicated branching system to the results, making the outcomes harder to predict.

PAGE 100
Translated as **lucky bastard** here, the term *riajuu* was originally used on the Japanese message board 2ch to describe people whose real life is good, implying that the poster does NOT have a good real life. It has since been co-opted by young people as a pejorative term for individuals they envy in some way.

PAGE 104
Hidden ball trick is an actual baseball phrase to describe the act of making it seem like the ball was thrown in order to draw a runner off base and tag them out.

PAGE112
PALGO is a parody of the fashion-forward Japanese department store chain Parco.

PAGE 115
Because of their shape, *momo*, the Japanese word for "peach," is often used to refer to buttocks or erotic merchandise, hence **"peaches."**

PAGE 123
Machino Okashi is a reference to the actual snack food brand Machi no Okashiya-san, a line of snacks sold by 7-11 in Japan.

PAGE 123
The character sheet Tomoko is writing up is based on the **Fate/stay night** universe, so the anime she was watching was *Fate/Zero*. In the story, seven mages each summon a Heroic Spirit from history or legend to fight each other for the Holy Grail. Here, Tomoko is imagining herself as an eighth mage who has summoned the famous Shinsengumi swordsman, Souji Okita.

PAGE 123
Mana is a common gaming term for magic power.

PAGE 125
In the original edition, Tomoko misunderstands the word for "urgent" in the announcement as the word for "womb."

PAGE 128
This entire page, including the way Tomoko is cursing out the guy, is a reference to the Studio Ghibli film *Mimi o sumaseba*, released in English as *Whisper of the Heart*.

PAGE 130
Restricted Rock-Paper-Scissors is a reference to a card game played in the gambling manga *Kaiji*.

A SPECIAL MESSAGE FROM

NICO TANIGAWA

TO READERS OF THE YEN PRESS EDITION!

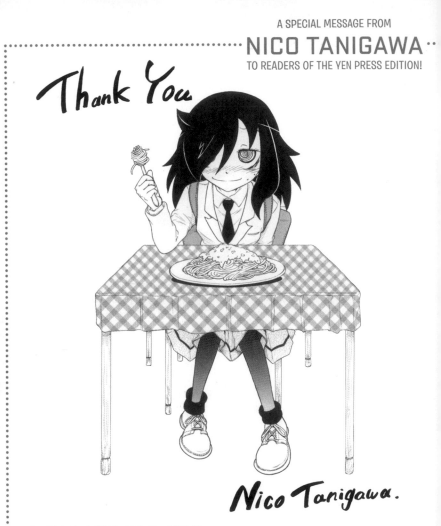

Thank You

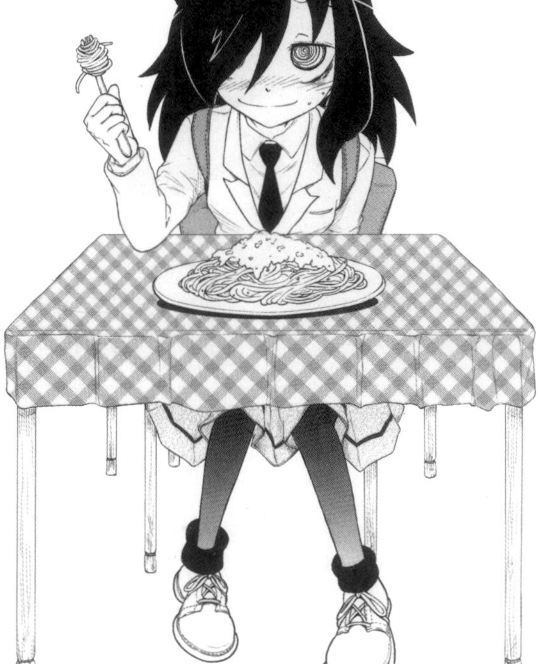

Nico Tanigawa.

NICO TANIGAWA HERE. NICE TO MEET YOU.

THANK YOU MUCHLY FOR PICKING UP THIS ENGLISH EDITION OF **WATAMOTE** (ABBR).

IT'S ALL THANKS TO THE PEOPLE WHO READ OUR WORK ON **GANGAN ONLINE** AND CHEERED US ON EVEN BEFORE THE BOOKS WERE IN PRINT THAT THIS TRANSLATED VERSION WAS POSSIBLE.

WE'RE REALLY, TRULY GRATEFUL FOR ALL THE SUPPORT WE'VE RECEIVED.

THE MANY COMMENTS AND D*CK PICS WE GOT FOLLOWING THE PUBLICATION OF VOLUME 1 IN JAPAN LIVE ON IN OUR HEARTS TO THIS VERY DAY!

WE'D BE THRILLED IF YOU'D CONTINUE TO SUPPORT THIS MANGA FROM HERE ON OUT.

WELL, LET'S MEET AGAIN IN VOLUME 2!

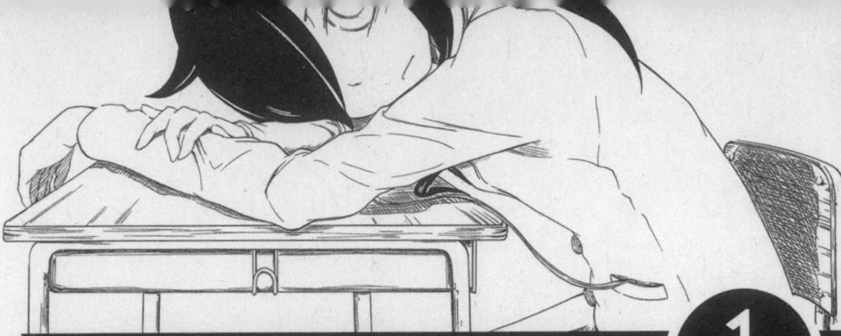

No Matter How I Look at It, It's You Guys' Fault I'm Not Popular!

1

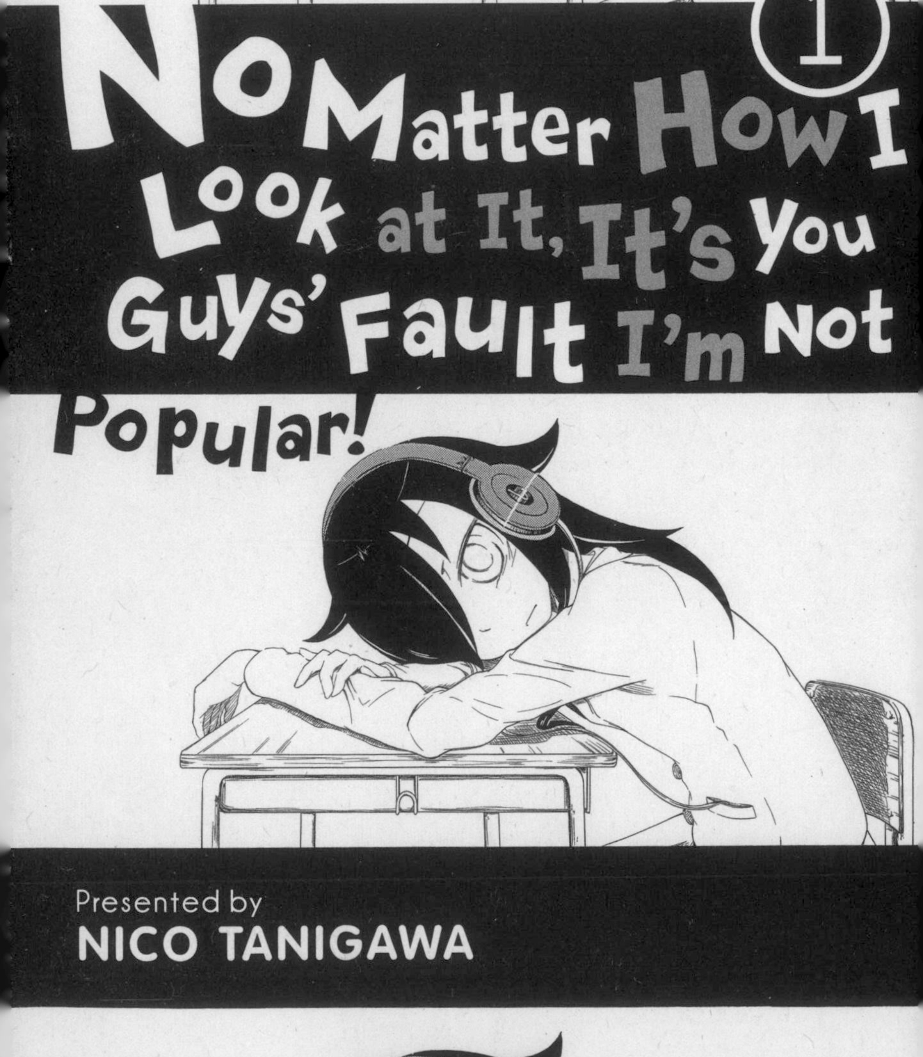

Presented by
NICO TANIGAWA

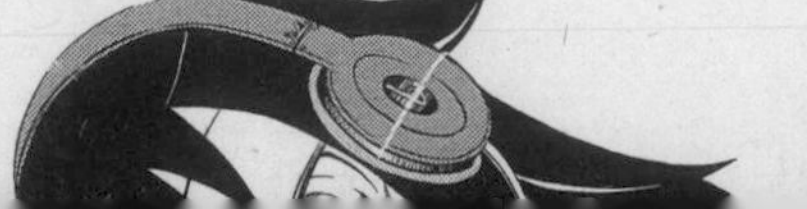

...AWW, IF I'D BEEN A WORM, I WOULD'VE HAD A MAN FROM THE GET-GO AND DEFINITELY HAVE HAD S●X, NOT TO MENTION KIDS...

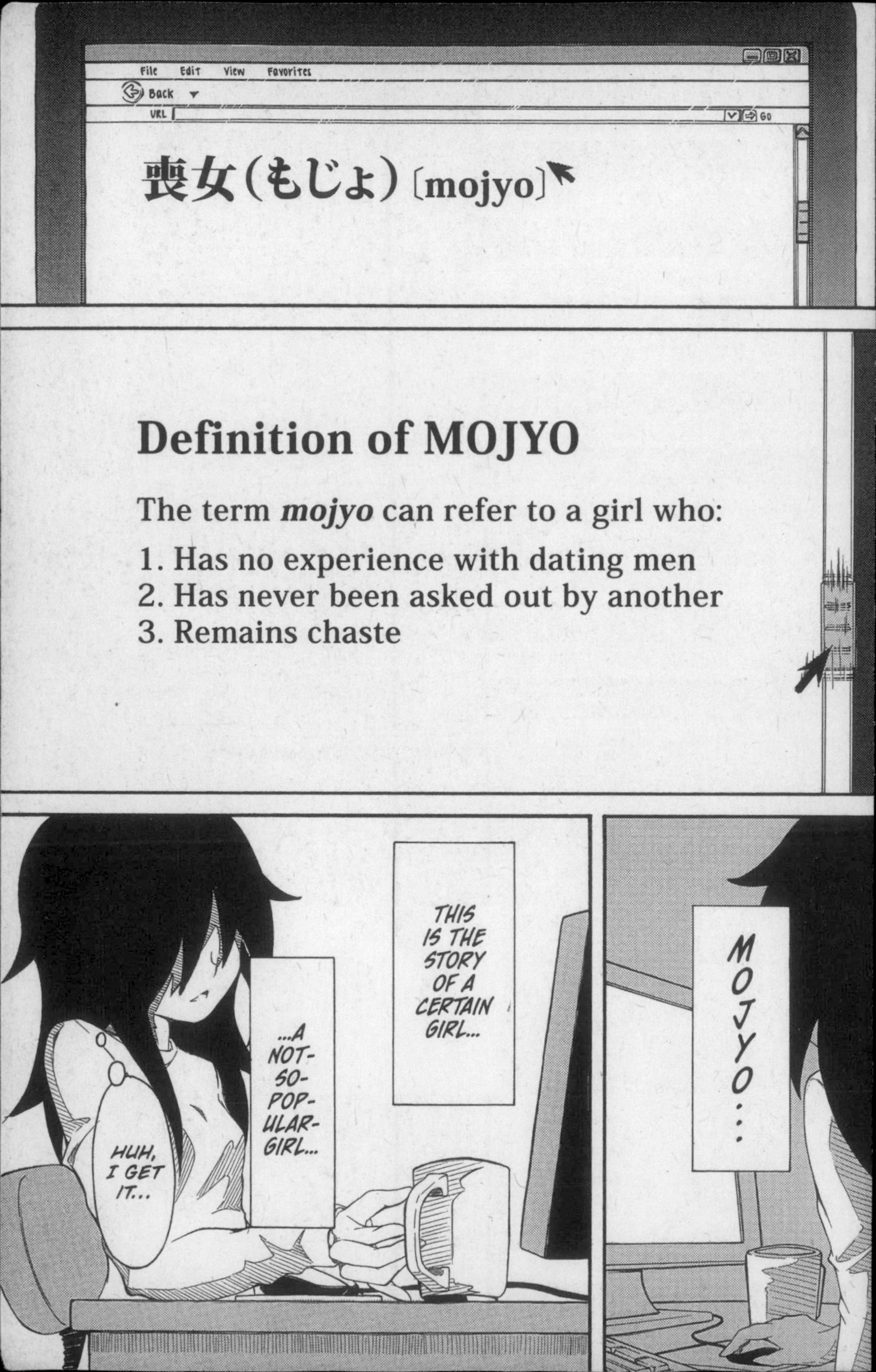
File Edit View Favorites
Back
URL
GO
喪女(もじょ)〔mojyo〕
Definition of MOJYO
The term mojyo can refer to a girl who:
1. Has no experience with dating men
2. Has never been asked out by another
3. Remains chaste
MOJYO...
THIS IS THE STORY OF A CERTAIN GIRL...
...A NOT-SO-POPULAR GIRL...
HUH, I GET IT...

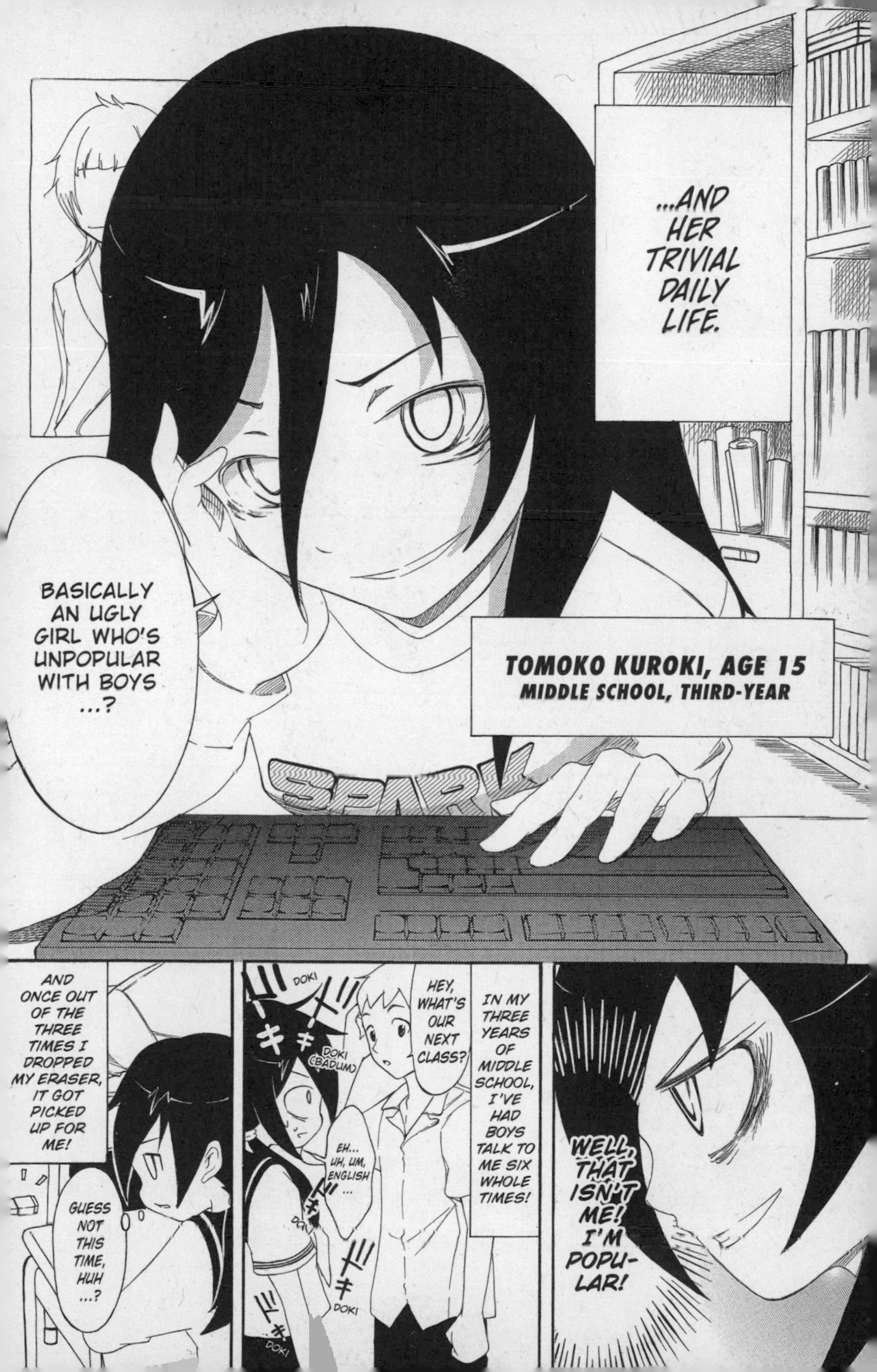
...AND HER TRIVIAL DAILY LIFE.
TOMOKO KUROKI, AGE 15
MIDDLE SCHOOL, THIRD-YEAR
BASICALLY AN UGLY GIRL WHO'S UNPOPULAR WITH BOYS ...?
WELL, THAT ISN'T ME! I'M POPU-LAR!
IN MY THREE YEARS OF MIDDLE SCHOOL, I'VE HAD BOYS TALK TO ME SIX WHOLE TIMES!
HEY, WHAT'S OUR NEXT CLASS?
DOKI
DOKI (BADUM)
EH... UH, UM, ENGLISH ...
DOKI
DOKI
AND ONCE OUT OF THE THREE TIMES I DROPPED MY ERASER, IT GOT PICKED UP FOR ME!
GUESS NOT THIS TIME, HUH ...?

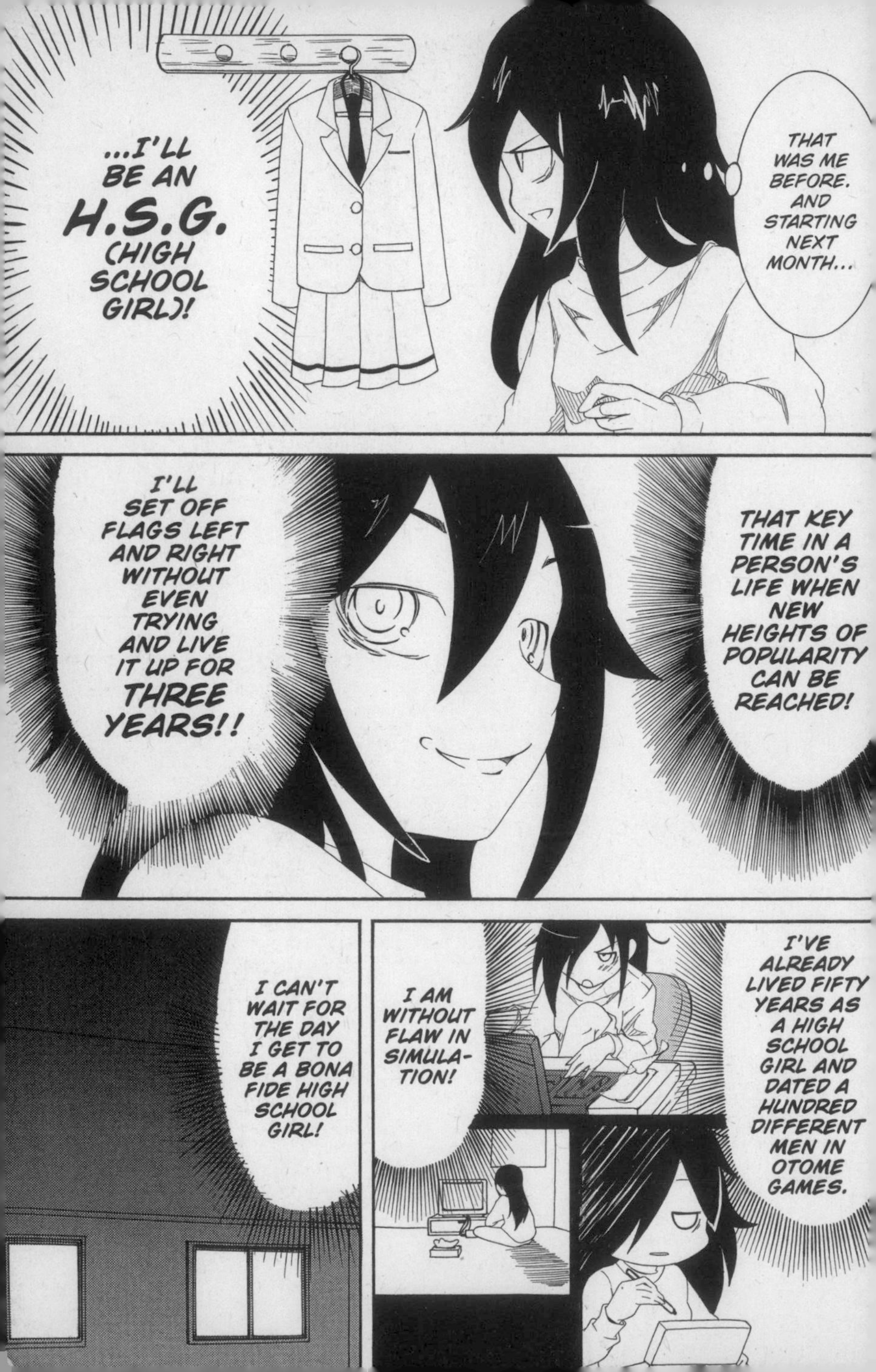
THAT WAS ME BEFORE. AND STARTING NEXT MONTH...
...I'LL BE AN H.S.G. (HIGH SCHOOL GIRL)!
THAT KEY TIME IN A PERSON'S LIFE WHEN NEW HEIGHTS OF POPULARITY CAN BE REACHED!
I'LL SET OFF FLAGS LEFT AND RIGHT WITHOUT EVEN TRYING AND LIVE IT UP FOR THREE YEARS!!
I'VE ALREADY LIVED FIFTY YEARS AS A HIGH SCHOOL GIRL AND DATED A HUNDRED DIFFERENT MEN IN OTOME GAMES.
I AM WITHOUT FLAW IN SIMULA-TION!
I CAN'T WAIT FOR THE DAY I GET TO BE A BONA FIDE HIGH SCHOOL GIRL!

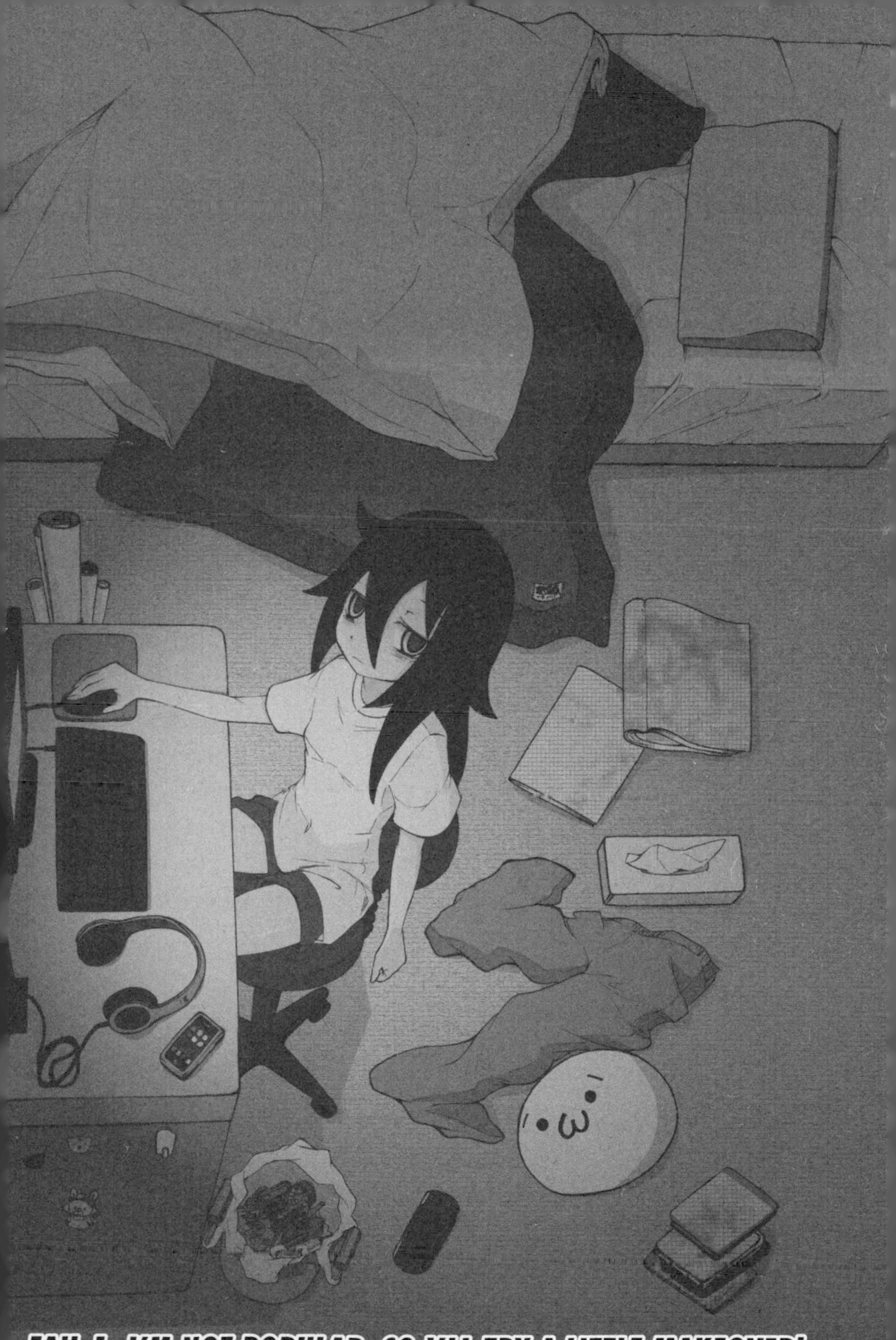

FAIL 1: I'M NOT POPULAR, SO I'LL TRY A LITTLE MAKEOVER!

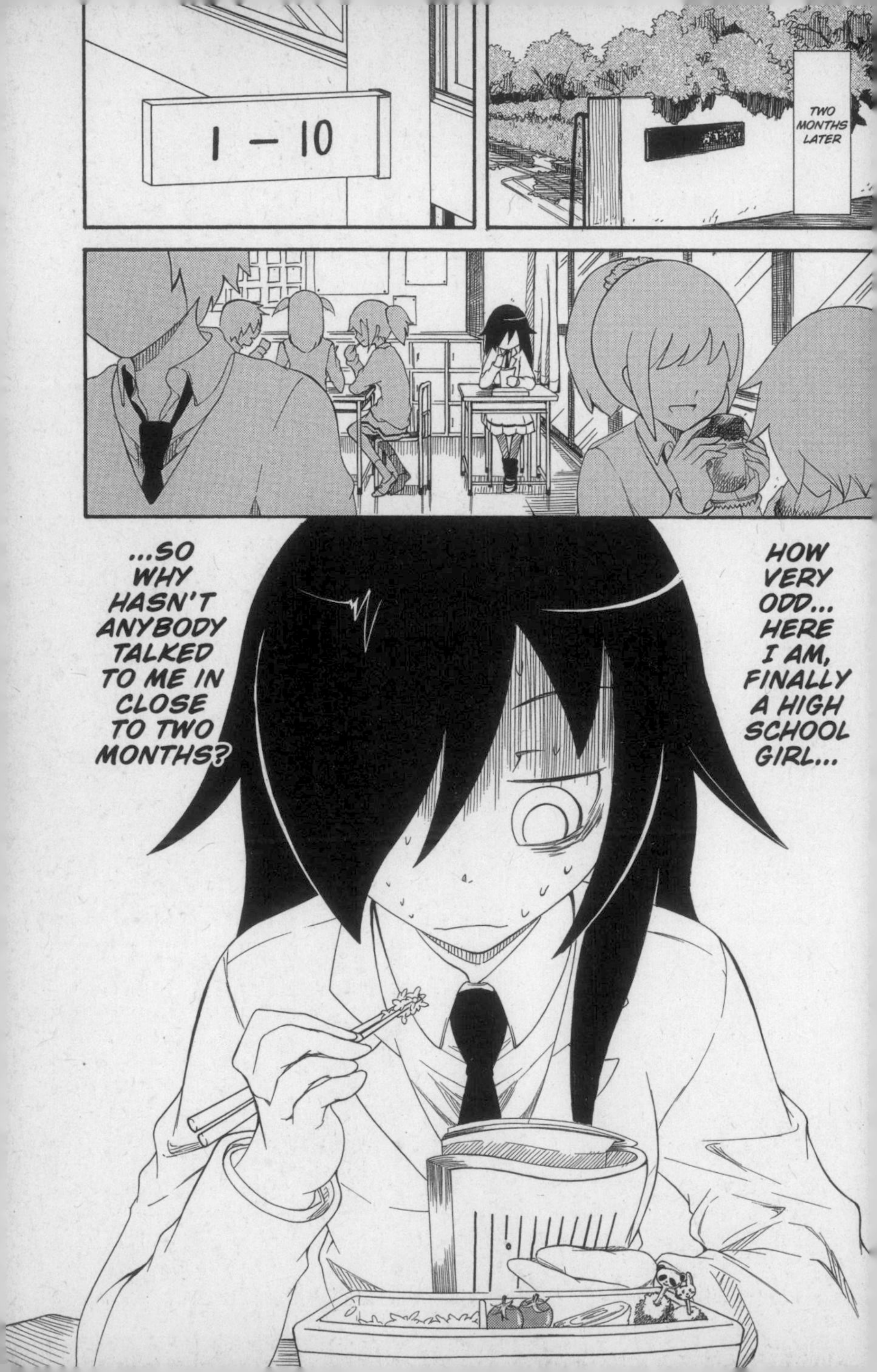

TWO MONTHS LATER
1 — 10
HOW VERY ODD... HERE I AM, FINALLY A HIGH SCHOOL GIRL...
...SO WHY HASN'T ANYBODY TALKED TO ME IN CLOSE TO TWO MONTHS?

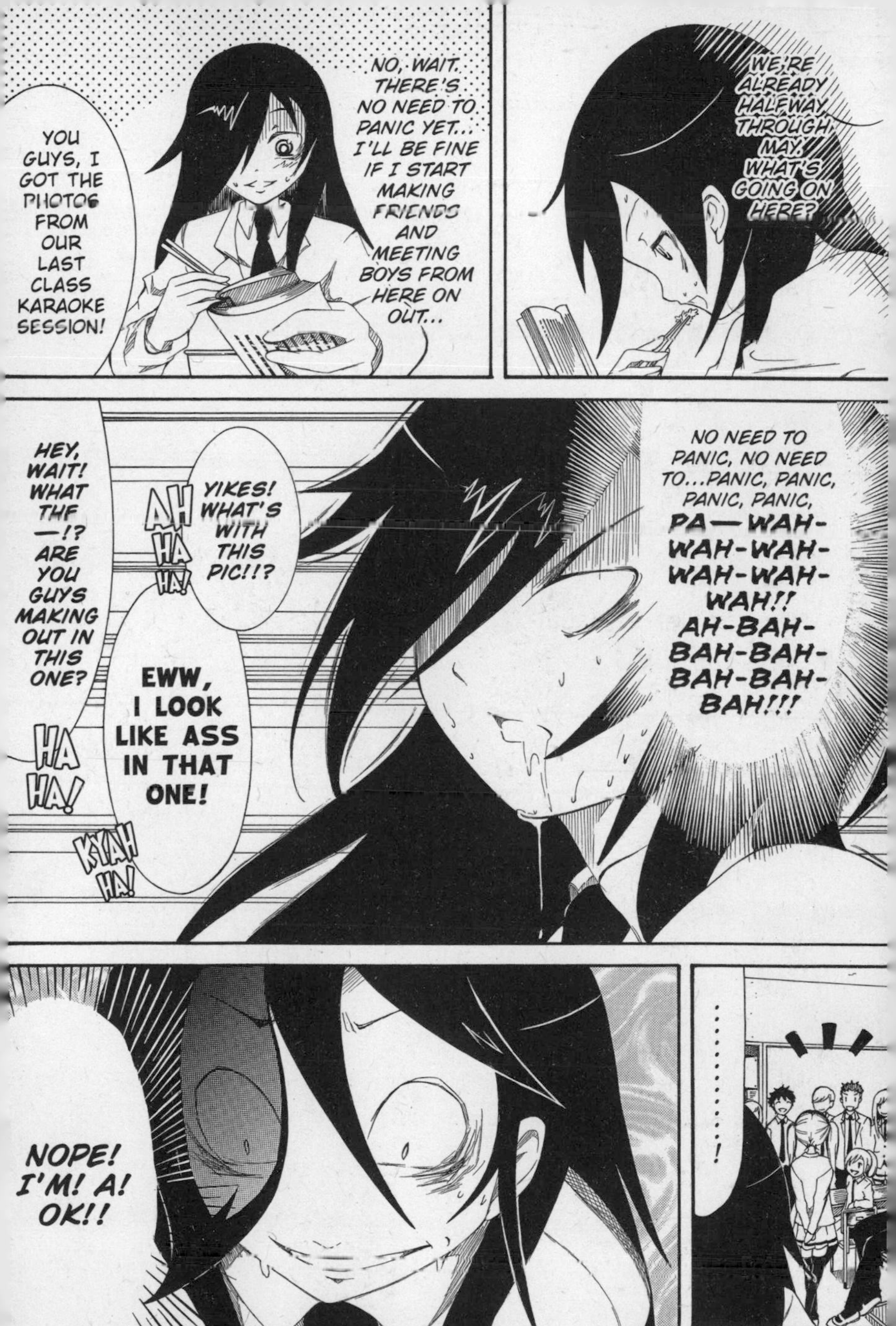
WE'RE ALREADY HALFWAY THROUGH MAY. WHAT'S GOING ON HERE?
NO, WAIT. THERE'S NO NEED TO PANIC YET... I'LL BE FINE IF I START MAKING FRIENDS AND MEETING BOYS FROM HERE ON OUT...
YOU GUYS, I GOT THE PHOTOS FROM OUR LAST CLASS KARAOKE SESSION!
NO NEED TO PANIC, NO NEED TO...PANIC, PANIC, PANIC, PANIC, PA—WAH-WAH-WAH-WAH-WAH-WAH!! AH-BAH-BAH-BAH-BAH-BAH-BAH!!!
YIKES! WHAT'S WITH THIS PIC!!?
AH HA HA!
HEY, WAIT! WHAT THE—!? ARE YOU GUYS MAKING OUT IN THIS ONE?
EWW, I LOOK LIKE ASS IN THAT ONE!
HA HA!
KYAH HA!
......!
NOPE! I'M! A! OK!!

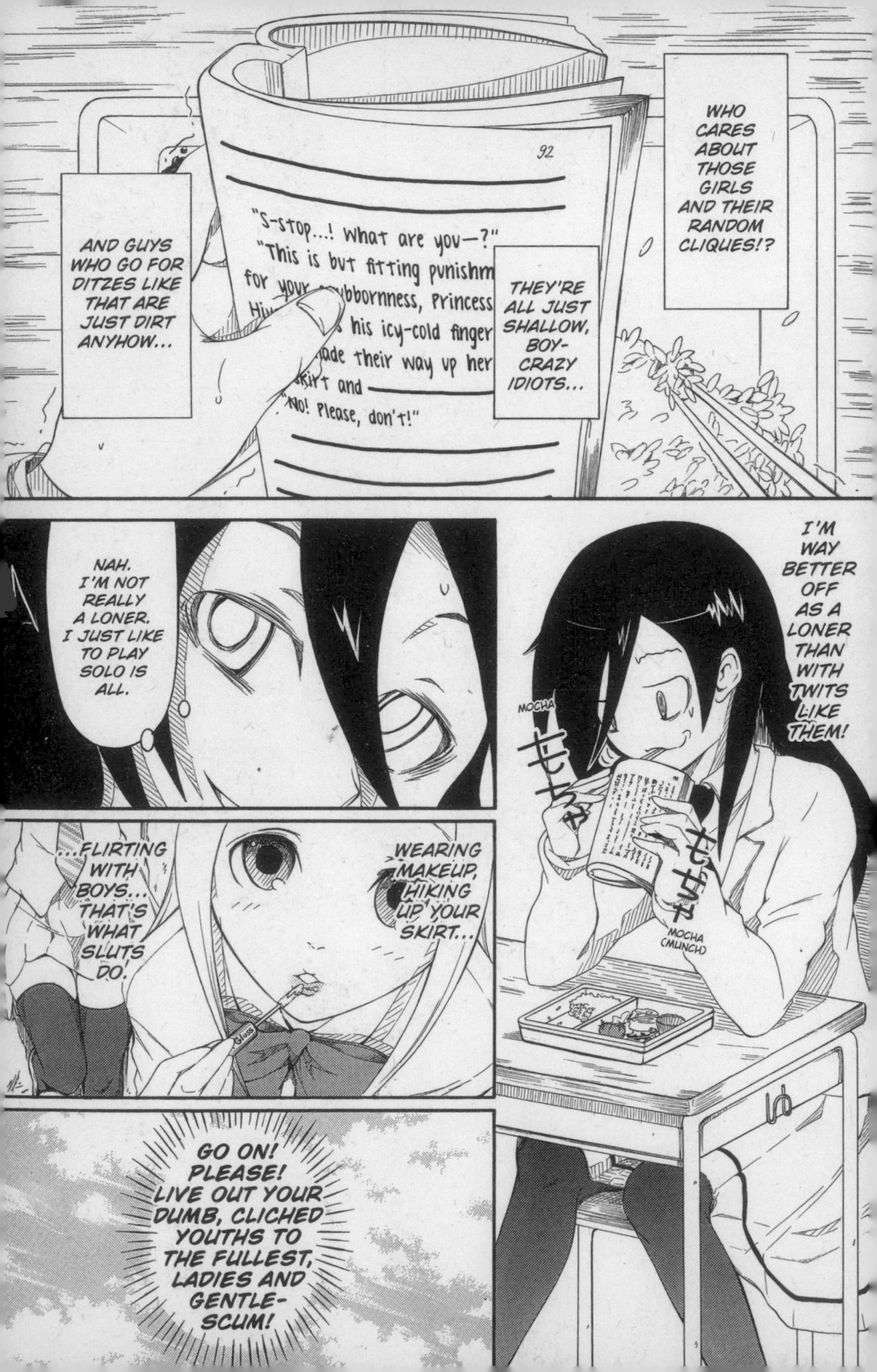
WHO CARES ABOUT THOSE GIRLS AND THEIR RANDOM CLIQUES!?
THEY'RE ALL JUST SHALLOW, BOY-CRAZY IDIOTS...
92
"S-stop...! What are you—?"
"This is but fitting punishm
for your
bbornness, Princess
his icy-cold finger
ade their way up her
skirt and
"No! Please, don't!"
AND GUYS WHO GO FOR DITZES LIKE THAT ARE JUST DIRT ANYHOW...
I'M WAY BETTER OFF AS A LONER THAN WITH TWITS LIKE THEM!
MOCHA
MOCHA (MUNCH)
NAH. I'M NOT REALLY A LONER. I JUST LIKE TO PLAY SOLO IS ALL.
WEARING MAKEUP, HIKING UP YOUR SKIRT...
...FLIRTING WITH BOYS... THAT'S WHAT SLUTS DO!
Gloss
GO ON! PLEASE! LIVE OUT YOUR DUMB, CLICHED YOUTHS TO THE FULLEST, LADIES AND GENTLE-SCUM!

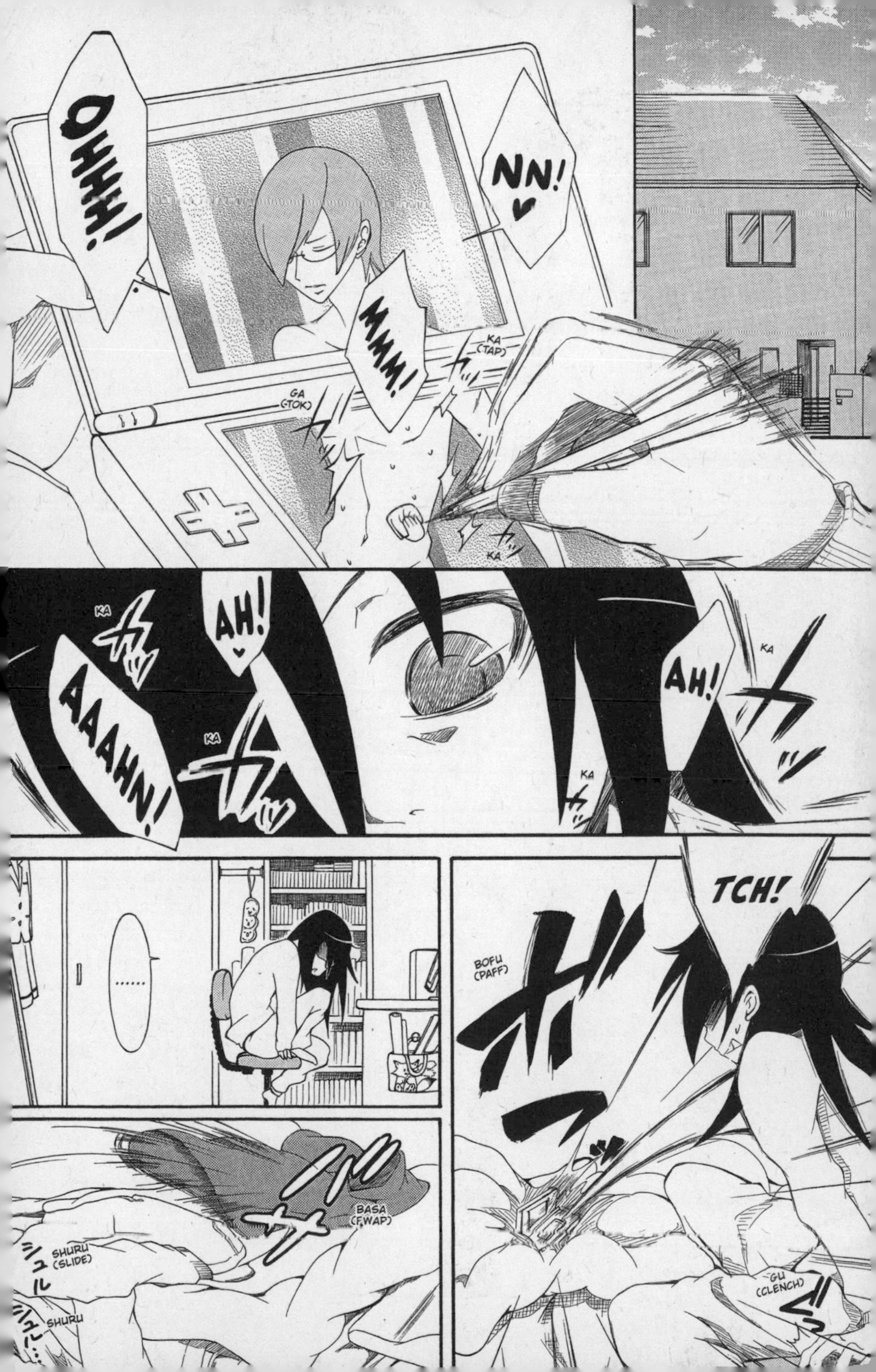
NN! ♥
KA (TAP)
MMM!
GA (TOK)
KA
OHHH!
AH!
KA
KA
AH! ♥
KA
AAAHN!
TCH!
BOFU (PAFF)
GU (CLENCH)
......
BASA (FWAP)
SHURU (SLIDE)
シュル
SHURU
シュル…

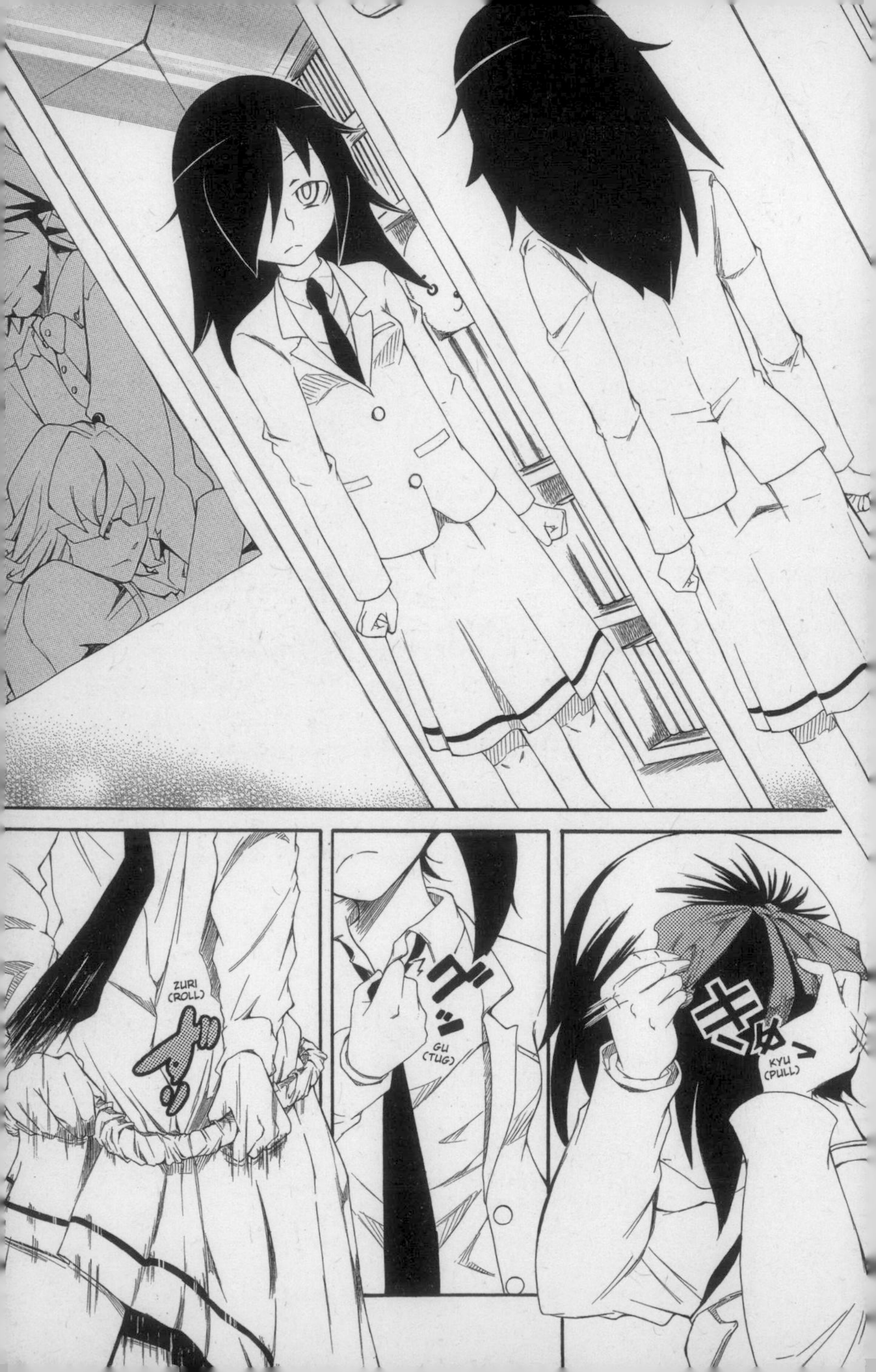
KYU
(PULL)
GU
(TUG)
ZURI
(ROLL)

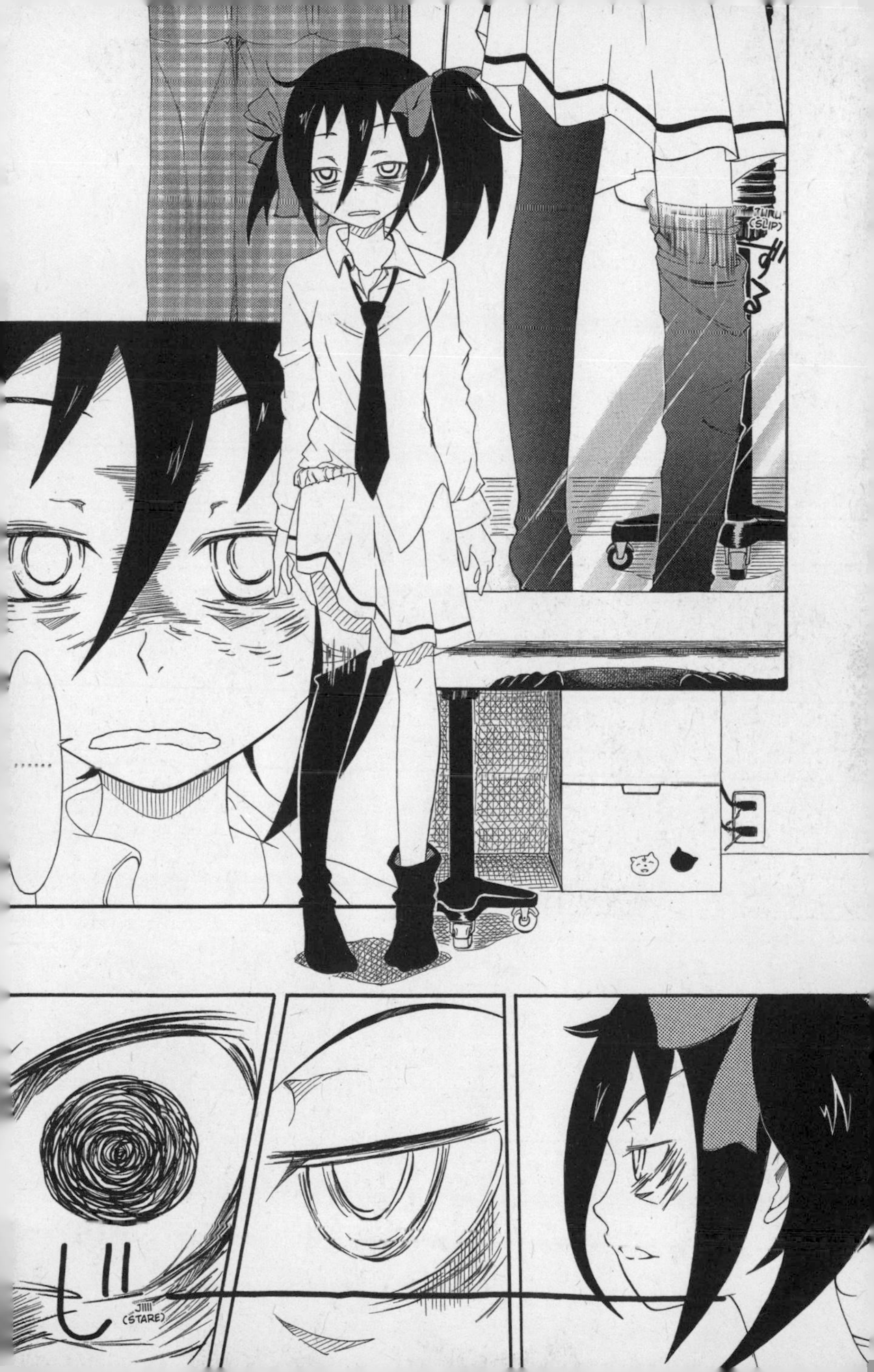
ZURU
(SLIP)
ずるっ
......
じーー
JIIII
(STARE)

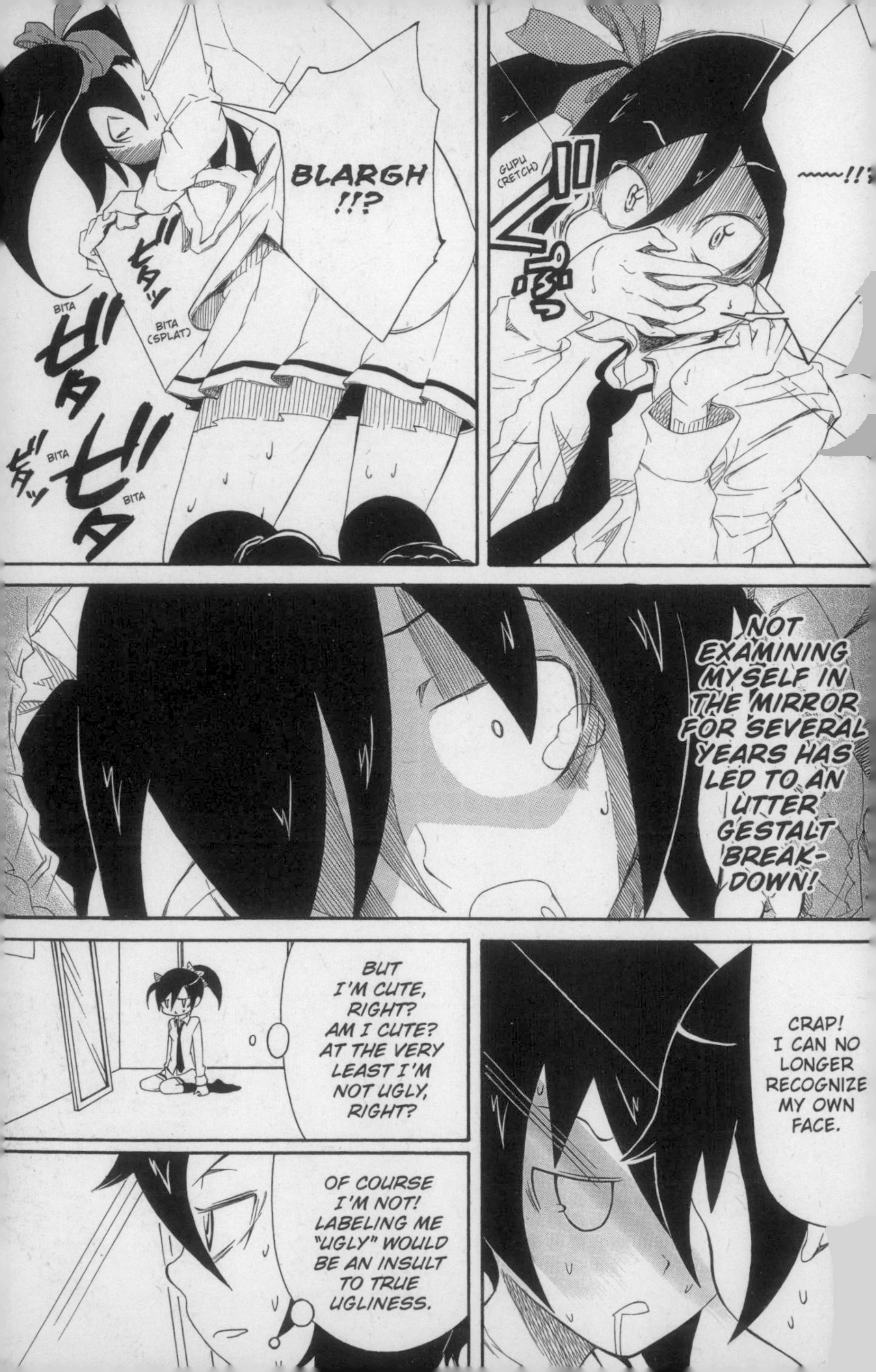
GUPU (RETCH)
~~~~!!?
BLARGH !!?
BITA (SPLAT)
BITA
BITA
BITA
NOT EXAMINING MYSELF IN THE MIRROR FOR SEVERAL YEARS HAS LED TO AN UTTER GESTALT BREAK-DOWN!
CRAP! I CAN NO LONGER RECOGNIZE MY OWN FACE.
BUT I'M CUTE, RIGHT? AM I CUTE? AT THE VERY LEAST I'M NOT UGLY, RIGHT?
OF COURSE I'M NOT! LABELING ME "UGLY" WOULD BE AN INSULT TO TRUE UGLINESS.
~~~~

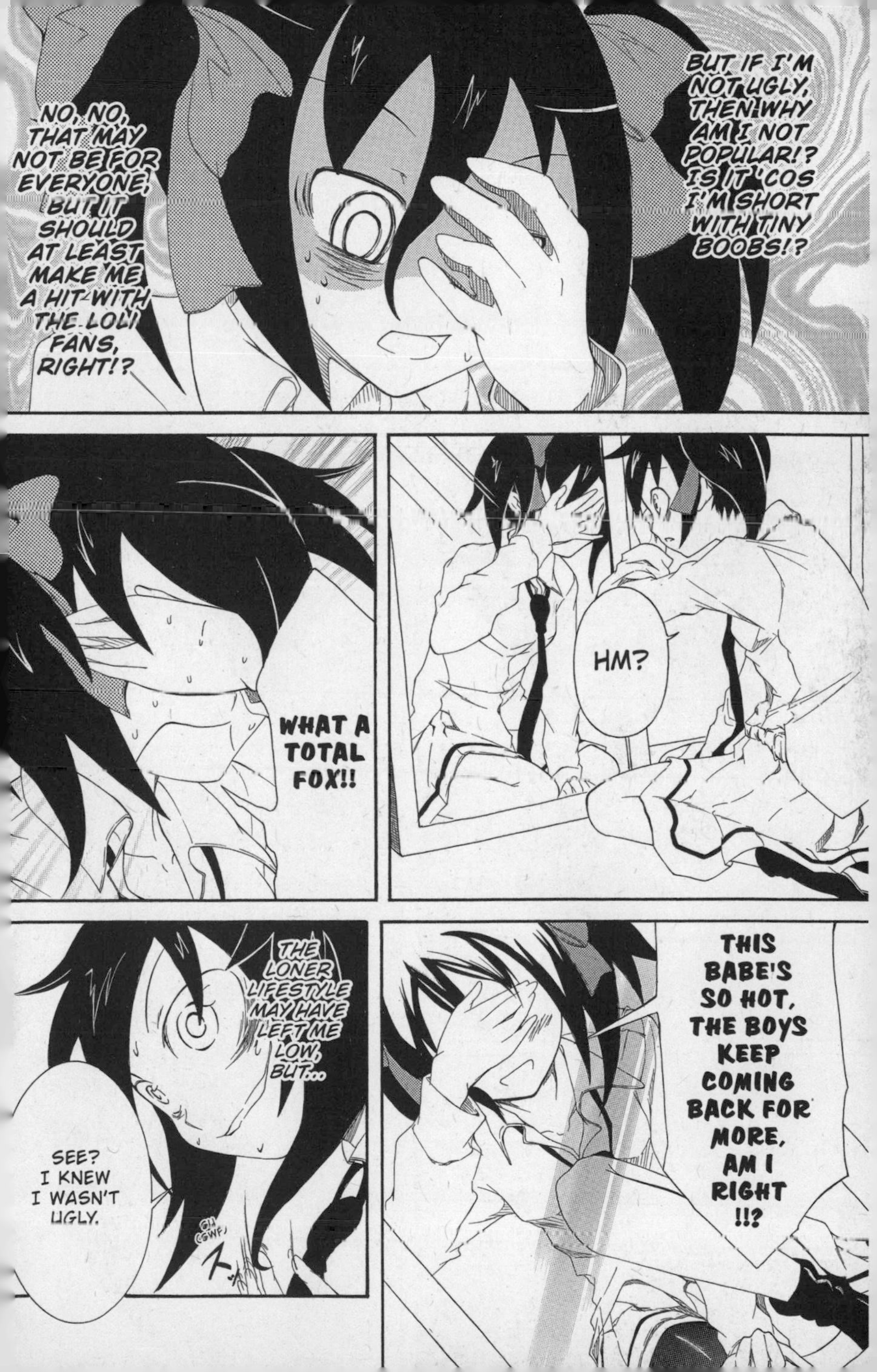
BUT IF I'M NOT UGLY, THEN WHY AM I NOT POPULAR!? IS IT 'COS I'M SHORT WITH TINY BOOBS!?
NO, NO, THAT MAY NOT BE FOR EVERYONE, BUT IT SHOULD AT LEAST MAKE ME A HIT WITH THE LOLI FANS, RIGHT!?
HM?
WHAT A TOTAL FOX!!
THIS BABE'S SO HOT, THE BOYS KEEP COMING BACK FOR MORE, AM I RIGHT !!?
THE LONER LIFESTYLE MAY HAVE LEFT ME LOW, BUT...
SEE? I KNEW I WASN'T UGLY.

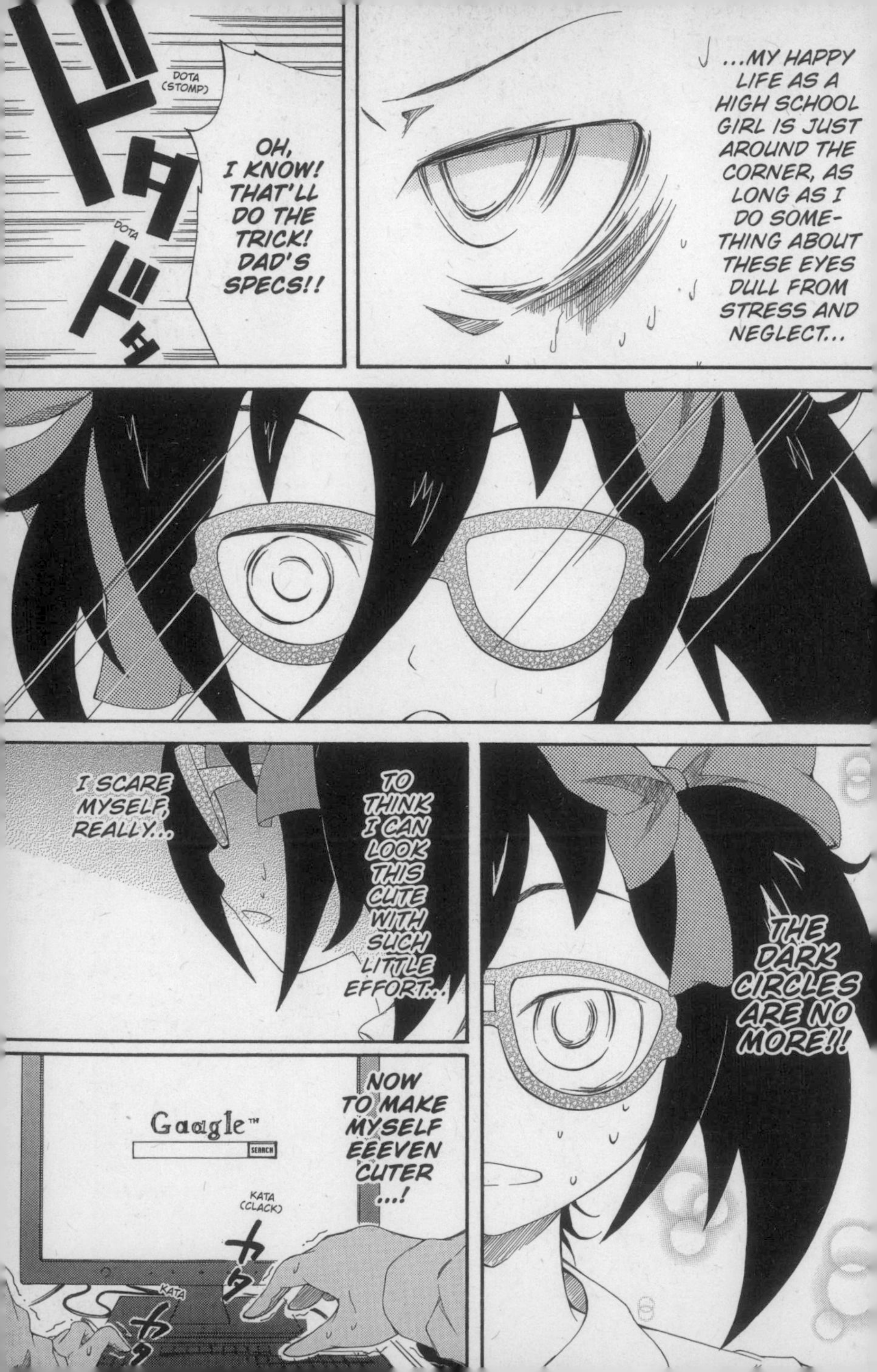
...MY HAPPY LIFE AS A HIGH SCHOOL GIRL IS JUST AROUND THE CORNER, AS LONG AS I DO SOME-THING ABOUT THESE EYES DULL FROM STRESS AND NEGLECT...
OH, I KNOW! THAT'LL DO THE TRICK! DAD'S SPECS!!
ドタ
DOTA (STOMP)
ドタ
DOTA
THE DARK CIRCLES ARE NO MORE!!
TO THINK I CAN LOOK THIS CUTE WITH SUCH LITTLE EFFORT...
I SCARE MYSELF, REALLY...
NOW TO MAKE MYSELF EEEVEN CUTER ...!
Gaagle™
SEARCH
カタ
KATA (CLACK)
カタ
KATA

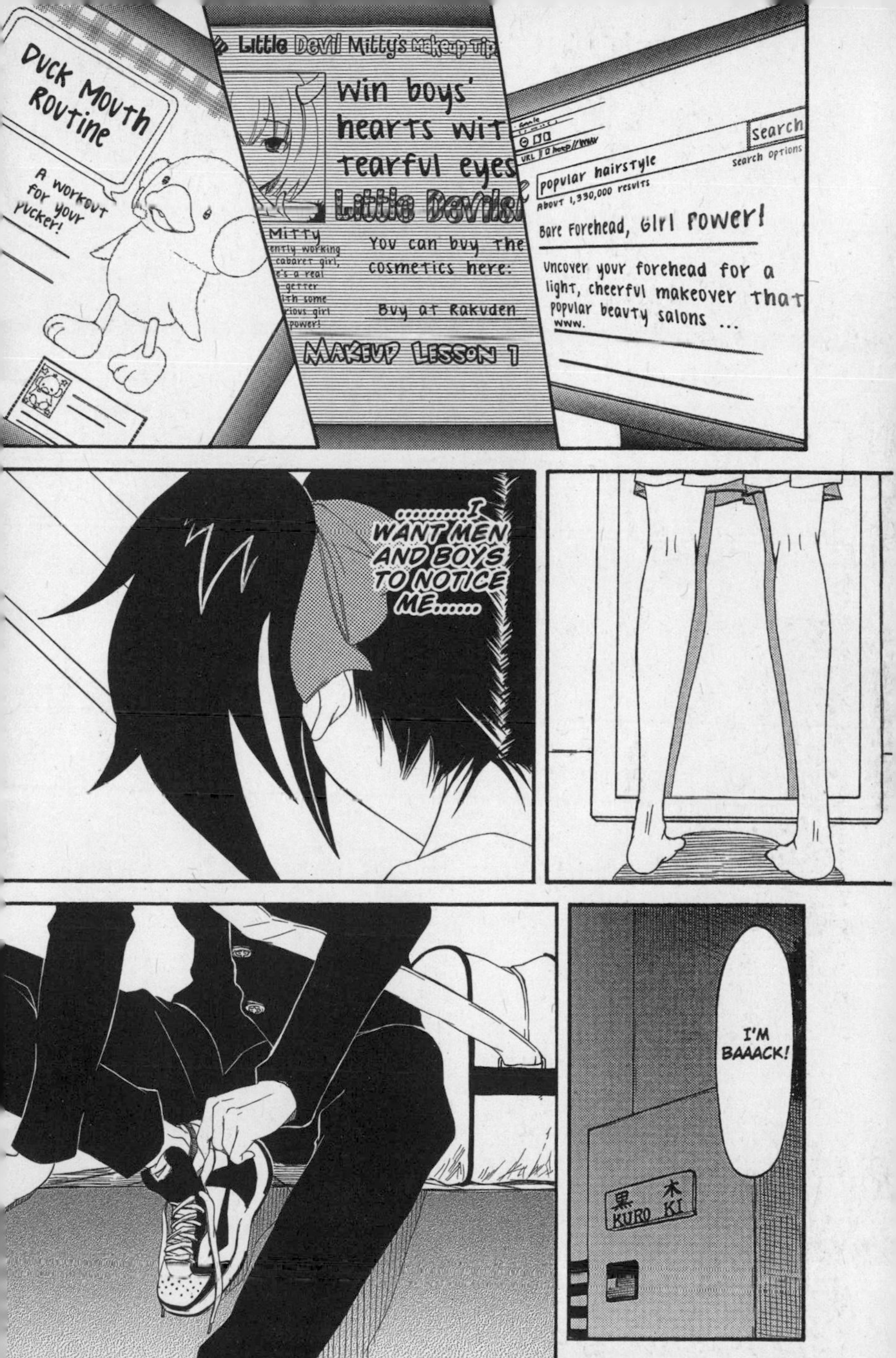
Search
Search Options
popular hairstyle
About 1,330,000 results
Bare Forehead, Girl Power!
Uncover your forehead for a light, cheerful makeover that popular beauty salons ...
Little Devil Mitty's Makeup Tips
Win boys' hearts wit tearful eyes
Little Devils!
Mitty
You can buy the cosmetics here:
Buy at Rakuden
MAKEUP LESSON 1
Duck Mouth Routine
A workout for your pucker!
..........I WANT MEN AND BOYS TO NOTICE ME......
I'M BAAACK!
黒 木
KURO KI

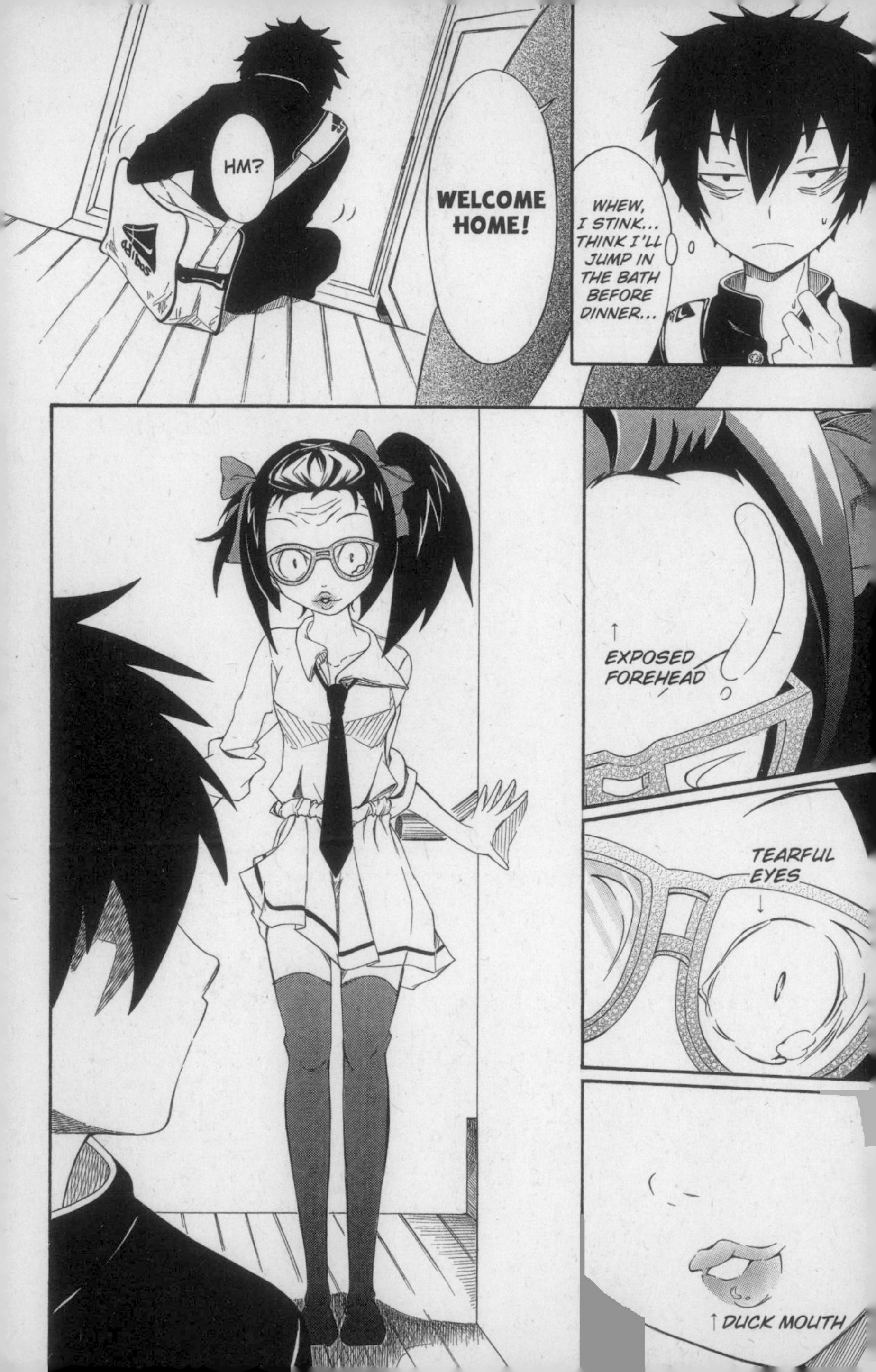
WHEW, I STINK... THINK I'LL JUMP IN THE BATH BEFORE DINNER...
WELCOME HOME!
HM?
EXPOSED FOREHEAD
TEARFUL EYES
DUCK MOUTH

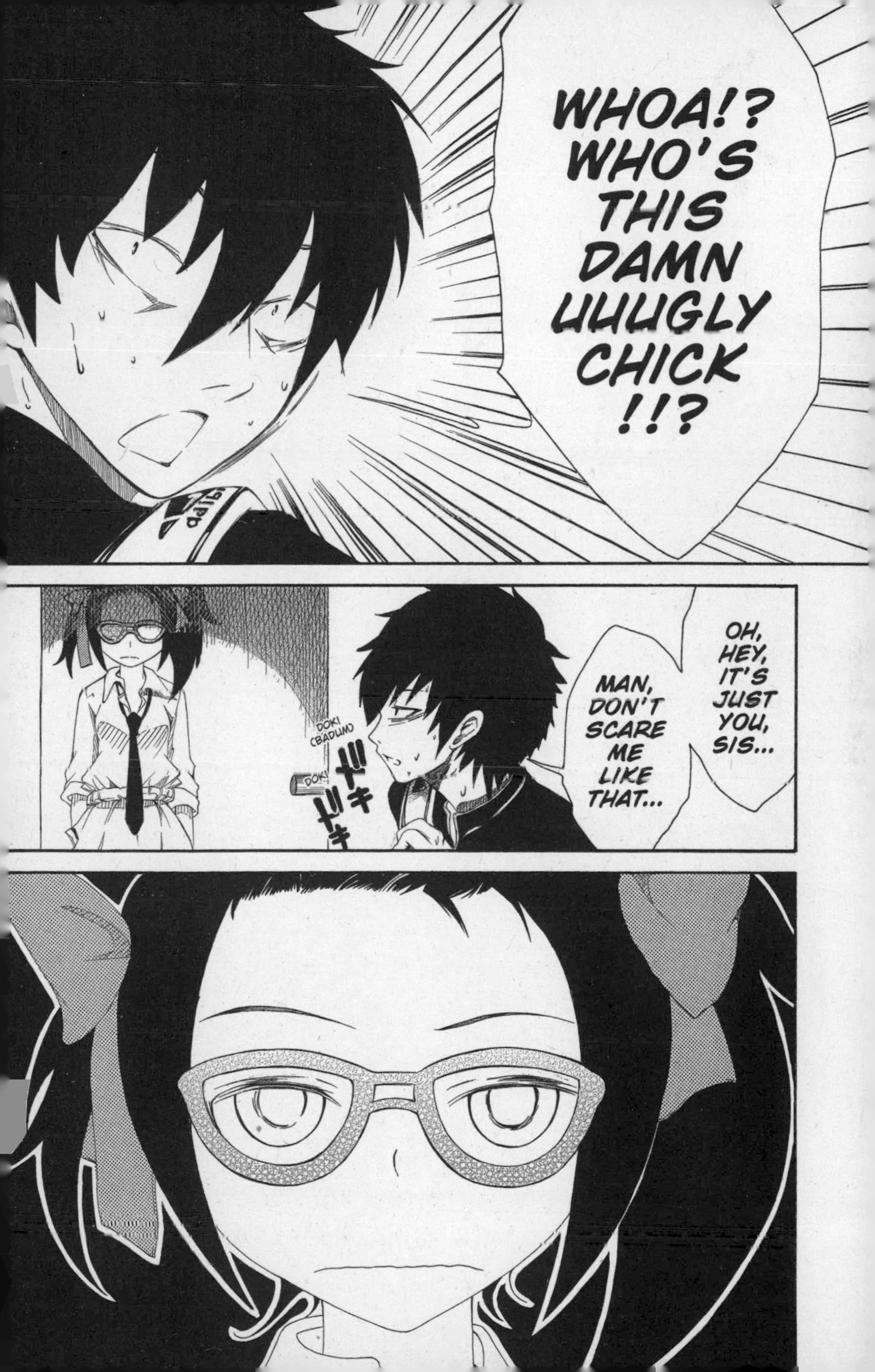
WHOA!? WHO'S THIS DAMN UUUGLY CHICK !!?
OH, HEY, IT'S JUST YOU, SIS...
MAN, DON'T SCARE ME LIKE THAT...
DOKI (BADUM)
DOKI
ドキ
ドキ

No Matter How I Look at It, It's You Guys' Fault I'm Not Popular!

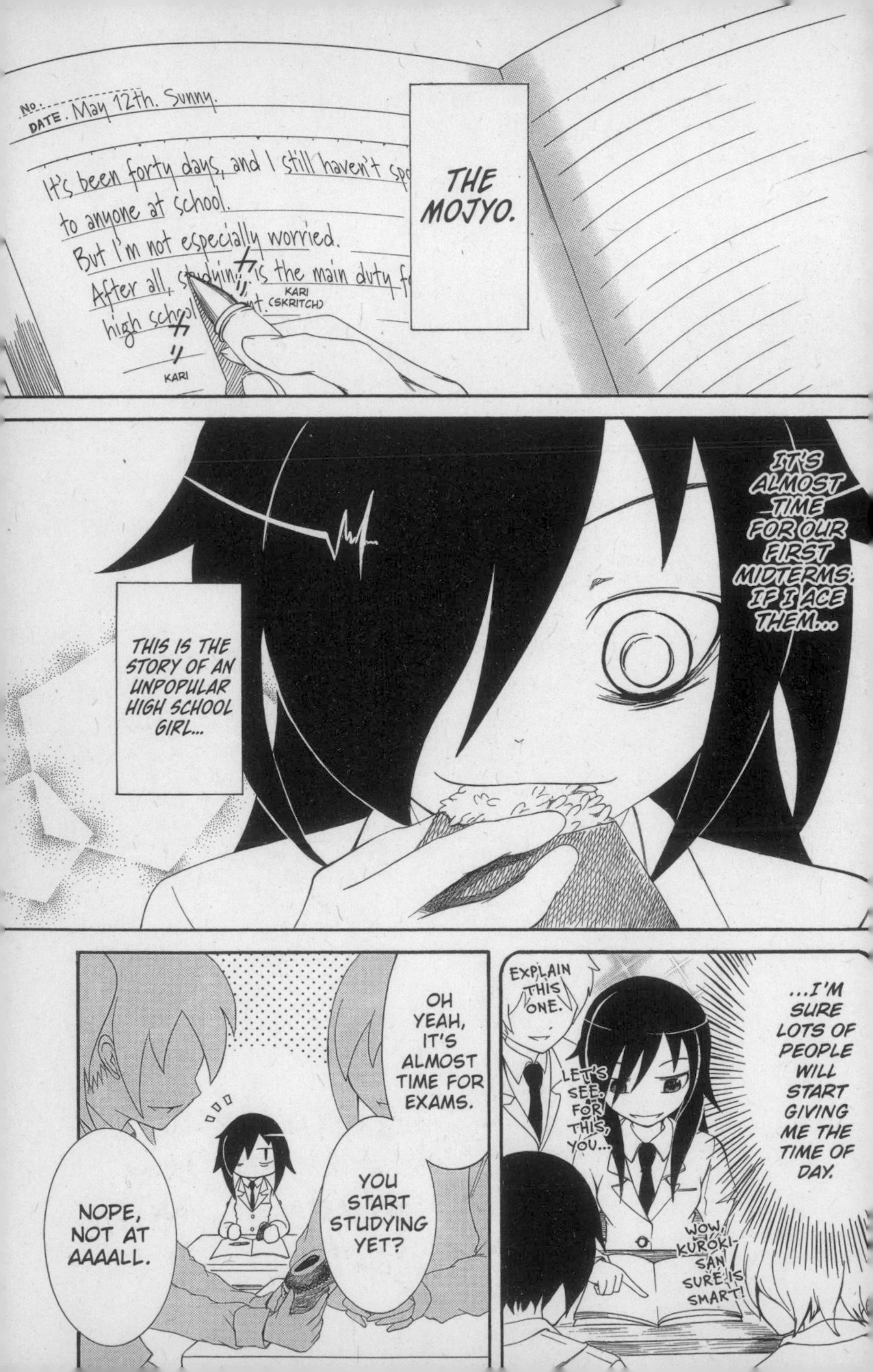

No.
DATE. May 12th. Sunny.
It's been forty days, and I still haven't sp
to anyone at school.
But I'm not especially worried.
After all, studyin is the main duty f
high schoo
KARI (SKRITCH)
KARI
THE MOJYO.
IT'S ALMOST TIME FOR OUR FIRST MIDTERMS. IF I ACE THEM...
THIS IS THE STORY OF AN UNPOPULAR HIGH SCHOOL GIRL...
...I'M SURE LOTS OF PEOPLE WILL START GIVING ME THE TIME OF DAY.
EXPLAIN THIS ONE.
LET'S SEE. FOR THIS, YOU...
WOW, KUROKI-SAN SURE IS SMART!
OH YEAH, IT'S ALMOST TIME FOR EXAMS.
YOU START STUDYING YET?
NOPE, NOT AT AAAALL.

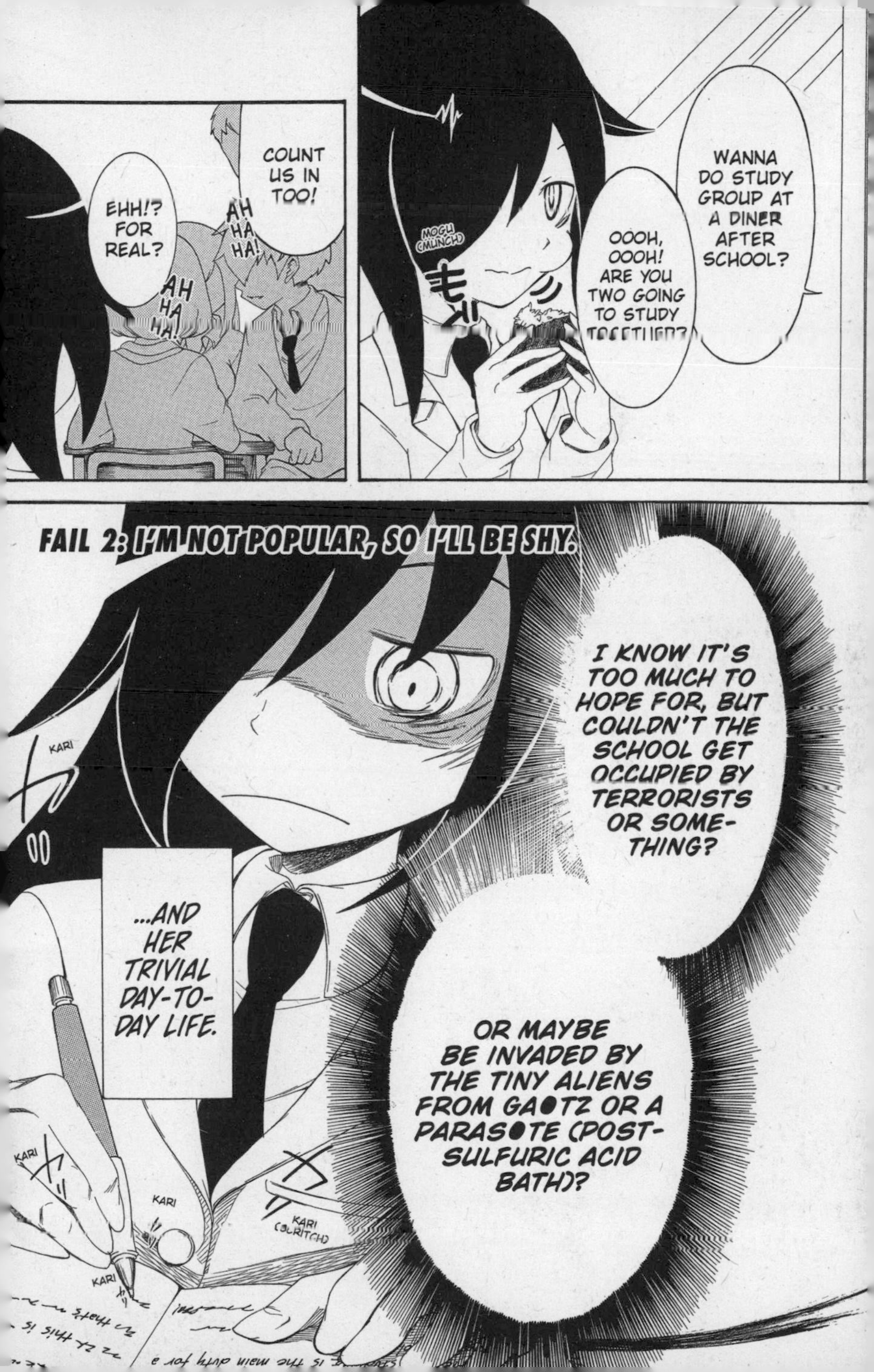
WANNA DO STUDY GROUP AT A DINER AFTER SCHOOL?
OOOH, OOOH! ARE YOU TWO GOING TO STUDY TOGETHER?
MOGU (MUNCH)
COUNT US IN TOO!
AH HA HA!
EHH!? FOR REAL?
AH HA HA!
FAIL 2: I'M NOT POPULAR, SO I'LL BE SHY.
I KNOW IT'S TOO MUCH TO HOPE FOR, BUT COULDN'T THE SCHOOL GET OCCUPIED BY TERRORISTS OR SOME-THING?
OR MAYBE BE INVADED BY THE TINY ALIENS FROM GAOTZ OR A PARASOTE (POST-SULFURIC ACID BATH)?
KARI
KARI (SCRITCH)
KARI
KARI
KARI
...AND HER TRIVIAL DAY-TO-DAY LIFE.

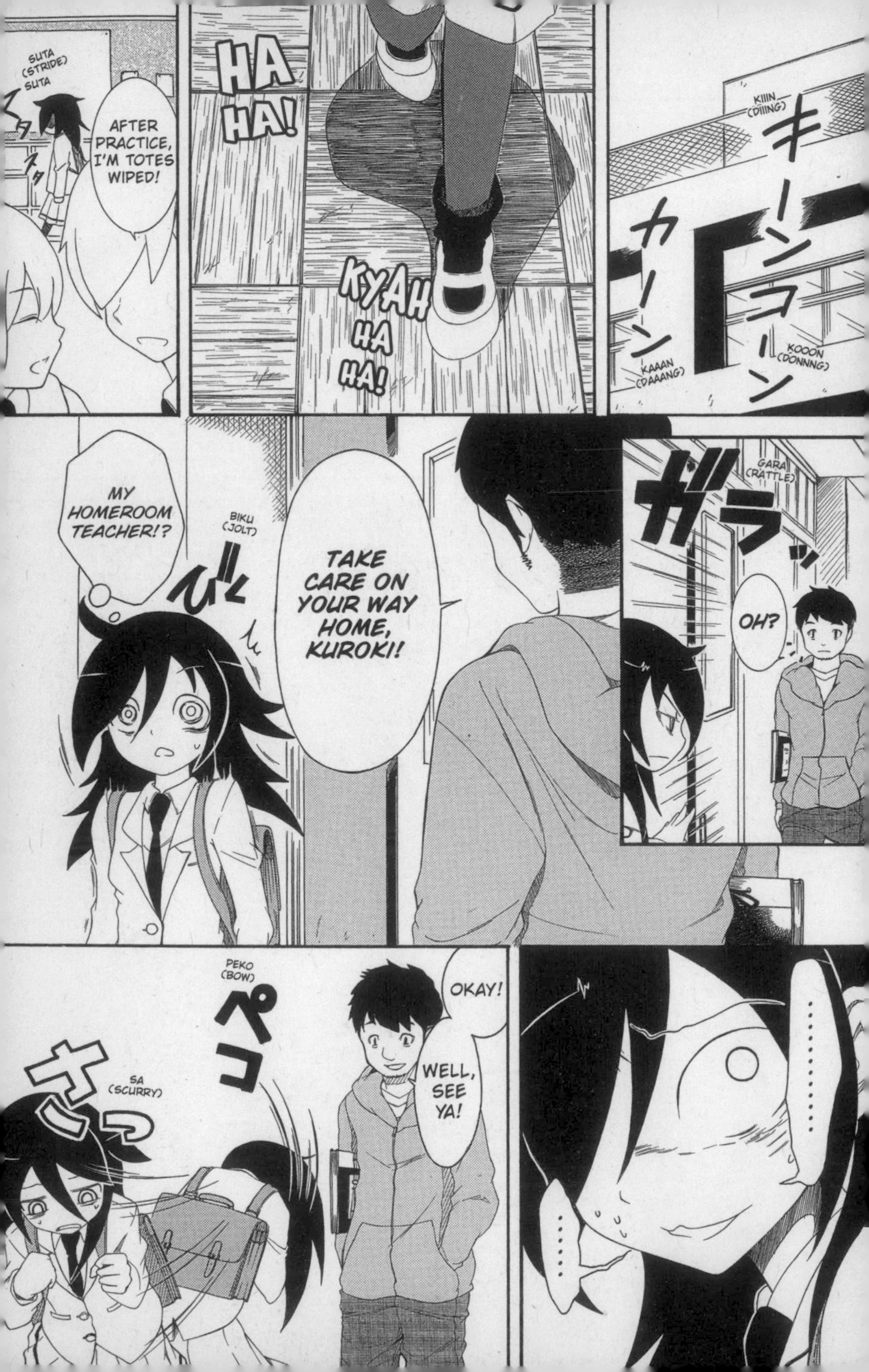
KIIN (DIIING)
KOOON (DONNNG)
KAAAN (DAAANG)
HA HA!
KYAH HA HA!
SUTA (STRIDE) SUTA
AFTER PRACTICE, I'M TOTES WIPED!
GARA (RATTLE)
OH?
TAKE CARE ON YOUR WAY HOME, KUROKI!
BIKU (JOLT)
MY HOMEROOM TEACHER!?
......
......
OKAY!
WELL, SEE YA!
PEKO (BOW)
SA (SCURRY)

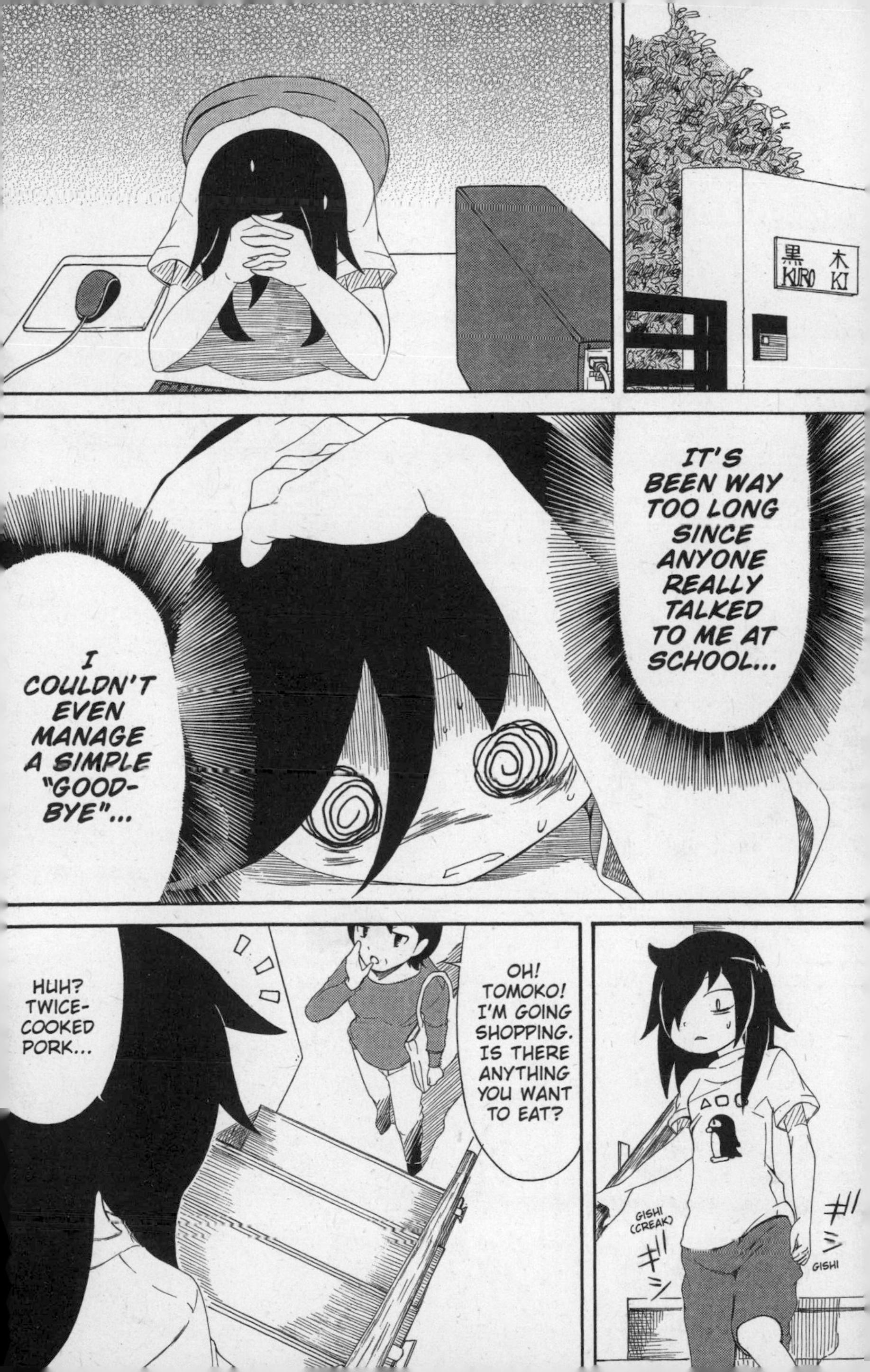
黒 木
KURO KI
IT'S BEEN WAY TOO LONG SINCE ANYONE REALLY TALKED TO ME AT SCHOOL...
I COULDN'T EVEN MANAGE A SIMPLE "GOOD-BYE"...
ギシ
GISHI
GISHI (CREAK)
ギシ
OH! TOMOKO! I'M GOING SHOPPING. IS THERE ANYTHING YOU WANT TO EAT?
HUH? TWICE-COOKED PORK...

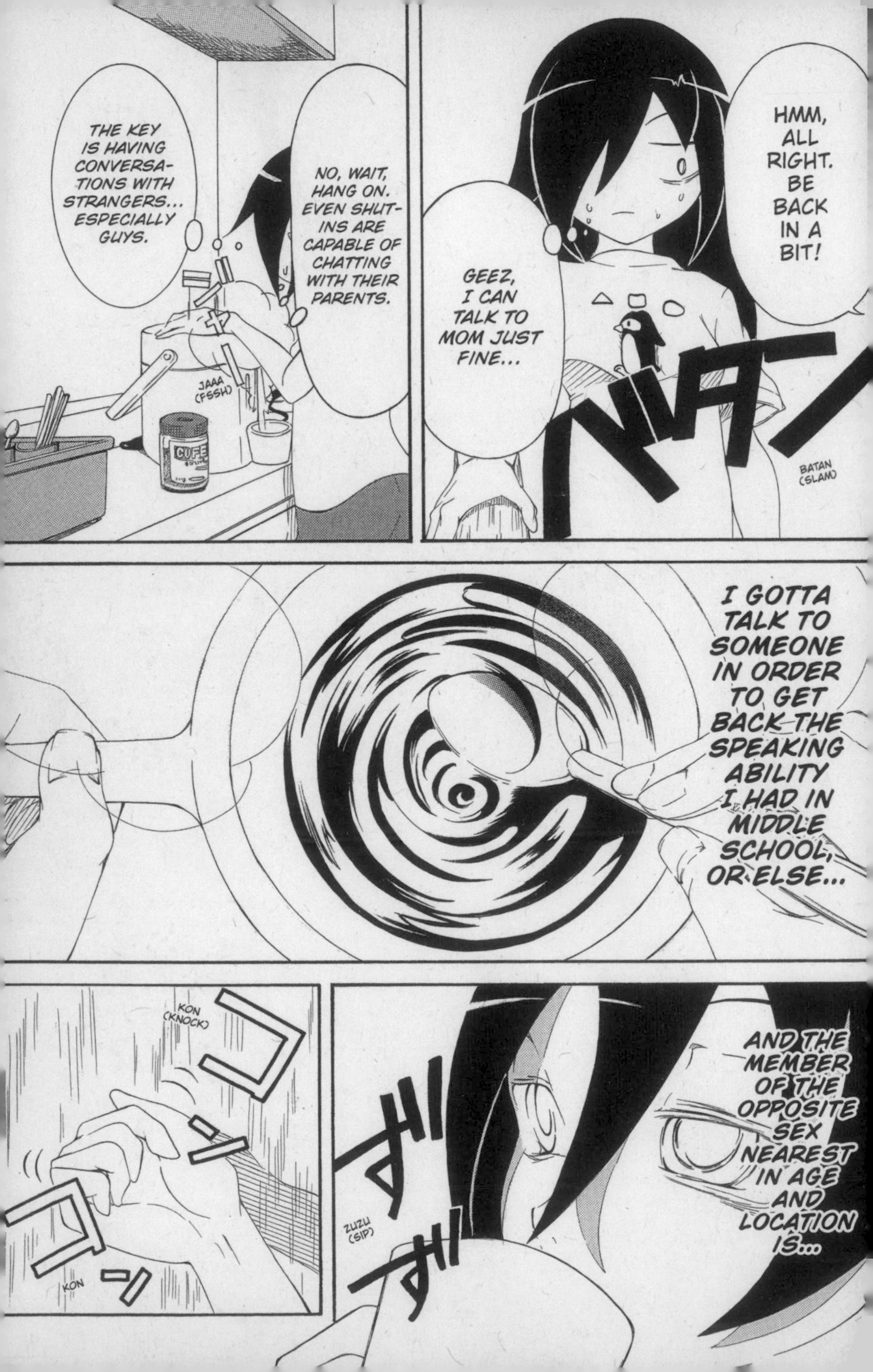
HMM, ALL RIGHT. BE BACK IN A BIT!
GEEZ, I CAN TALK TO MOM JUST FINE...
BATAN (SLAM)
NO, WAIT, HANG ON. EVEN SHUT-INS ARE CAPABLE OF CHATTING WITH THEIR PARENTS.
THE KEY IS HAVING CONVERSA-TIONS WITH STRANGERS... ESPECIALLY GUYS.
JAAA (FSSH)
I GOTTA TALK TO SOMEONE IN ORDER TO GET BACK THE SPEAKING ABILITY I HAD IN MIDDLE SCHOOL, OR ELSE...
AND THE MEMBER OF THE OPPOSITE SEX NEAREST IN AGE AND LOCATION IS...
ZUZU (SIP)
KON (KNOCK)
KON

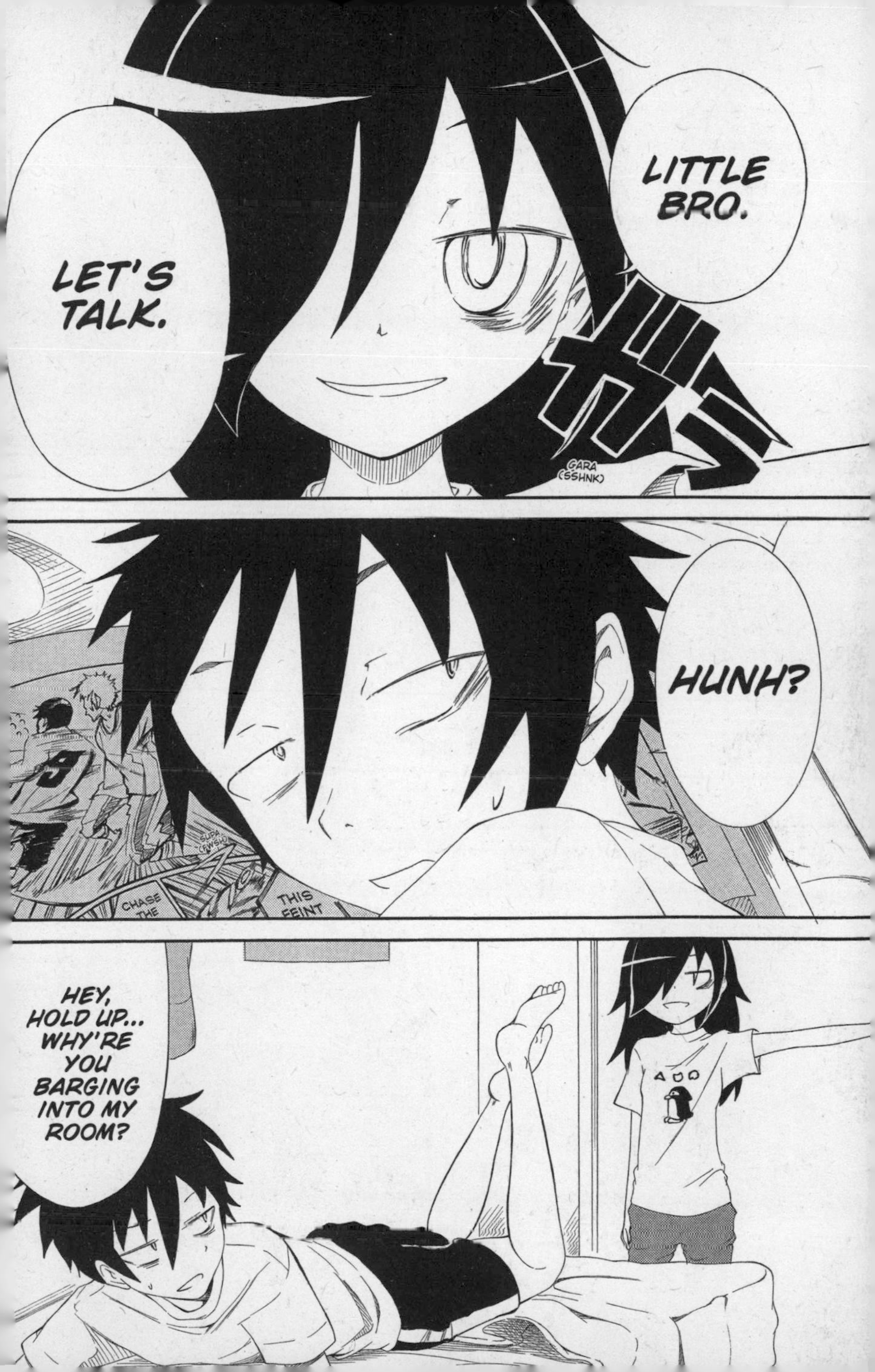
LITTLE BRO.
LET'S TALK.
GARA (SSHNK)
HUNH?
SUPA (FWSH)
THIS FEINT
CHASE THE
HEY, HOLD UP... WHY'RE YOU BARGING INTO MY ROOM?

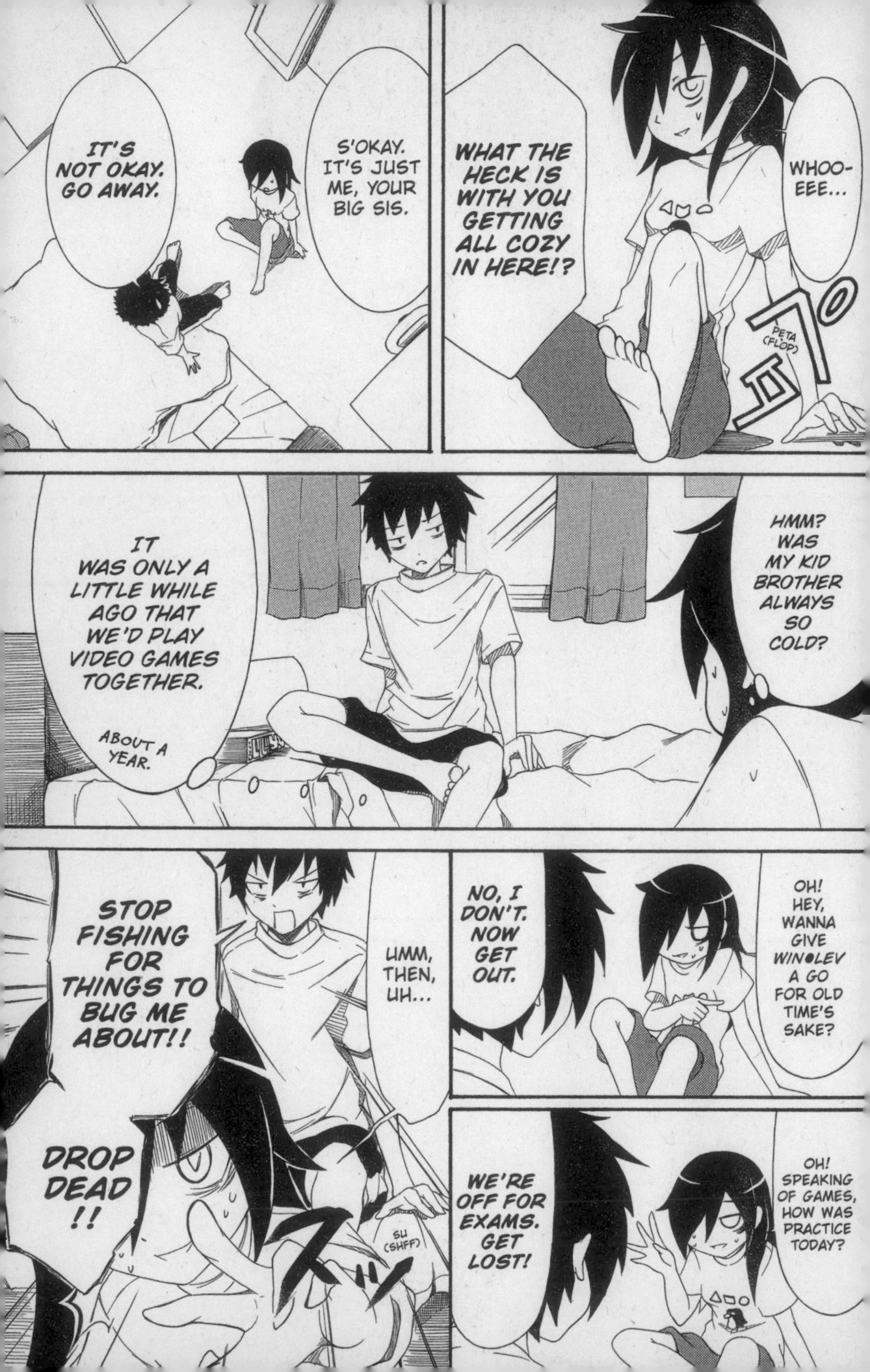
WHOO-EEE...
PETA (FLOP)
WHAT THE HECK IS WITH YOU GETTING ALL COZY IN HERE!?
S'OKAY. IT'S JUST ME, YOUR BIG SIS.
IT'S NOT OKAY. GO AWAY.
HMM? WAS MY KID BROTHER ALWAYS SO COLD?
IT WAS ONLY A LITTLE WHILE AGO THAT WE'D PLAY VIDEO GAMES TOGETHER.
ABOUT A YEAR.
OH! HEY, WANNA GIVE WIN●LEV A GO FOR OLD TIME'S SAKE?
NO, I DON'T. NOW GET OUT.
OH! SPEAKING OF GAMES, HOW WAS PRACTICE TODAY?
WE'RE OFF FOR EXAMS. GET LOST!
UMM, THEN, UH...
STOP FISHING FOR THINGS TO BUG ME ABOUT!!
DROP DEAD!!
SU (SHFF)

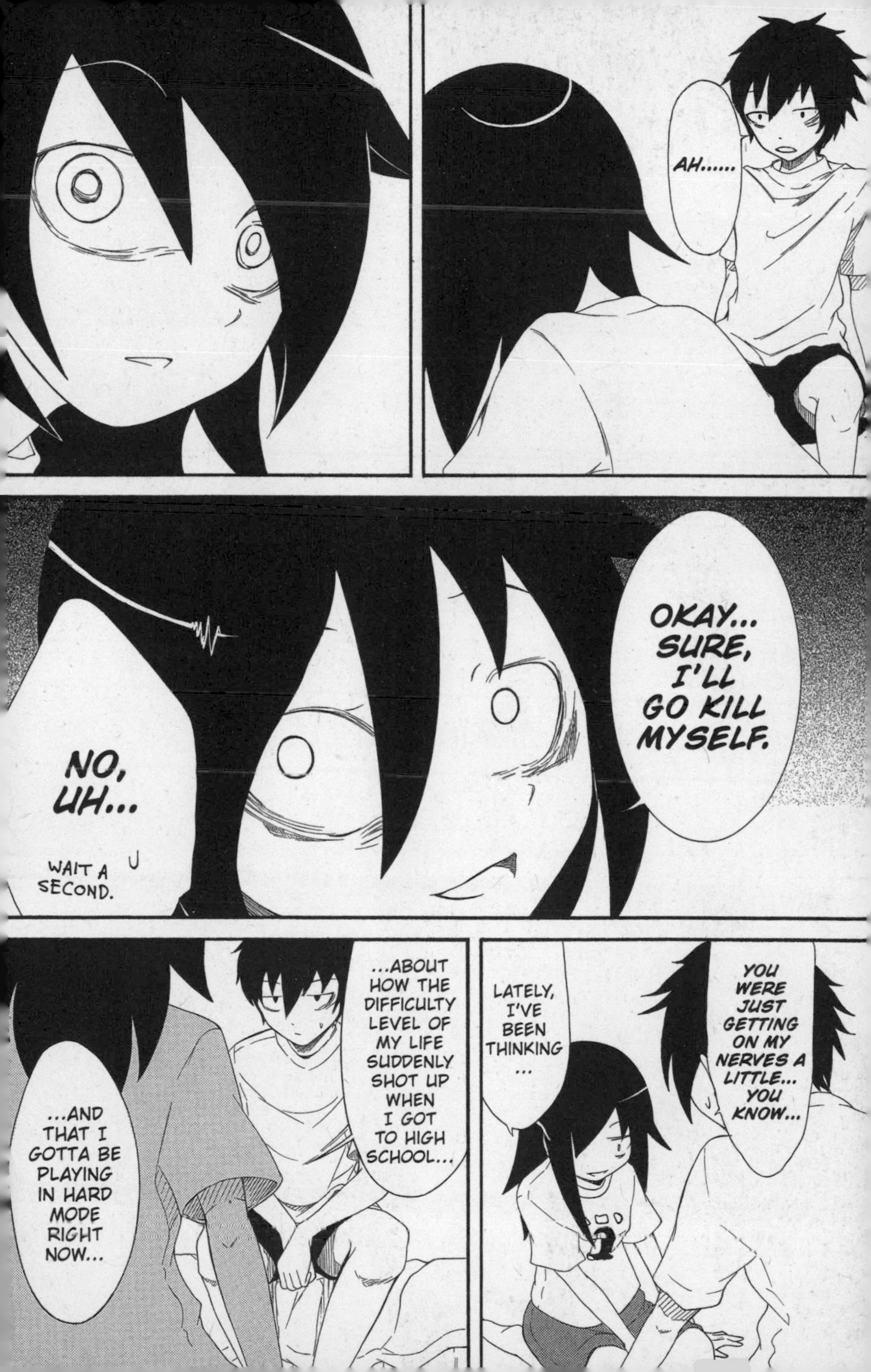
AH......
OKAY... SURE, I'LL GO KILL MYSELF.
NO, UH...
WAIT A SECOND.
YOU WERE JUST GETTING ON MY NERVES A LITTLE... YOU KNOW...
LATELY, I'VE BEEN THINKING ...
...ABOUT HOW THE DIFFICULTY LEVEL OF MY LIFE SUDDENLY SHOT UP WHEN I GOT TO HIGH SCHOOL...
...AND THAT I GOTTA BE PLAYING IN HARD MODE RIGHT NOW...

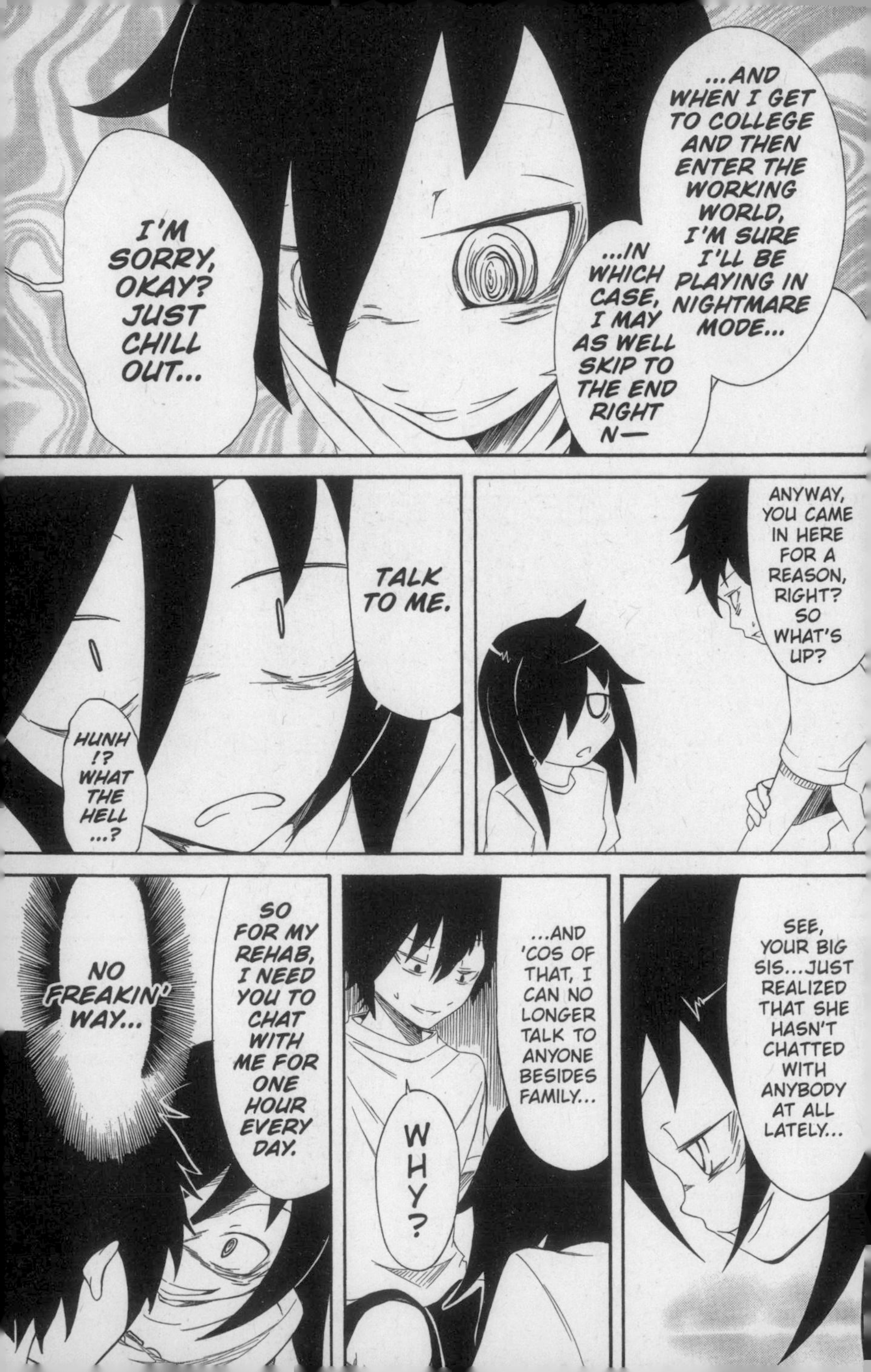
...AND WHEN I GET TO COLLEGE AND THEN ENTER THE WORKING WORLD, I'M SURE I'LL BE PLAYING IN NIGHTMARE MODE...
...IN WHICH CASE, I MAY AS WELL SKIP TO THE END RIGHT N—
I'M SORRY, OKAY? JUST CHILL OUT...
ANYWAY, YOU CAME IN HERE FOR A REASON, RIGHT? SO WHAT'S UP?
TALK TO ME.
HUNH!? WHAT THE HELL...?
SEE, YOUR BIG SIS...JUST REALIZED THAT SHE HASN'T CHATTED WITH ANYBODY AT ALL LATELY...
...AND 'COS OF THAT, I CAN NO LONGER TALK TO ANYONE BESIDES FAMILY...
WHY?
SO FOR MY REHAB, I NEED YOU TO CHAT WITH ME FOR ONE HOUR EVERY DAY.
NO FREAKIN' WAY...

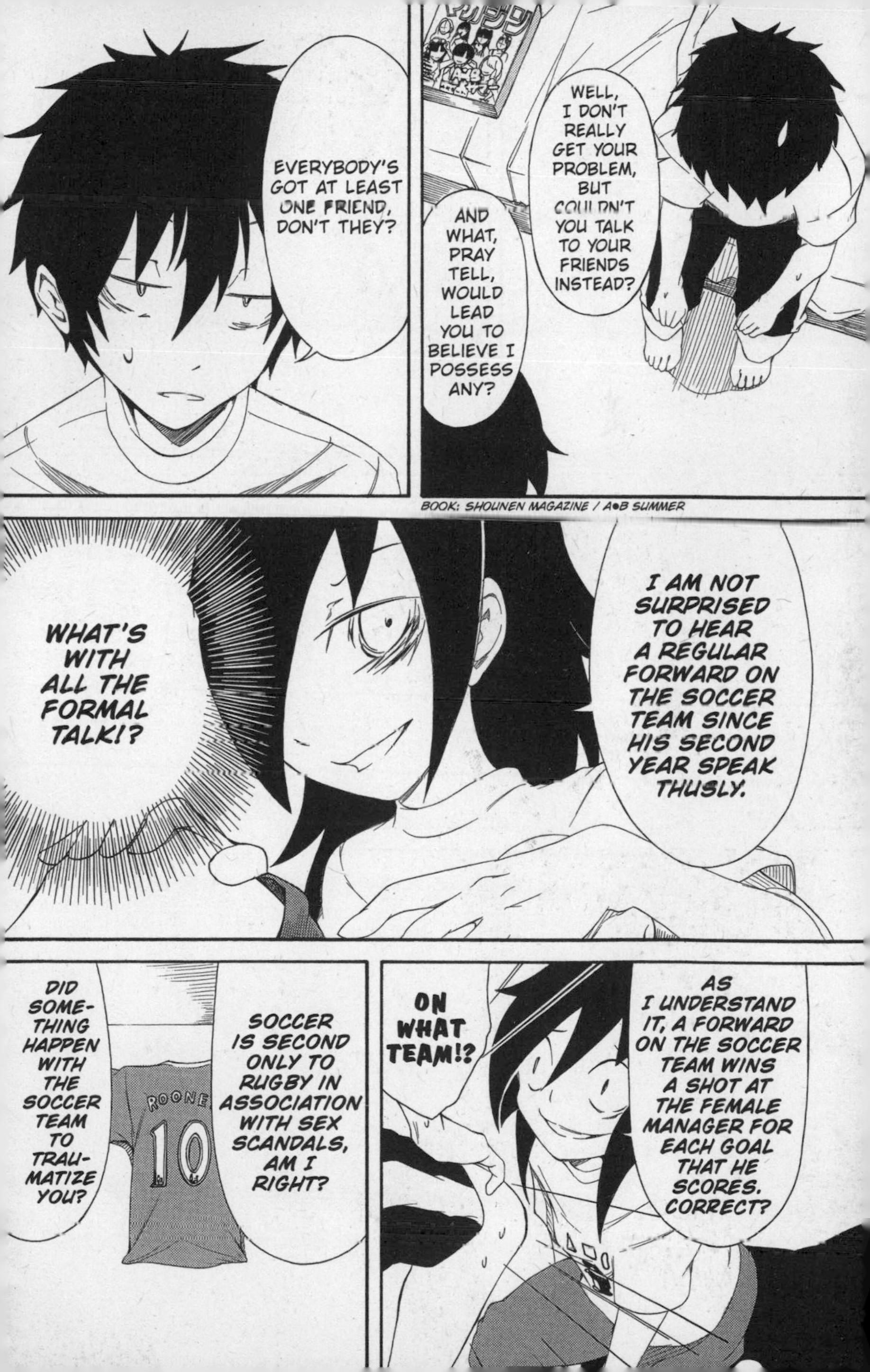
WELL, I DON'T REALLY GET YOUR PROBLEM, BUT COULDN'T YOU TALK TO YOUR FRIENDS INSTEAD?
AND WHAT, PRAY TELL, WOULD LEAD YOU TO BELIEVE I POSSESS ANY?
EVERYBODY'S GOT AT LEAST ONE FRIEND, DON'T THEY?
BOOK: SHOUNEN MAGAZINE / A•B SUMMER
I AM NOT SURPRISED TO HEAR A REGULAR FORWARD ON THE SOCCER TEAM SINCE HIS SECOND YEAR SPEAK THUSLY.
WHAT'S WITH ALL THE FORMAL TALK!?
AS I UNDERSTAND IT, A FORWARD ON THE SOCCER TEAM WINS A SHOT AT THE FEMALE MANAGER FOR EACH GOAL THAT HE SCORES. CORRECT?
ON WHAT TEAM!?
SOCCER IS SECOND ONLY TO RUGBY IN ASSOCIATION WITH SEX SCANDALS, AM I RIGHT?
ROONE
10
DID SOMETHING HAPPEN WITH THE SOCCER TEAM TO TRAUMATIZE YOU?

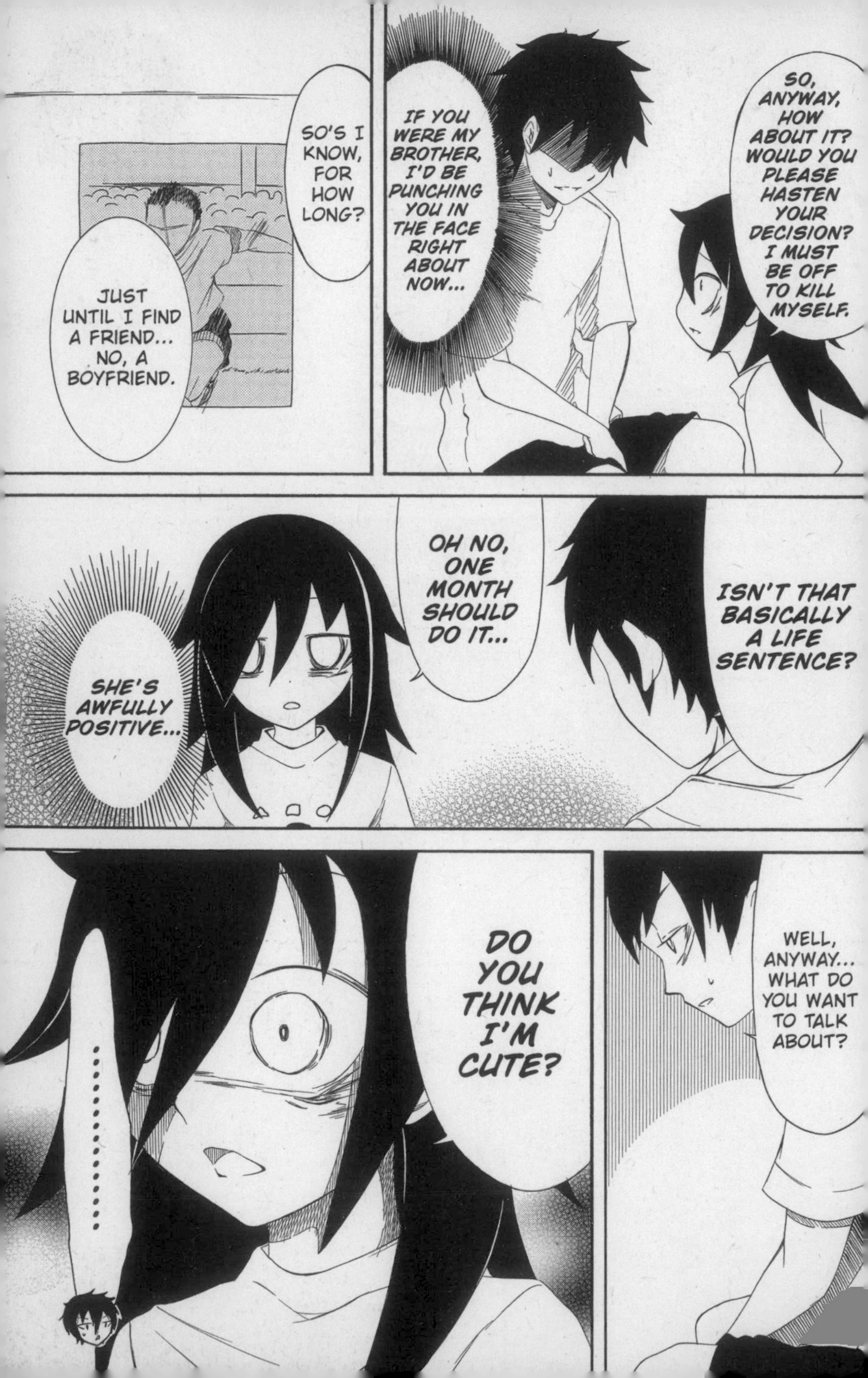
SO, ANYWAY, HOW ABOUT IT? WOULD YOU PLEASE HASTEN YOUR DECISION? I MUST BE OFF TO KILL MYSELF.
IF YOU WERE MY BROTHER, I'D BE PUNCHING YOU IN THE FACE RIGHT ABOUT NOW...
SO'S I KNOW, FOR HOW LONG?
JUST UNTIL I FIND A FRIEND... NO, A BOYFRIEND.
ISN'T THAT BASICALLY A LIFE SENTENCE?
OH NO, ONE MONTH SHOULD DO IT...
SHE'S AWFULLY POSITIVE...
WELL, ANYWAY... WHAT DO YOU WANT TO TALK ABOUT?
DO YOU THINK I'M CUTE?
......

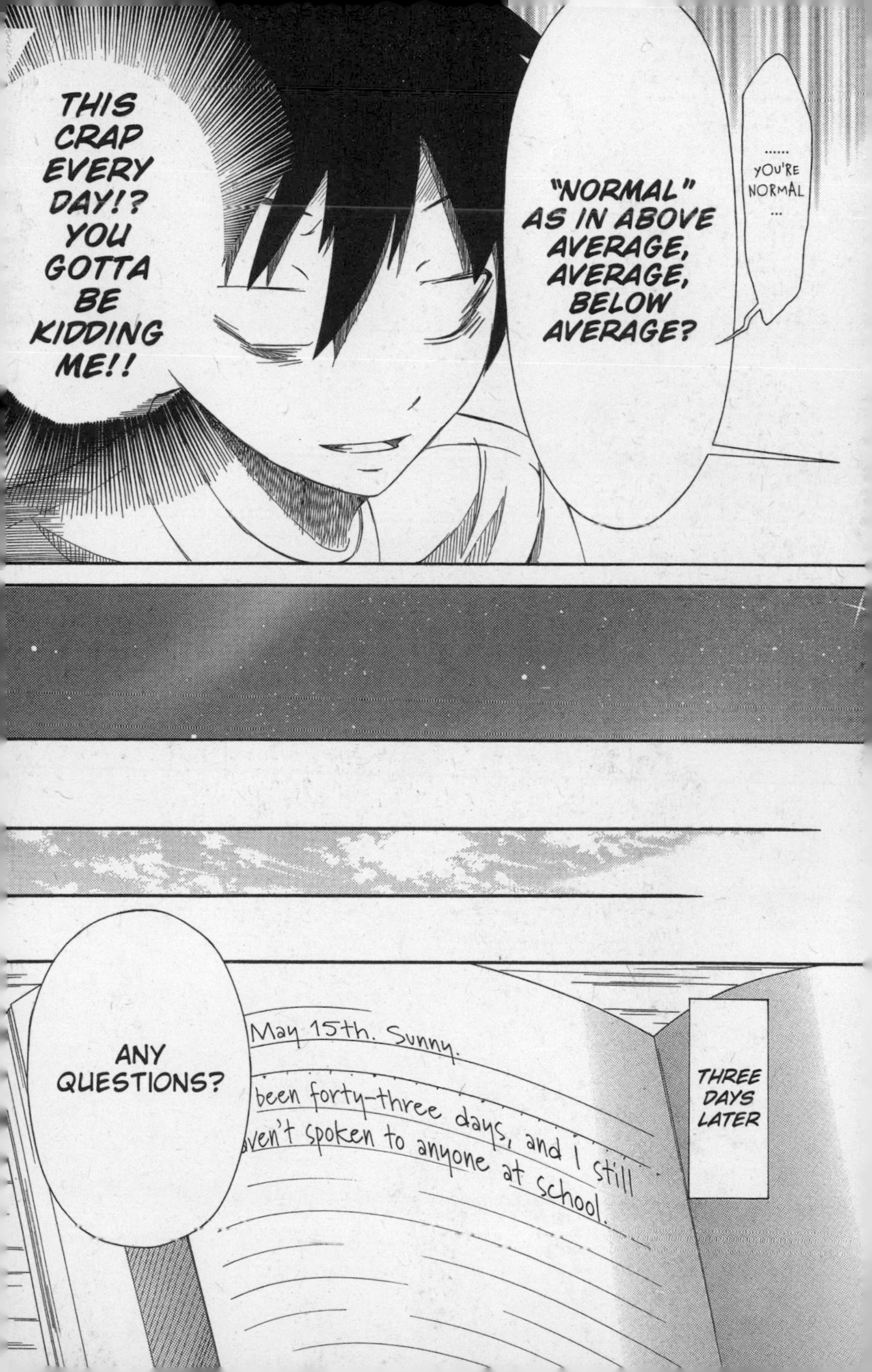
......YOU'RE NORMAL...
"NORMAL" AS IN ABOVE AVERAGE, AVERAGE, BELOW AVERAGE?
THIS CRAP EVERY DAY!? YOU GOTTA BE KIDDING ME!!
THREE DAYS LATER
May 15th. Sunny.
been forty-three days, and I still
aven't spoken to anyone at school.
ANY QUESTIONS?

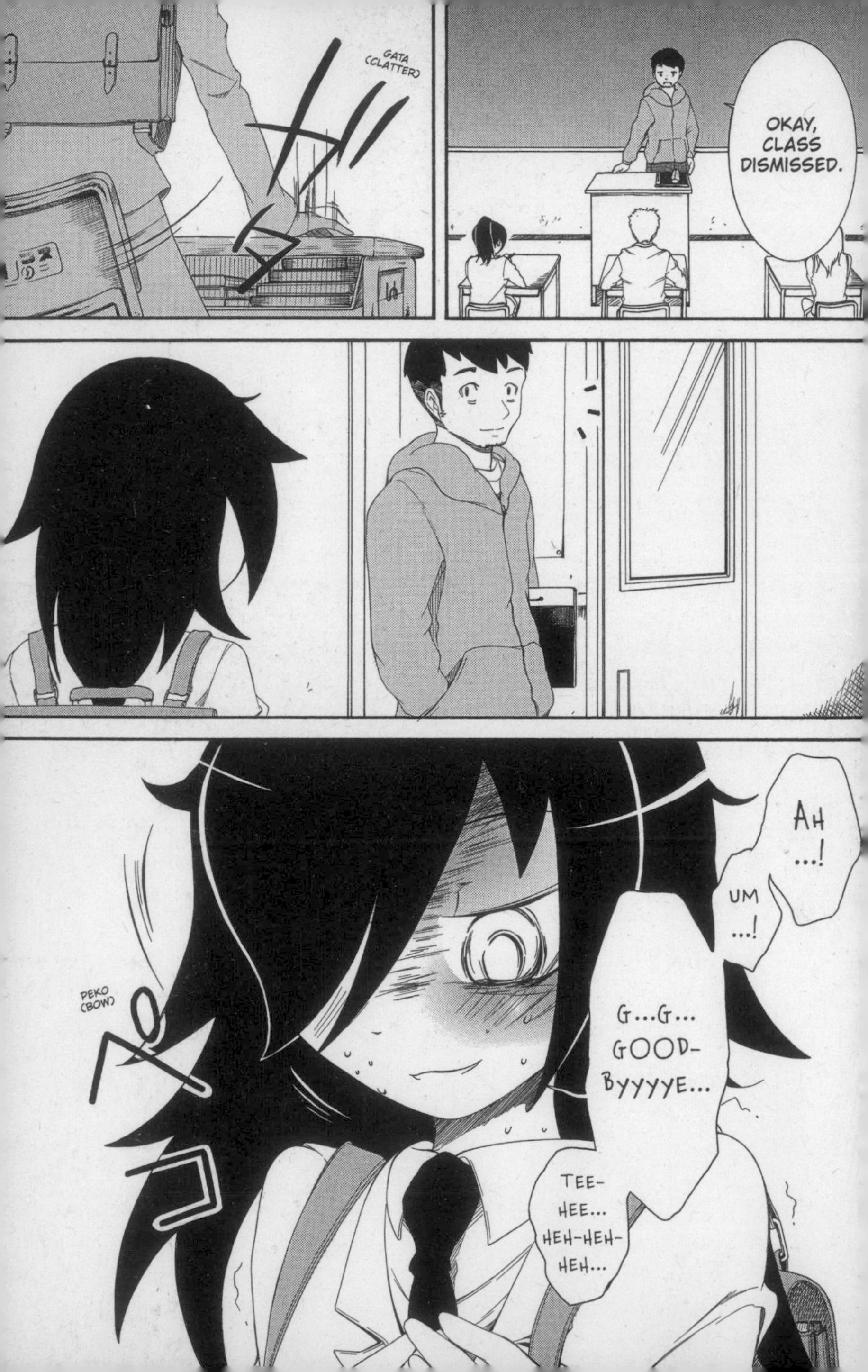
OKAY, CLASS DISMISSED.
GATA (CLATTER)
AH ...!
UM ...!
G...G... GOOD-BYYYYE...
TEE-HEE... HEH-HEH-HEH...
PEKO (BOW)

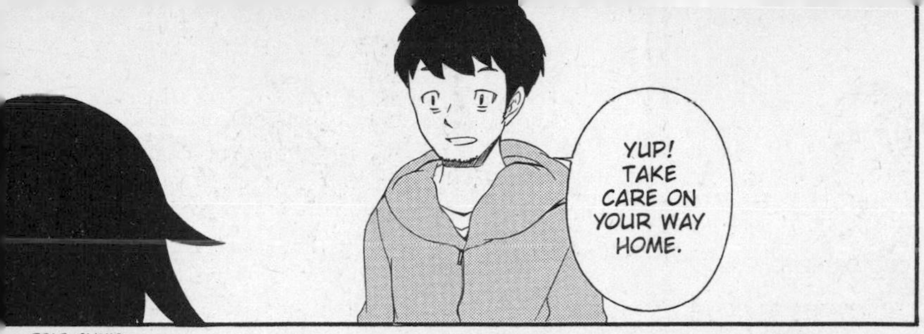
YUP! TAKE CARE ON YOUR WAY HOME.
POLE: CLINIC

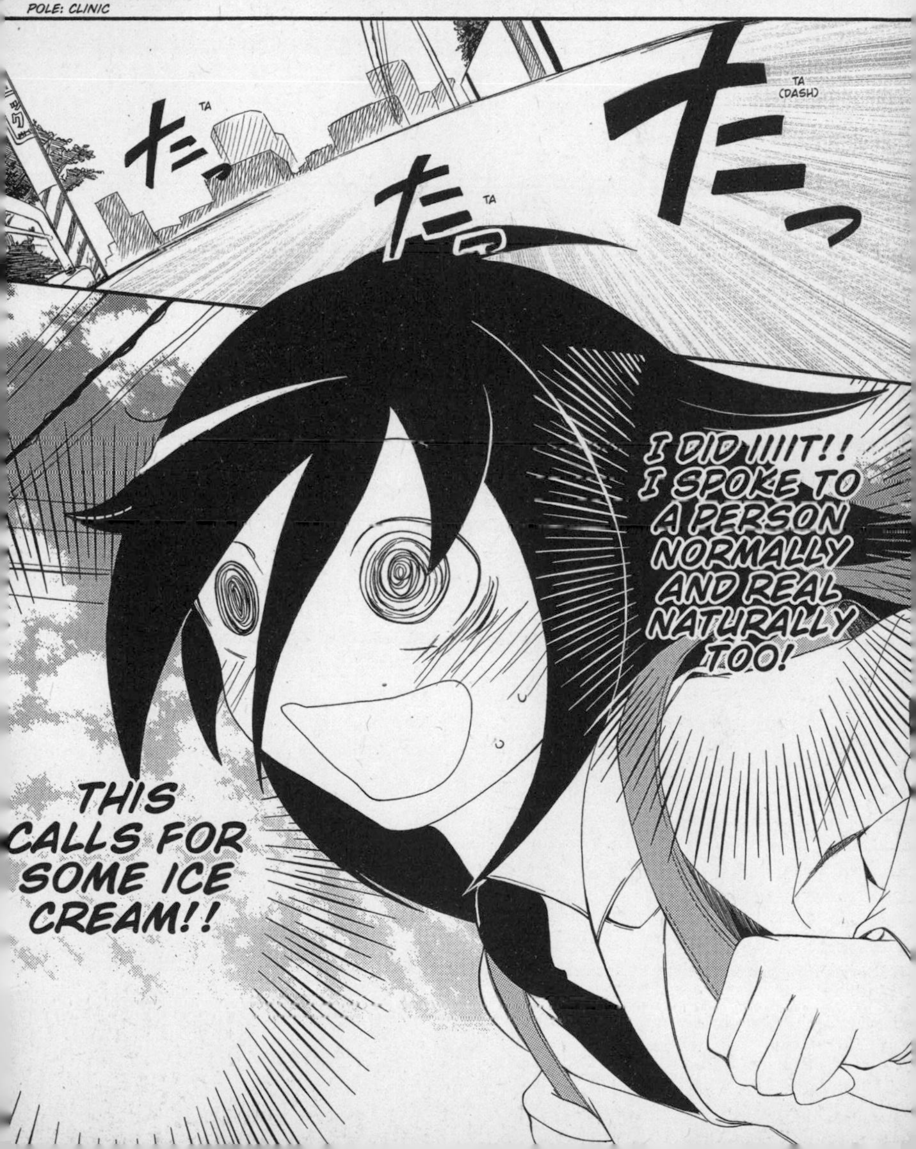
TA (DASH)
TA
TA
I DID IIIIT!! I SPOKE TO A PERSON NORMALLY AND REAL NATURALLY TOO!
THIS CALLS FOR SOME ICE CREAM!!

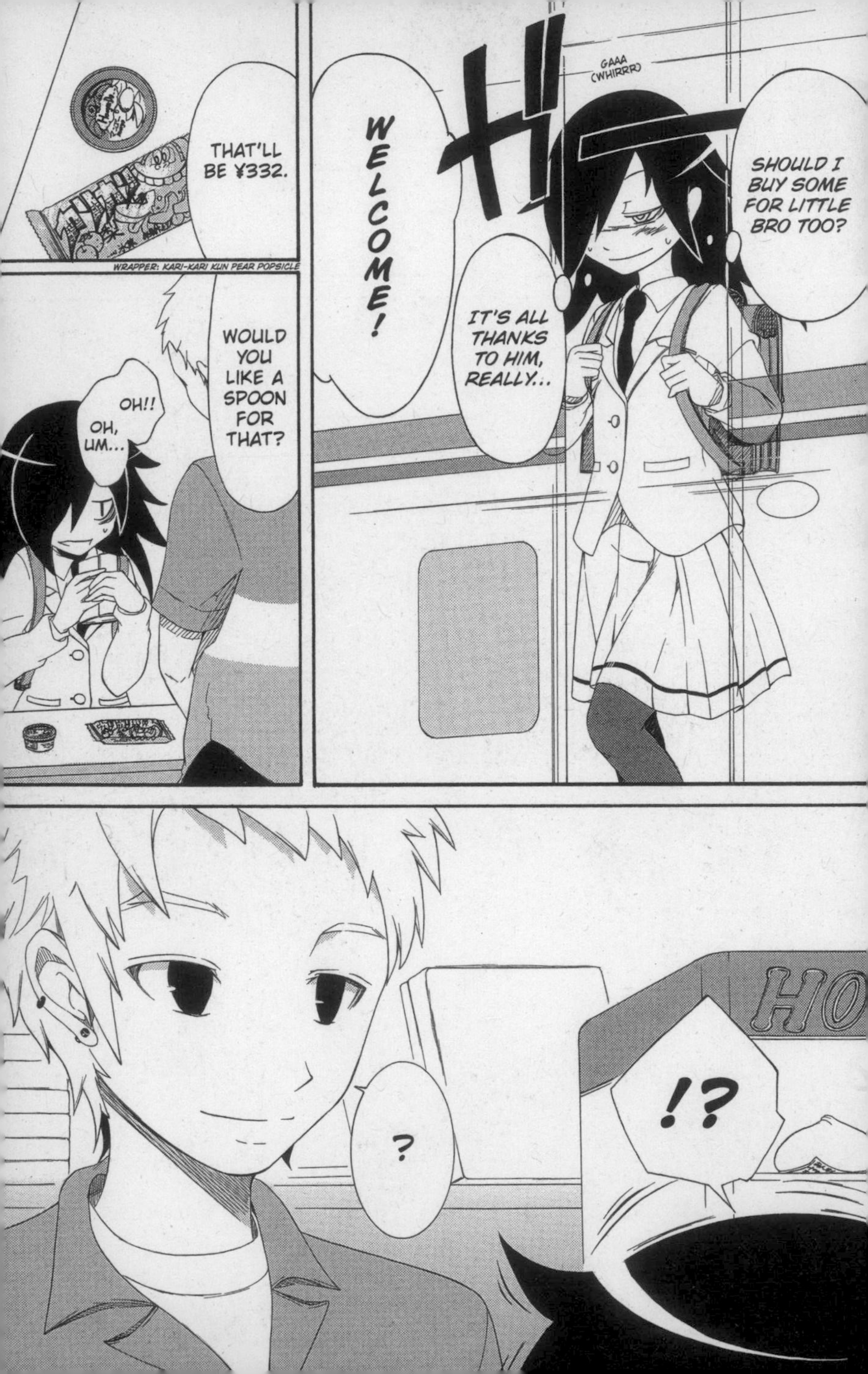
GAAA (WHIRRR)
SHOULD I BUY SOME FOR LITTLE BRO TOO?
IT'S ALL THANKS TO HIM, REALLY...
WELCOME!
THAT'LL BE ¥332.
WRAPPER: KARI-KARI KUN PEAR POPSICLE
WOULD YOU LIKE A SPOON FOR THAT?
OH!! OH, UM...
!?
?

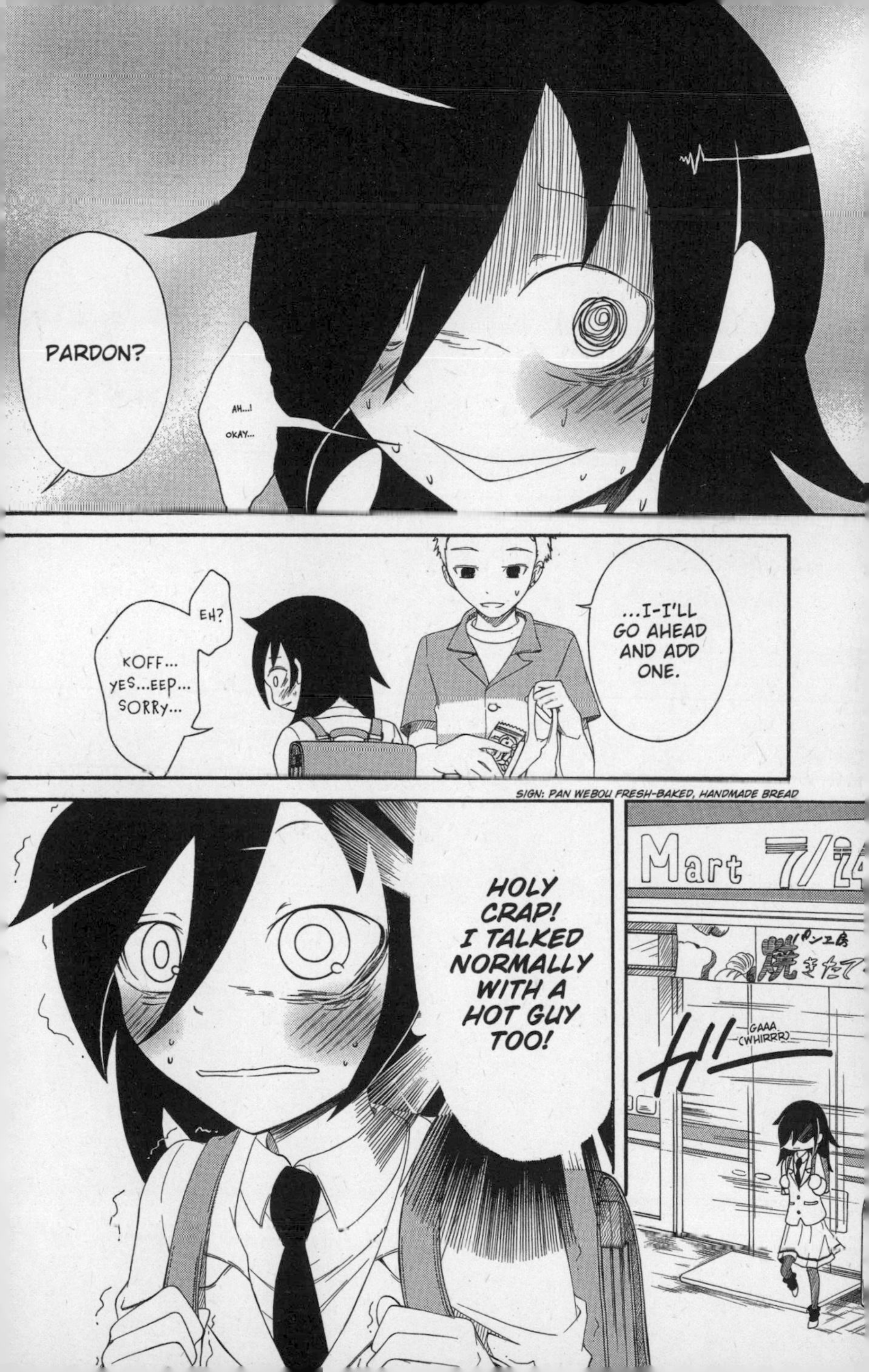
AH...!
OKAY...
PARDON?
...I-I'LL GO AHEAD AND ADD ONE.
EH?
KOFF... YES...EEP... SORRY...
SIGN: PAN WEBOU FRESH-BAKED, HANDMADE BREAD
Mart 7/24
パン工房
焼きたて
GAAA (WHIRRR)
HOLY CRAP! I TALKED NORMALLY WITH A HOT GUY TOO!

No Matter How I Look at It, It's You Guys' Fault I'm Not Popular!

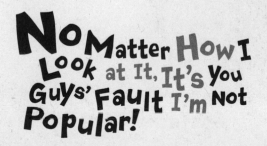

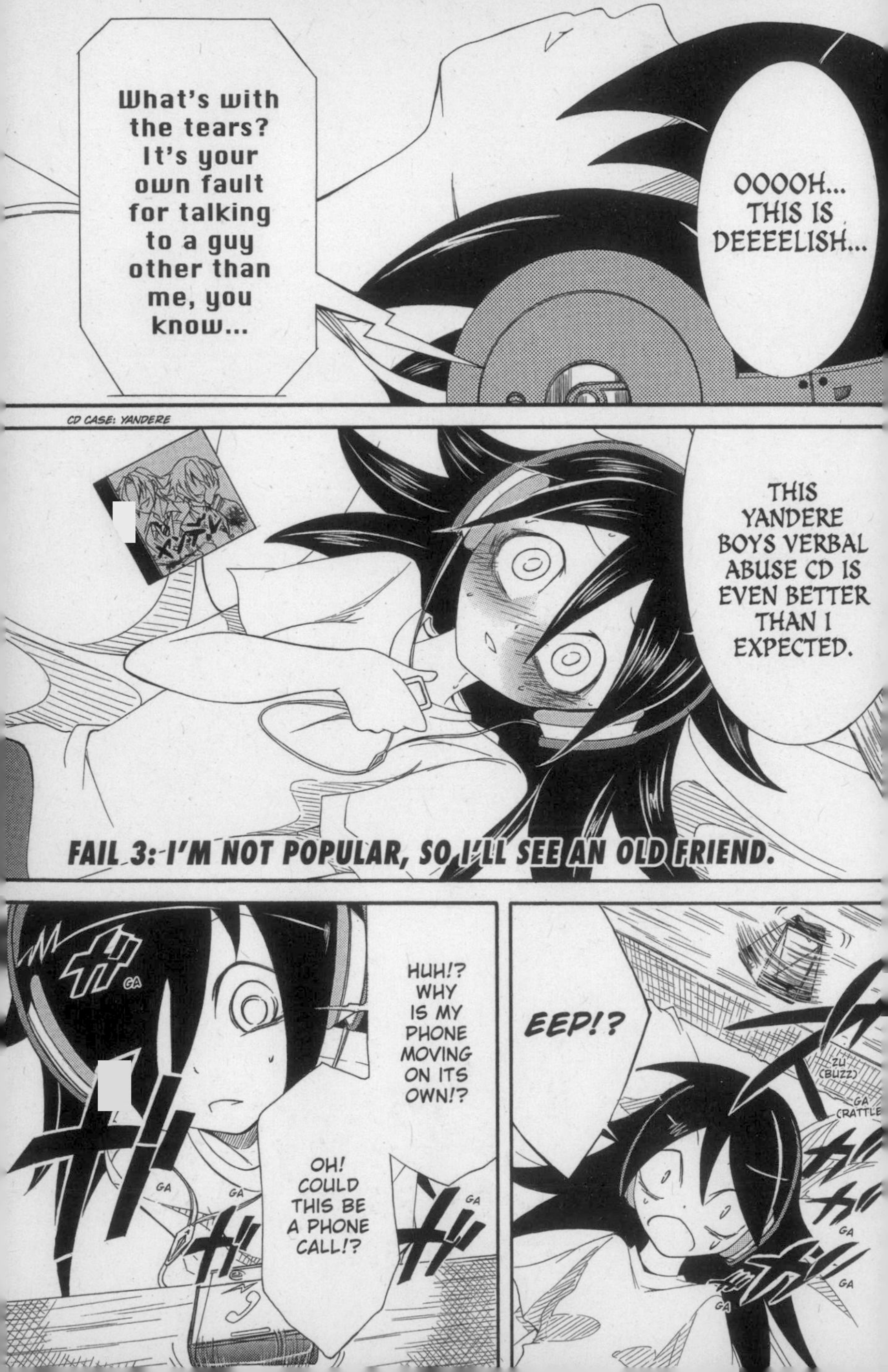

What's with the tears? It's your own fault for talking to a guy other than me, you know...
OOOOH... THIS IS DEEEELISH...
CD CASE: YANDERE
THIS YANDERE BOYS VERBAL ABUSE CD IS EVEN BETTER THAN I EXPECTED.
FAIL 3: I'M NOT POPULAR, SO I'LL SEE AN OLD FRIEND.
EEP!?
ZU (BUZZ)
GA (RATTLE)
GA
GA
GA
GA
HUH!? WHY IS MY PHONE MOVING ON ITS OWN!?
OH! COULD THIS BE A PHONE CALL!?
GA
GA
GA

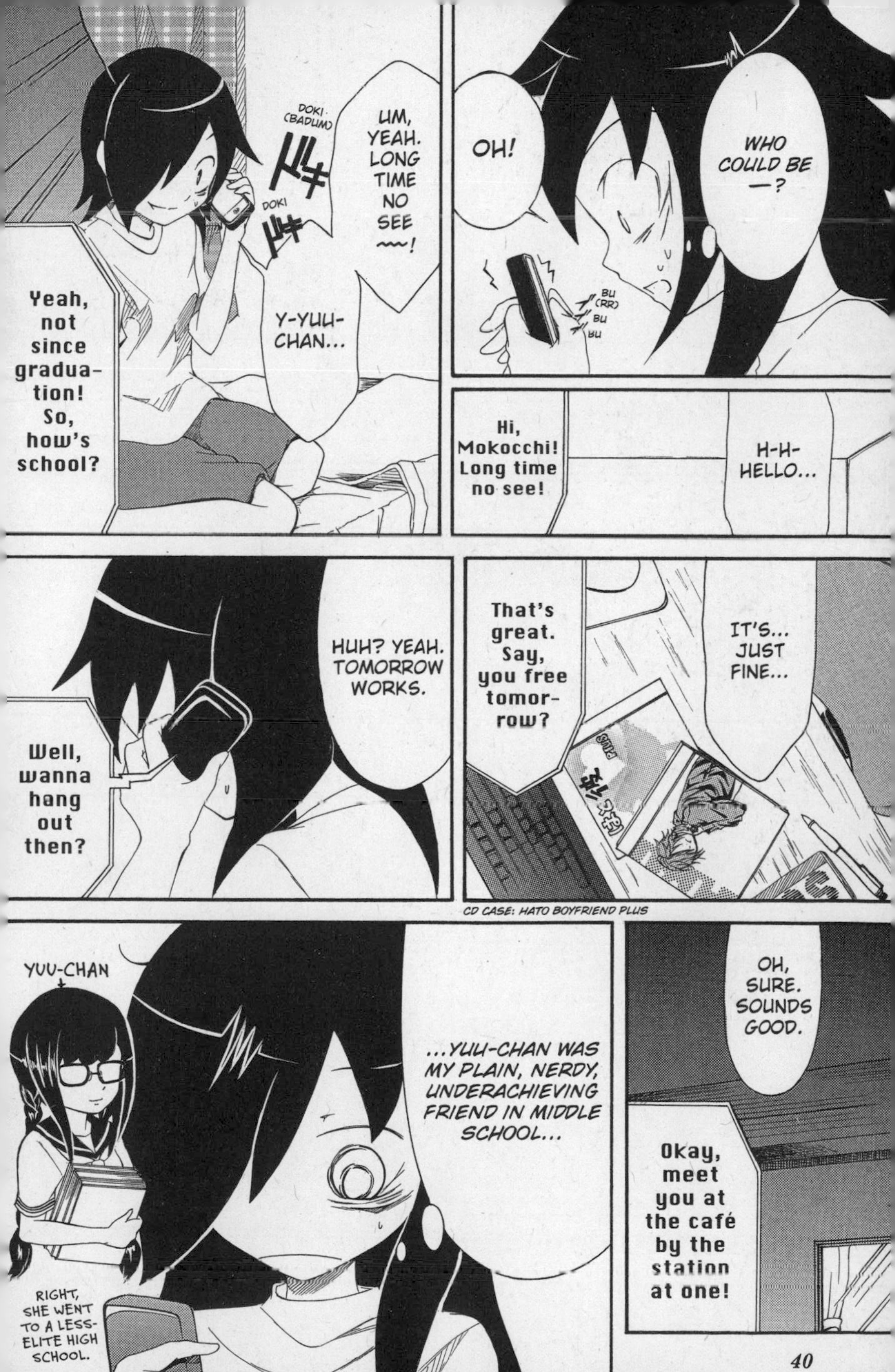

WHO COULD BE —?
OH!
BU (RR)
BU
BU
H-H-HELLO...
Hi, Mokocchi! Long time no see!
UM, YEAH. LONG TIME NO SEE~!
DOKI (BADUM)
DOKI
Y-YUU-CHAN...
Yeah, not since gradua-tion! So, how's school?
IT'S... JUST FINE...
That's great. Say, you free tomor-row?
CD CASE: HATO BOYFRIEND PLUS
HUH? YEAH. TOMORROW WORKS.
Well, wanna hang out then?
OH, SURE. SOUNDS GOOD.
Okay, meet you at the café by the station at one!
...YUU-CHAN WAS MY PLAIN, NERDY, UNDERACHIEVING FRIEND IN MIDDLE SCHOOL...
YUU-CHAN
RIGHT, SHE WENT TO A LESS-ELITE HIGH SCHOOL.

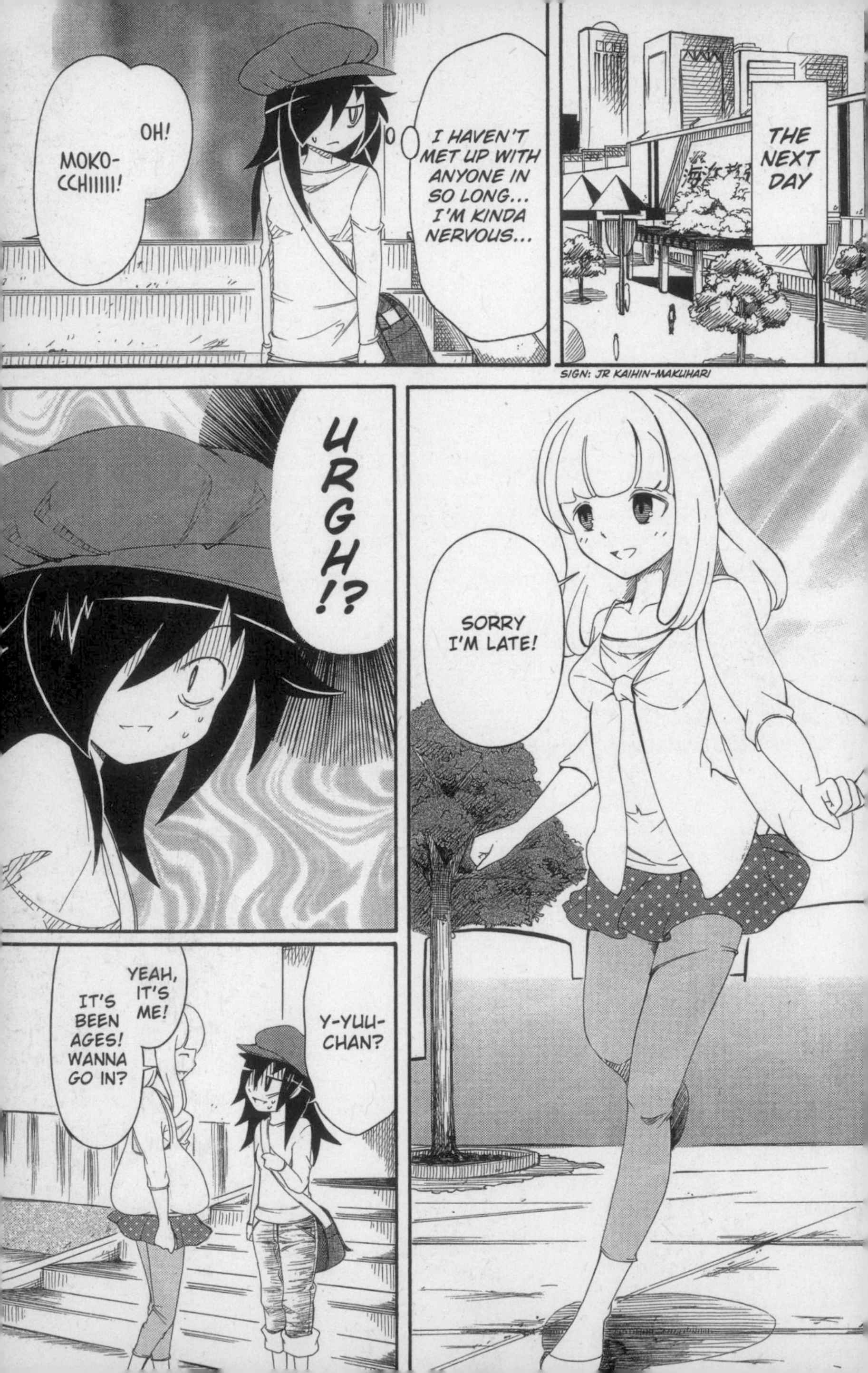
THE NEXT DAY
SIGN: JR KAIHIN-MAKUHARI
I HAVEN'T MET UP WITH ANYONE IN SO LONG... I'M KINDA NERVOUS...
OH! MOKO-CCHIIIIII!
SORRY I'M LATE!
URGH!?
Y-YUU-CHAN?
YEAH, IT'S ME! IT'S BEEN AGES! WANNA GO IN?

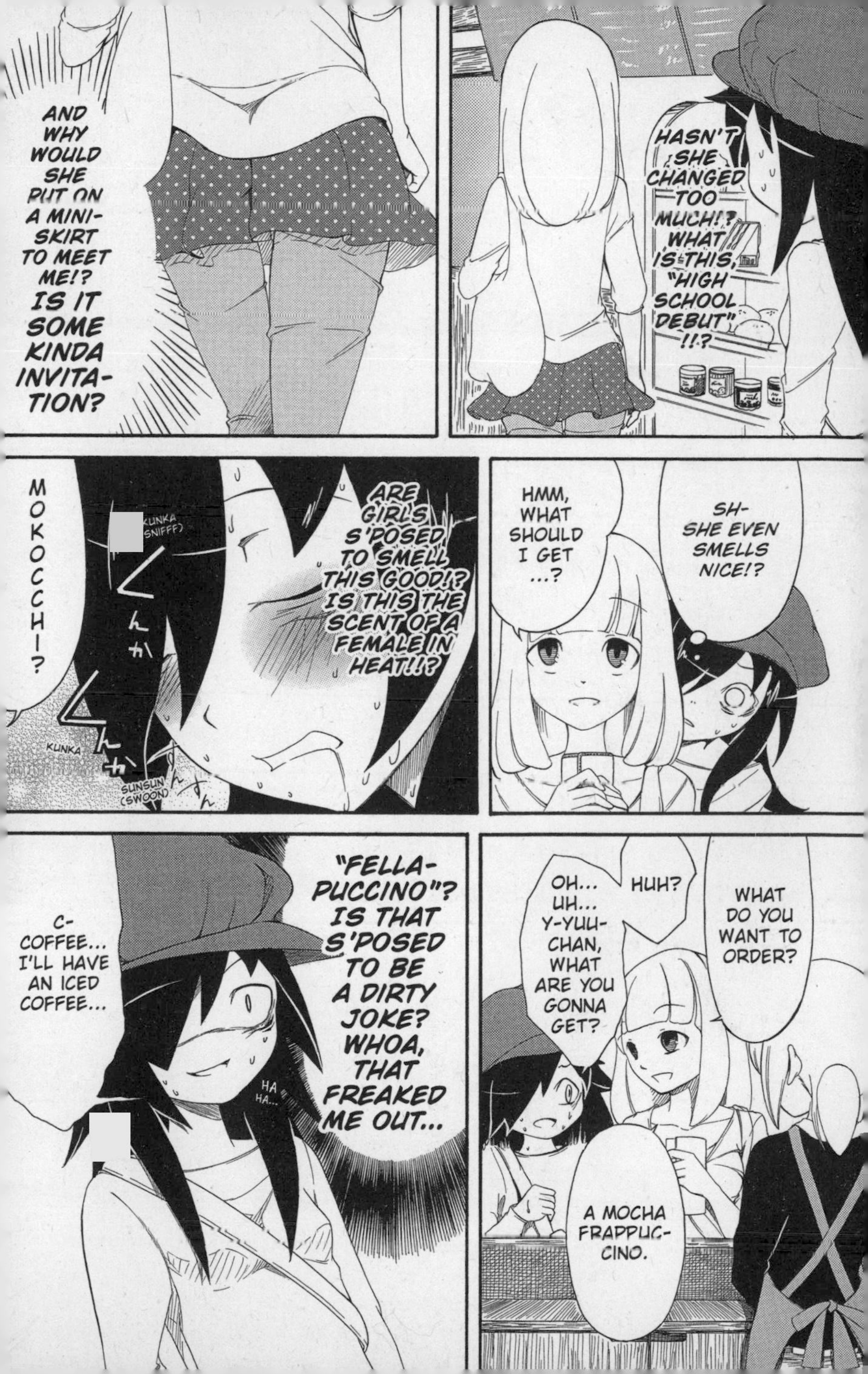
HASN'T SHE CHANGED TOO MUCH!? WHAT IS THIS, "HIGH SCHOOL DEBUT"!!?
AND WHY WOULD SHE PUT ON A MINI-SKIRT TO MEET ME!? IS IT SOME KINDA INVITATION?
SH- SHE EVEN SMELLS NICE!?
HMM, WHAT SHOULD I GET ...?
ARE GIRLS S'POSED TO SMELL THIS GOOD!? IS THIS THE SCENT OF A FEMALE IN HEAT!!?
KUNKA (SNIFFF)
MOKOCCHI-?
KUNKA
SUNSUN (SWOON)
WHAT DO YOU WANT TO ORDER?
HUH?
OH... UH... Y-YUU-CHAN, WHAT ARE YOU GONNA GET?
A MOCHA FRAPPUC-CINO.
"FELLA-PUCCINO"? IS THAT S'POSED TO BE A DIRTY JOKE? WHOA, THAT FREAKED ME OUT...
C-COFFEE... I'LL HAVE AN ICED COFFEE...
HA HA...

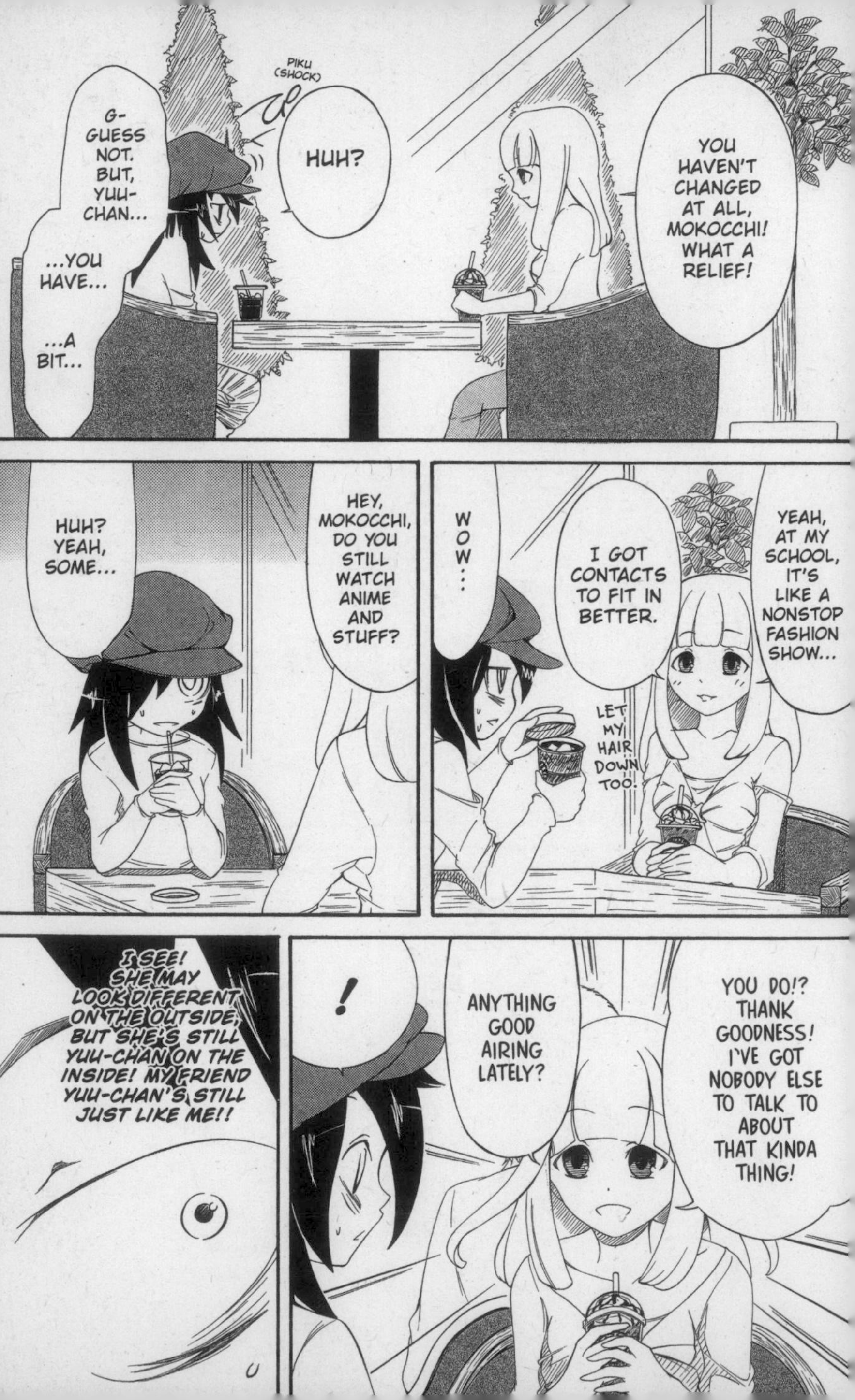
YOU HAVEN'T CHANGED AT ALL, MOKOCCHI! WHAT A RELIEF!
PIKU (SHOCK)
HUH?
G-GUESS NOT. BUT, YUU-CHAN...
...YOU HAVE...
...A BIT...
YEAH, AT MY SCHOOL, IT'S LIKE A NONSTOP FASHION SHOW...
I GOT CONTACTS TO FIT IN BETTER.
LET MY HAIR DOWN TOO.
WOW...
HEY, MOKOCCHI, DO YOU STILL WATCH ANIME AND STUFF?
HUH? YEAH, SOME...
YOU DO!? THANK GOODNESS! I'VE GOT NOBODY ELSE TO TALK TO ABOUT THAT KINDA THING!
ANYTHING GOOD AIRING LATELY?
!
I SEE! SHE MAY LOOK DIFFERENT ON THE OUTSIDE, BUT SHE'S STILL YUU-CHAN ON THE INSIDE! MY FRIEND YUU-CHAN'S STILL JUST LIKE ME!!

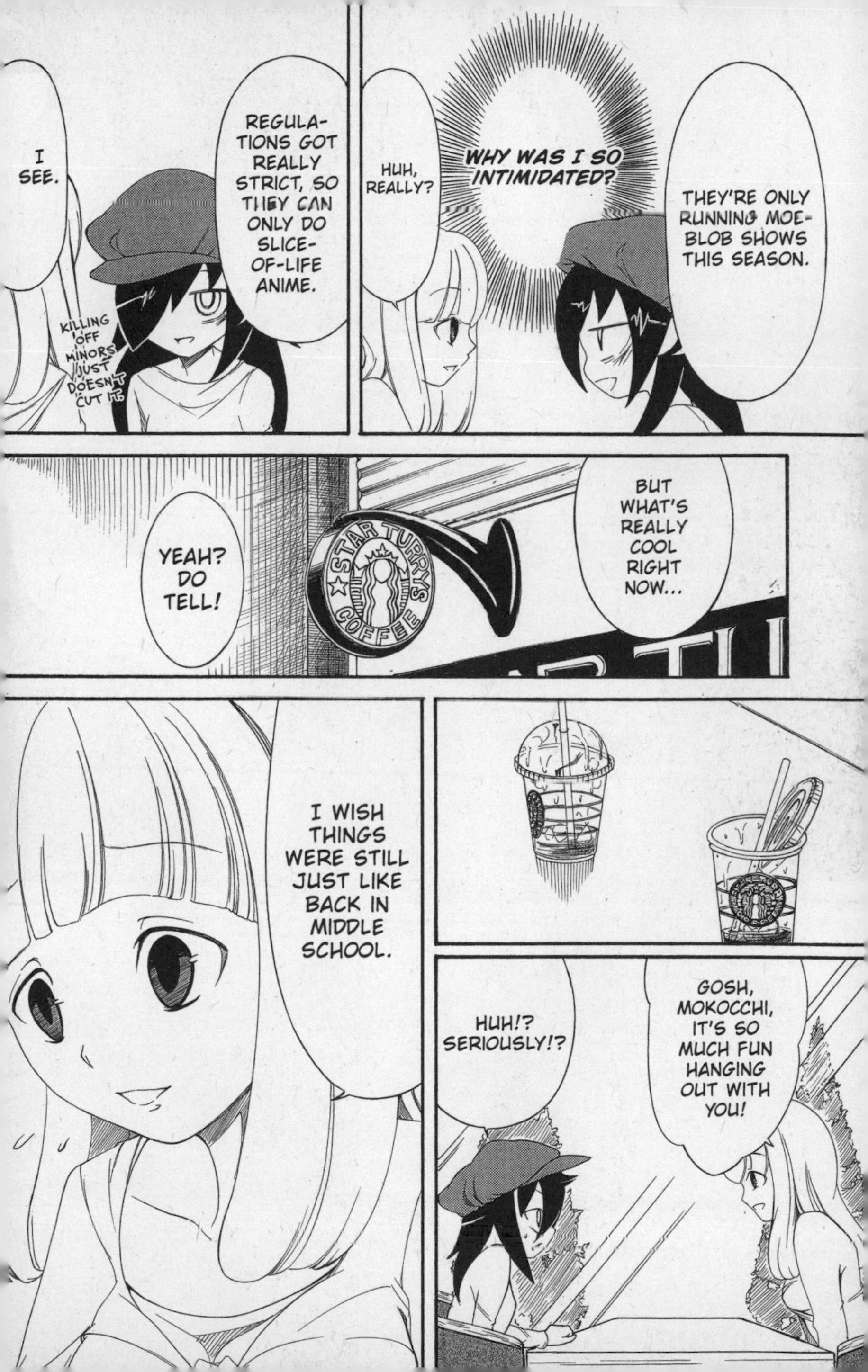
THEY'RE ONLY RUNNING MOE-BLOB SHOWS THIS SEASON.
WHY WAS I SO INTIMIDATED?
HUH, REALLY?
REGULATIONS GOT REALLY STRICT, SO THEY CAN ONLY DO SLICE-OF-LIFE ANIME.
I SEE.
KILLING OFF MINORS JUST DOESN'T CUT IT.
BUT WHAT'S REALLY COOL RIGHT NOW...
STAR TURRYS COFFEE
YEAH? DO TELL!
GOSH, MOKOCCHI, IT'S SO MUCH FUN HANGING OUT WITH YOU!
HUH!? SERIOUSLY!?
I WISH THINGS WERE STILL JUST LIKE BACK IN MIDDLE SCHOOL.

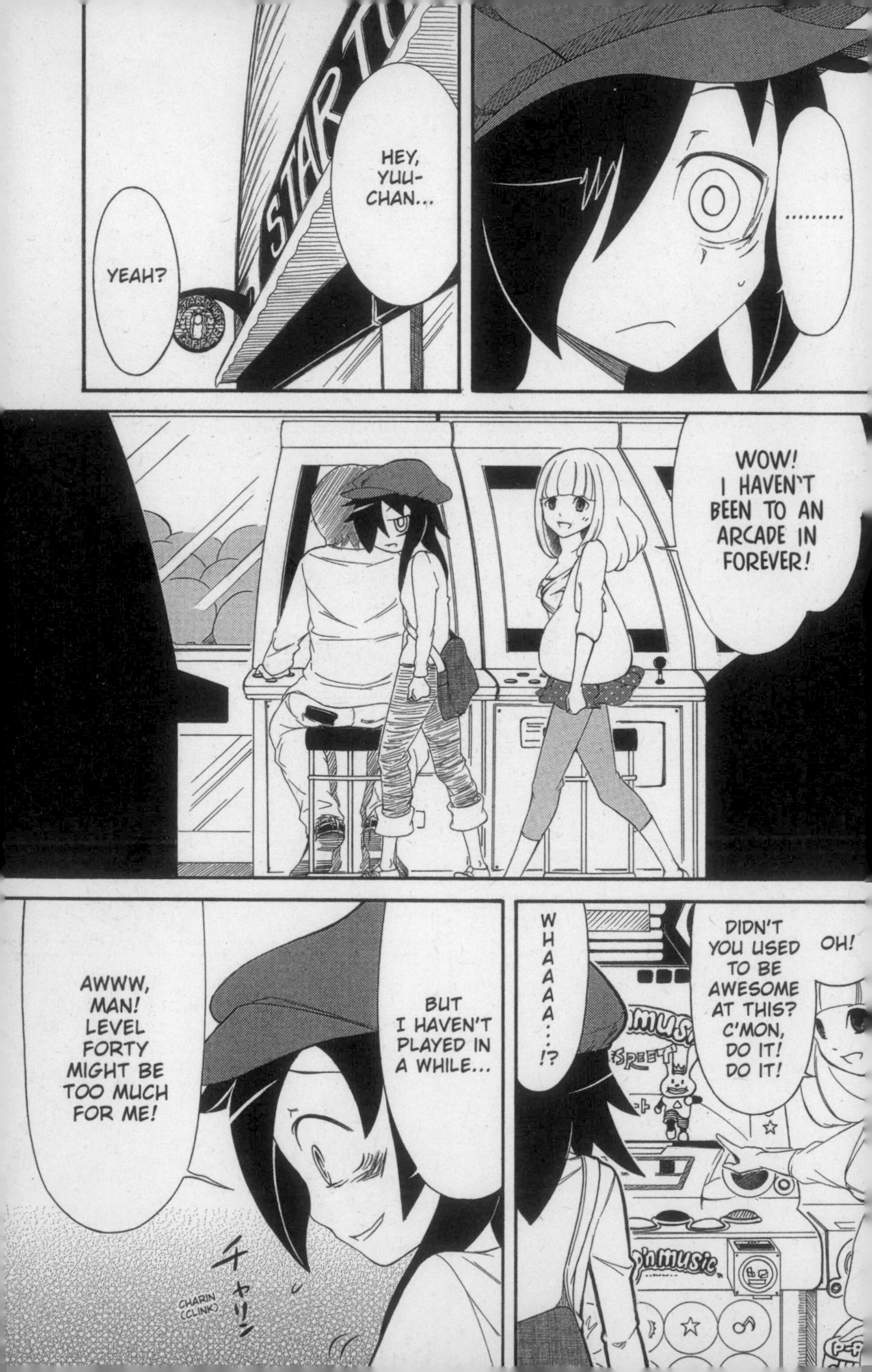
....
HEY, YUU-CHAN...
YEAH?
WOW! I HAVEN'T BEEN TO AN ARCADE IN FOREVER!
OH!
DIDN'T YOU USED TO BE AWESOME AT THIS? C'MON, DO IT! DO IT!
WHAAAAA...!?
pop'n music
BUT I HAVEN'T PLAYED IN A WHILE...
AWWW, MAN! LEVEL FORTY MIGHT BE TOO MUCH FOR ME!
チャリン
CHARIN (CLINK)

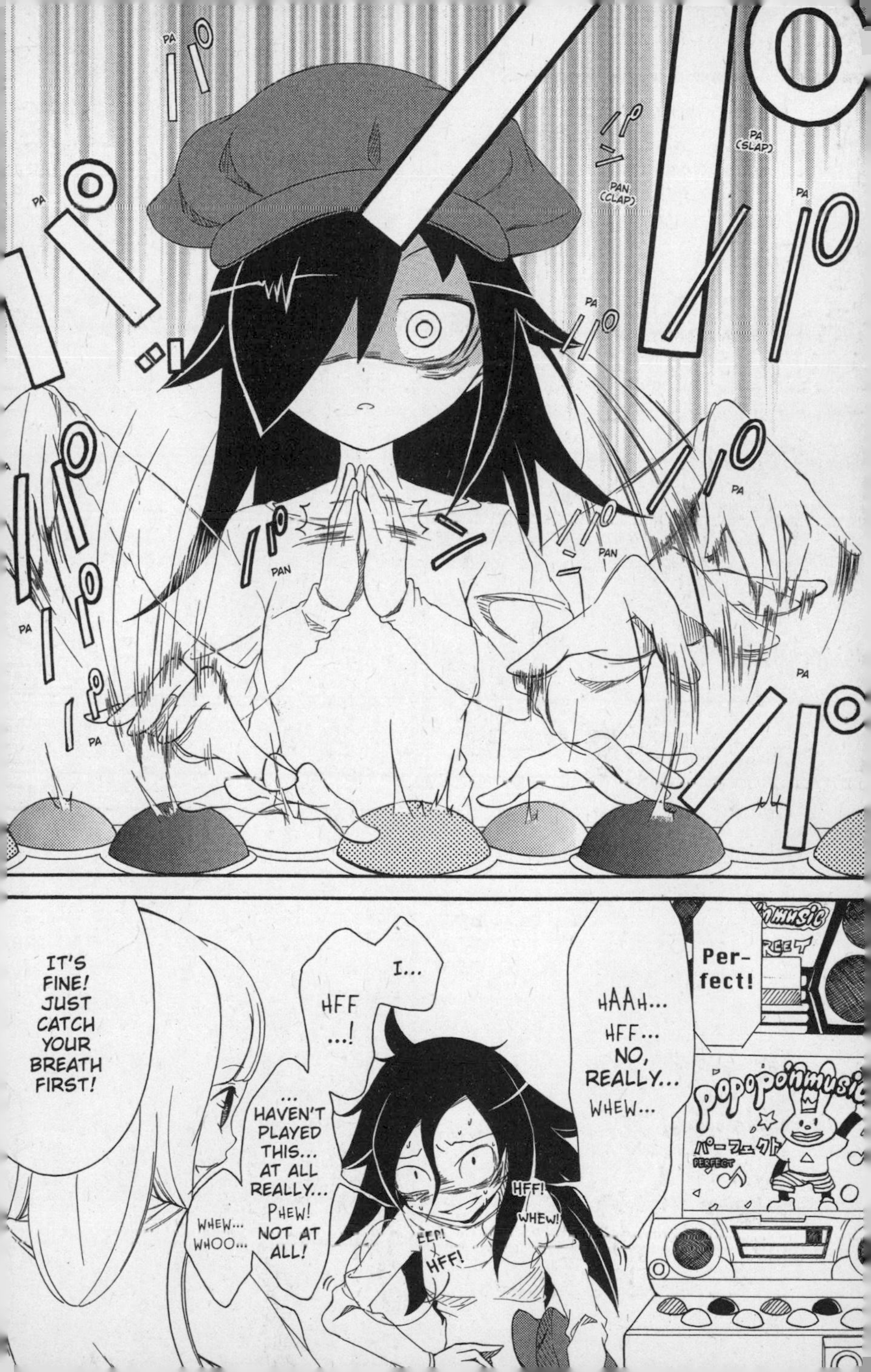
PA (SLAP)
PA
PAN (CLAP)
PA
PA
PA
PAN
PA
PAN
PA
PA
PA
Per-fect!
popopo'nmusic
パーフェクト
PERFECT
HAAH... HFF... NO, REALLY... WHEW...
I... HFF ...!
... HAVEN'T PLAYED THIS... AT ALL REALLY... PHEW! NOT AT ALL!
HFF!
WHEW!
EEP!
HFF!
WHEW... WHOO...
IT'S FINE! JUST CATCH YOUR BREATH FIRST!

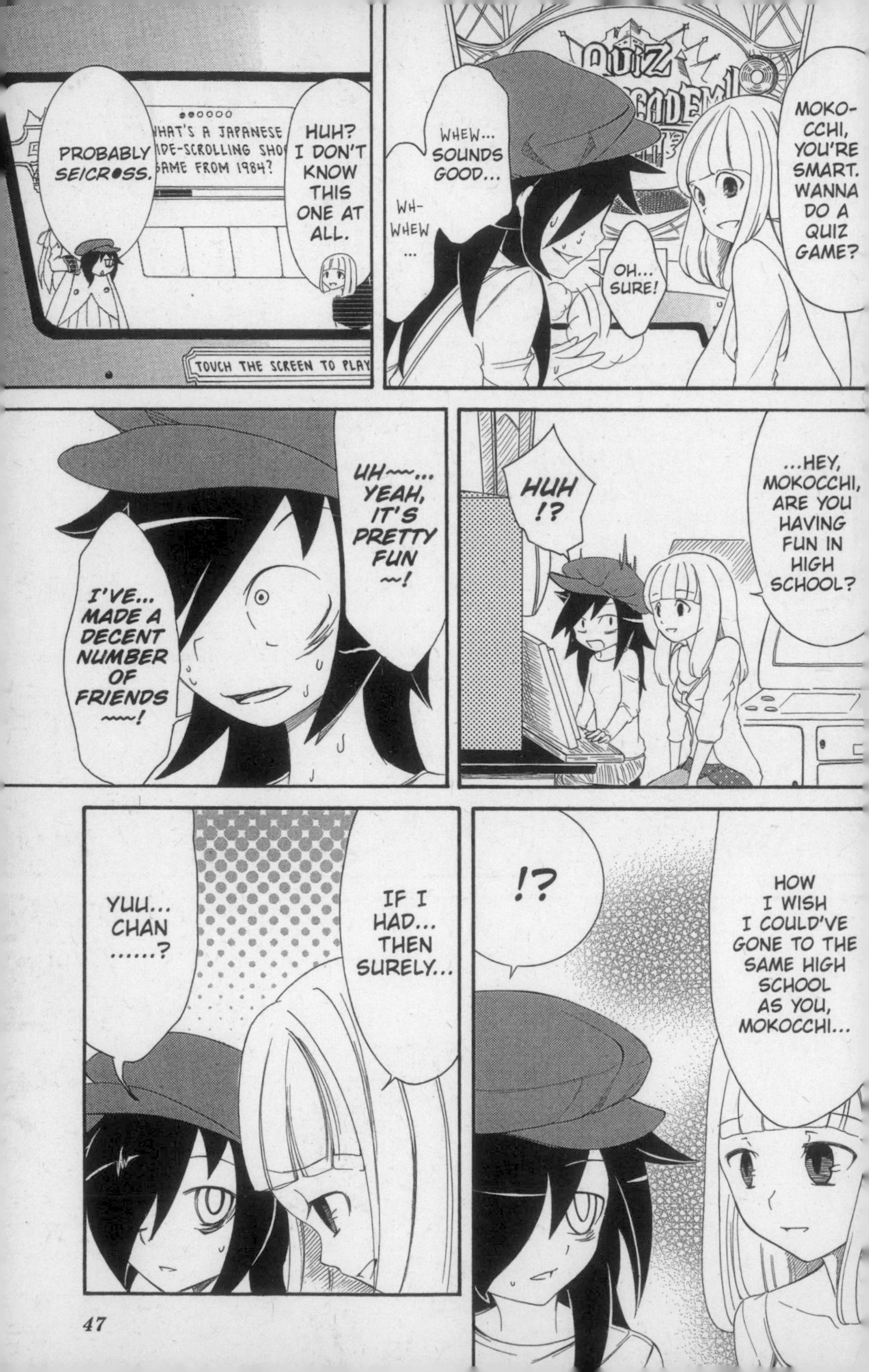
MOKOCCHI, YOU'RE SMART. WANNA DO A QUIZ GAME?
OH... SURE!
WHEW... SOUNDS GOOD...
WH-WHEW ...
HUH? I DON'T KNOW THIS ONE AT ALL.
WHAT'S A JAPANESE
IDE-SCROLLING SHO
GAME FROM 1984?
PROBABLY SEICROSS.
TOUCH THE SCREEN TO PLAY
...HEY, MOKOCCHI, ARE YOU HAVING FUN IN HIGH SCHOOL?
HUH !?
UH~~... YEAH, IT'S PRETTY FUN ~~!
I'VE... MADE A DECENT NUMBER OF FRIENDS ~~!
HOW I WISH I COULD'VE GONE TO THE SAME HIGH SCHOOL AS YOU, MOKOCCHI...
!?
IF I HAD... THEN SURELY...
YUU... CHAN ......?

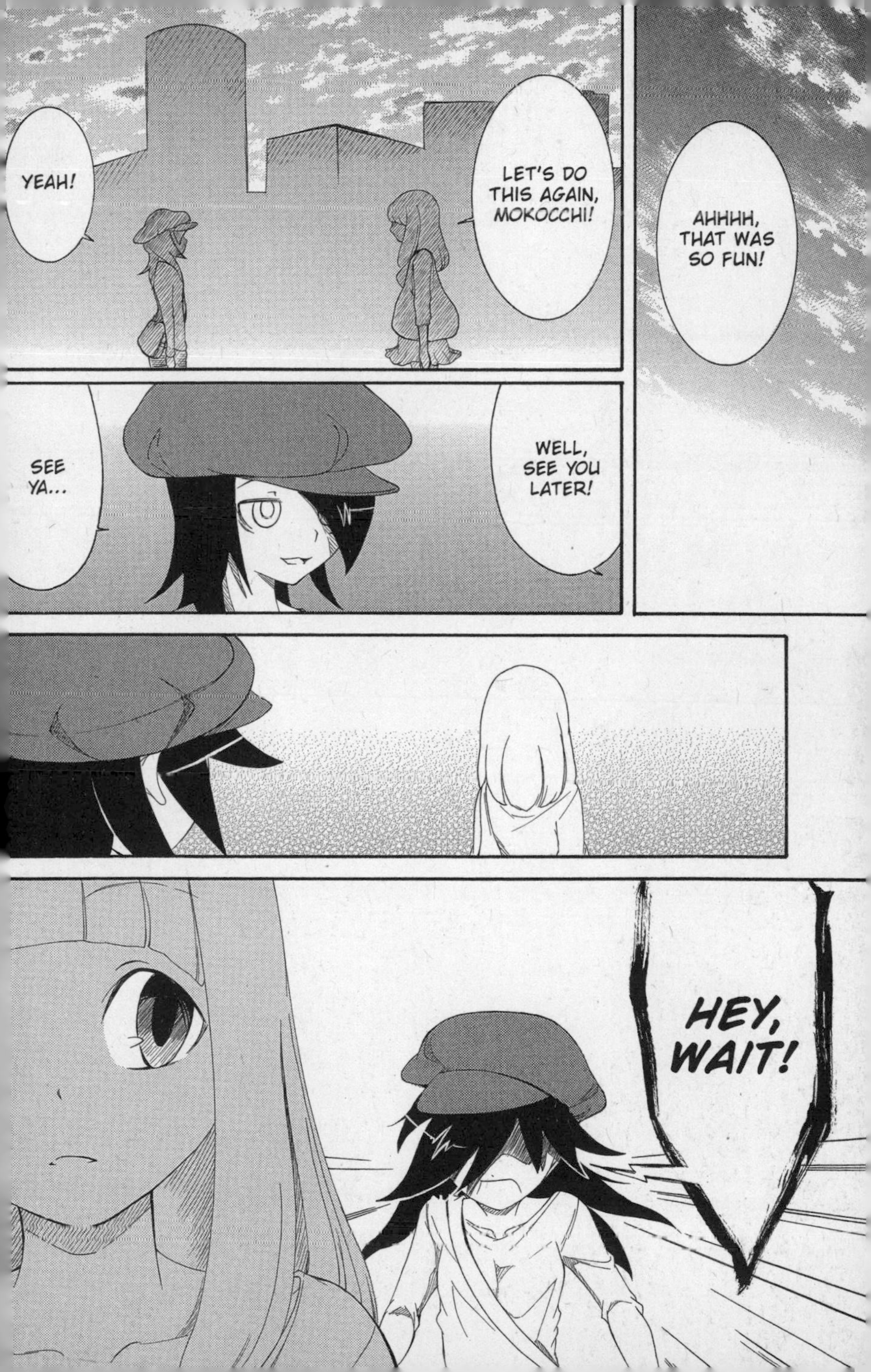
AHHHH, THAT WAS SO FUN!
LET'S DO THIS AGAIN, MOKOCCHI!
YEAH!
WELL, SEE YOU LATER!
SEE YA...
HEY, WAIT!

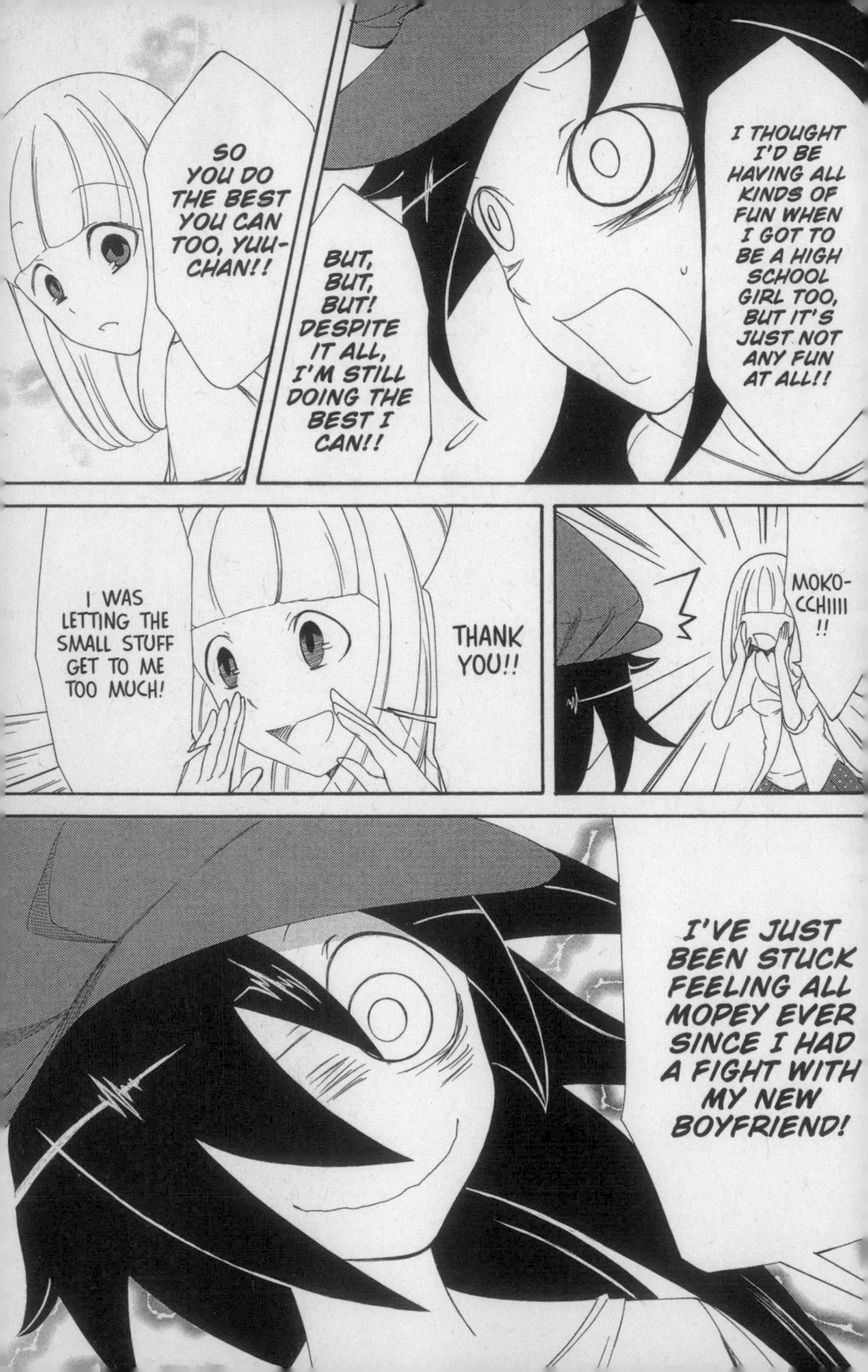
I THOUGHT I'D BE HAVING ALL KINDS OF FUN WHEN I GOT TO BE A HIGH SCHOOL GIRL TOO, BUT IT'S JUST NOT ANY FUN AT ALL!!
BUT, BUT, BUT! DESPITE IT ALL, I'M STILL DOING THE BEST I CAN!!
SO YOU DO THE BEST YOU CAN TOO, YUU-CHAN!!
MOKO-CCHIIII !!
THANK YOU!!
I WAS LETTING THE SMALL STUFF GET TO ME TOO MUCH!
I'VE JUST BEEN STUCK FEELING ALL MOPEY EVER SINCE I HAD A FIGHT WITH MY NEW BOYFRIEND!

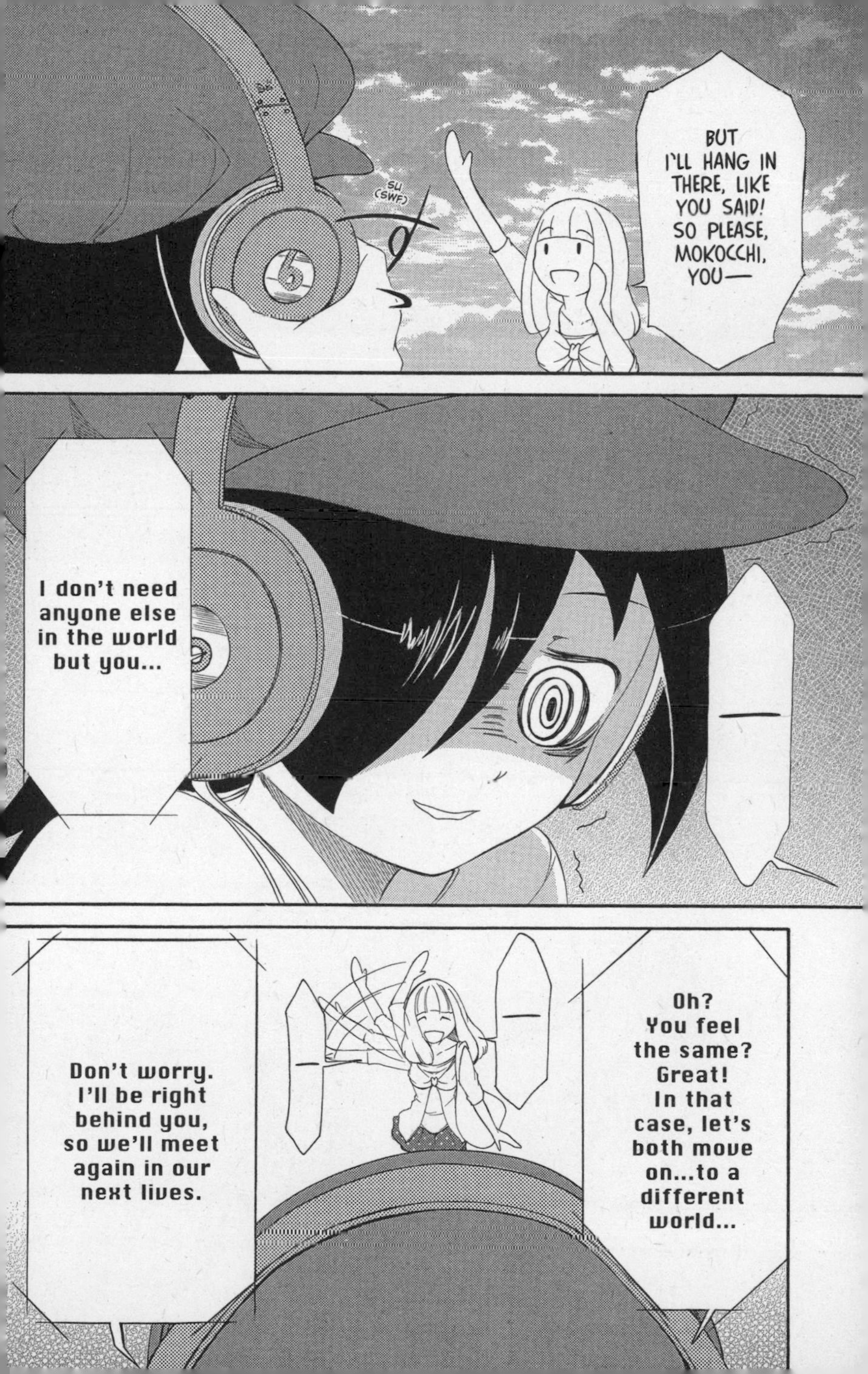
BUT I'LL HANG IN THERE, LIKE YOU SAID! SO PLEASE, MOKOCCHI, YOU—
SU (SWF)
—
I don't need anyone else in the world but you...
Oh? You feel the same? Great! In that case, let's both move on...to a different world...
—
—
Don't worry. I'll be right behind you, so we'll meet again in our next lives.

No Matter How I Look at It, It's You Guys' Fault I'm Not Popular!

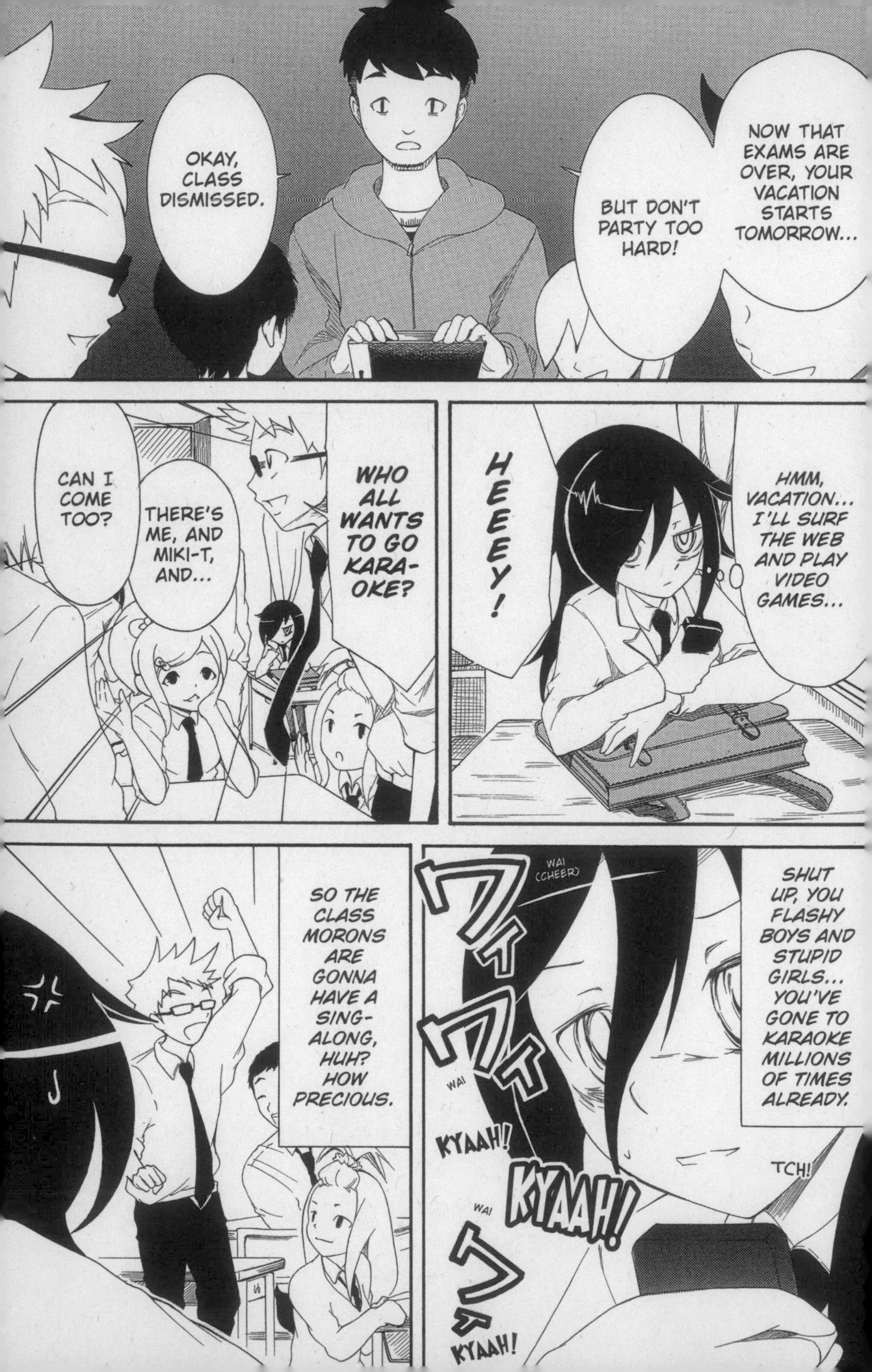
NOW THAT EXAMS ARE OVER, YOUR VACATION STARTS TOMORROW...
BUT DON'T PARTY TOO HARD!
OKAY, CLASS DISMISSED.
HMM, VACATION... I'LL SURF THE WEB AND PLAY VIDEO GAMES...
HEEEY!
WHO ALL WANTS TO GO KARAOKE?
THERE'S ME, AND MIKI-T, AND...
CAN I COME TOO?
SHUT UP, YOU FLASHY BOYS AND STUPID GIRLS... YOU'VE GONE TO KARAOKE MILLIONS OF TIMES ALREADY.
WAI (CHEER)
WAI
KYAAH!
KYAAH!
WAI
KYAAH!
TCH!
SO THE CLASS MORONS ARE GONNA HAVE A SING-ALONG, HUH? HOW PRECIOUS.

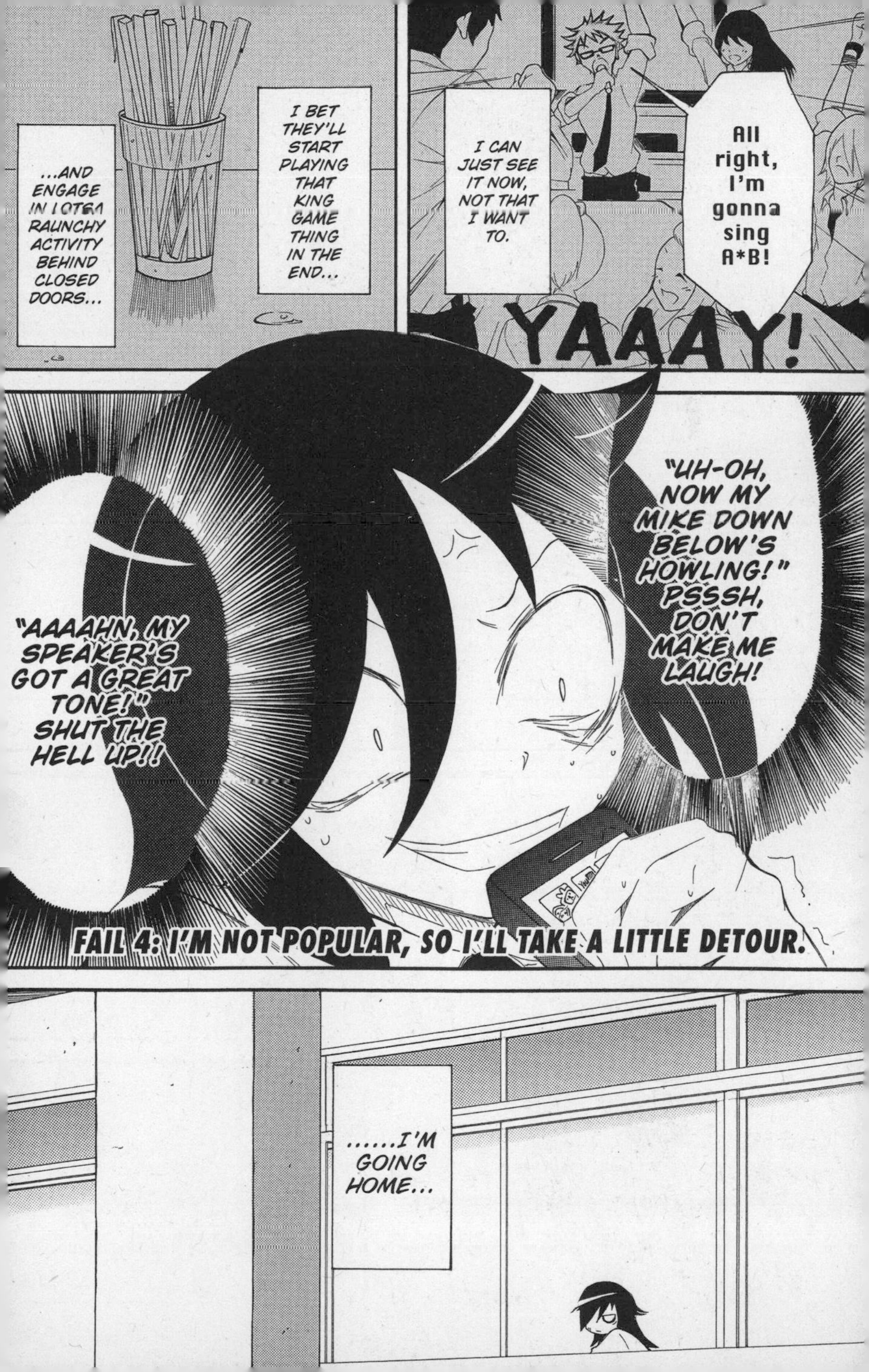
All right, I'm gonna sing A*B!
I CAN JUST SEE IT NOW, NOT THAT I WANT TO.
YAAAY!
I BET THEY'LL START PLAYING THAT KING GAME THING IN THE END...
...AND ENGAGE IN LOTSA RAUNCHY ACTIVITY BEHIND CLOSED DOORS...
"UH-OH, NOW MY MIKE DOWN BELOW'S HOWLING!" PSSSH, DON'T MAKE ME LAUGH!
"AAAAHN, MY SPEAKER'S GOT A GREAT TONE!" SHUT THE HELL UP!!
FAIL 4: I'M NOT POPULAR, SO I'LL TAKE A LITTLE DETOUR.
......I'M GOING HOME...

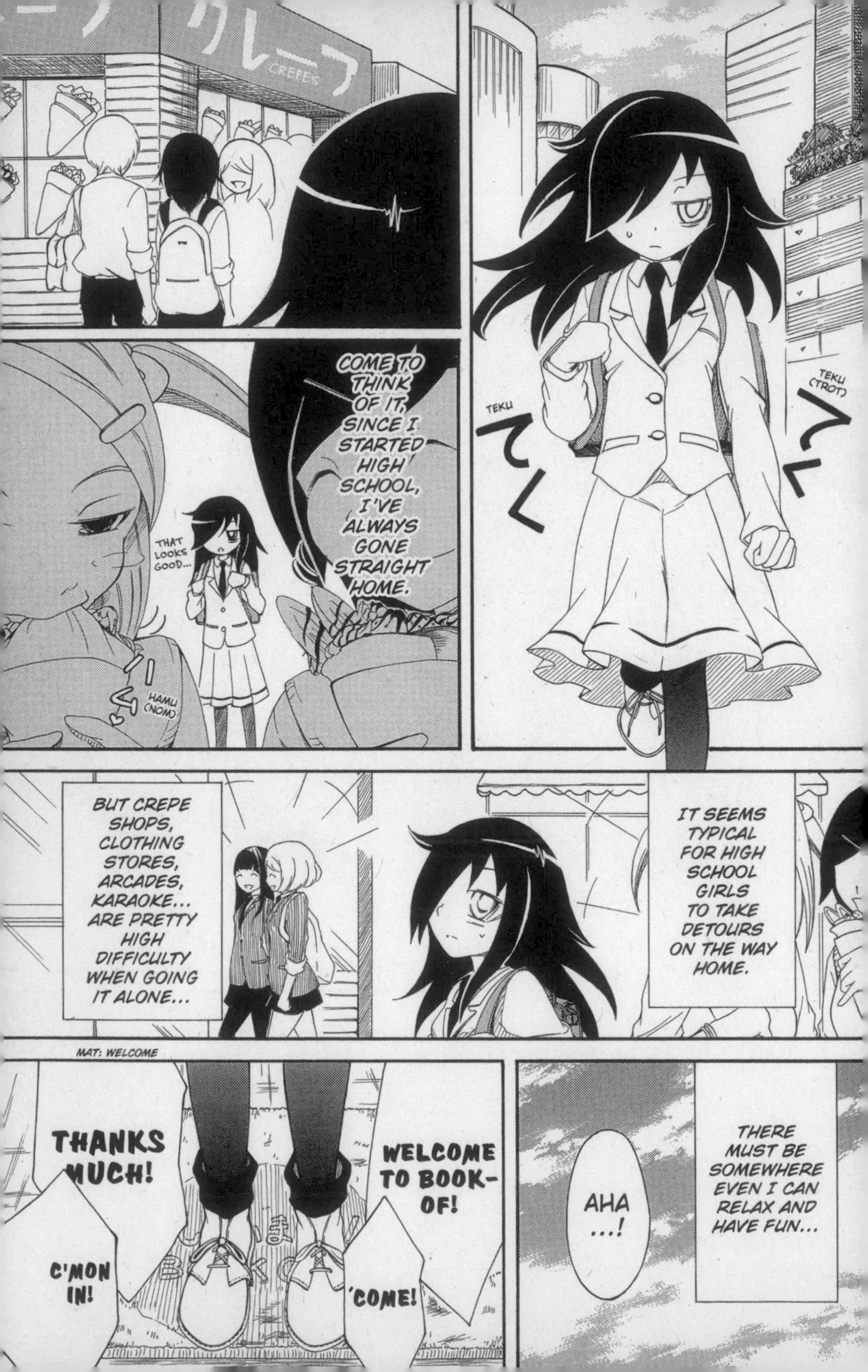
TEKU (TROT)
TEKU
CREPES
COME TO THINK OF IT, SINCE I STARTED HIGH SCHOOL, I'VE ALWAYS GONE STRAIGHT HOME.
THAT LOOKS GOOD...
HAMU (NOM)
IT SEEMS TYPICAL FOR HIGH SCHOOL GIRLS TO TAKE DETOURS ON THE WAY HOME.
BUT CREPE SHOPS, CLOTHING STORES, ARCADES, KARAOKE... ARE PRETTY HIGH DIFFICULTY WHEN GOING IT ALONE...
THERE MUST BE SOMEWHERE EVEN I CAN RELAX AND HAVE FUN...
AHA ...!
WELCOME TO BOOK-OF!
THANKS MUCH!
'COME!
C'MON IN!
MAT: WELCOME

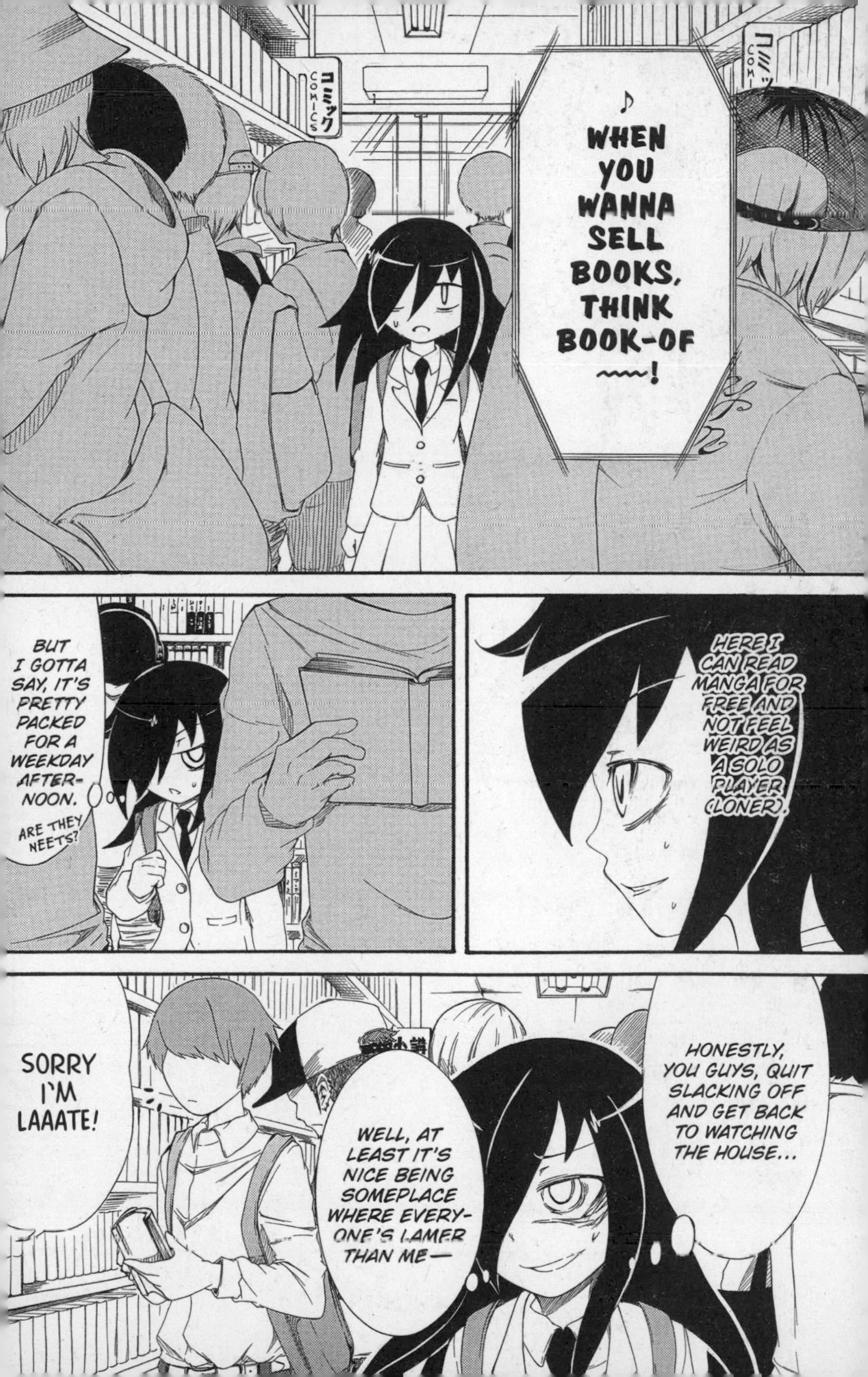
♪ WHEN YOU WANNA SELL BOOKS, THINK BOOK-OF ~~~!
HERE I CAN READ MANGA FOR FREE AND NOT FEEL WEIRD AS A SOLO PLAYER (LONER).
BUT I GOTTA SAY, IT'S PRETTY PACKED FOR A WEEKDAY AFTER-NOON.
ARE THEY NEETS?
HONESTLY, YOU GUYS, QUIT SLACKING OFF AND GET BACK TO WATCHING THE HOUSE...
WELL, AT LEAST IT'S NICE BEING SOMEPLACE WHERE EVERY-ONE'S LAMER THAN ME—
SORRY I'M LAAATE!

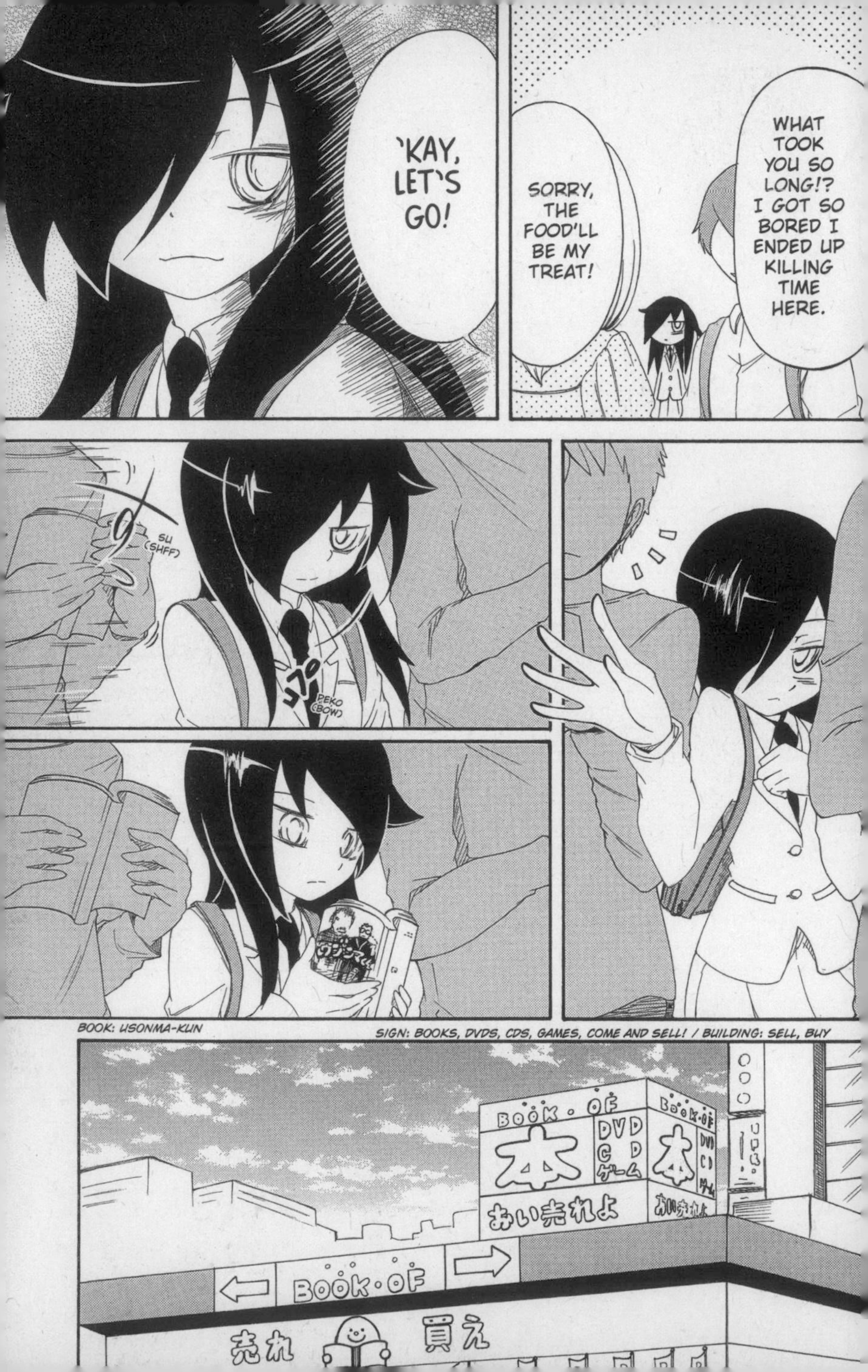
WHAT TOOK YOU SO LONG!? I GOT SO BORED I ENDED UP KILLING TIME HERE.
SORRY, THE FOOD'LL BE MY TREAT!
'KAY, LET'S GO!
SU (SHFF)
PEKO (BOW)
BOOK: USONMA-KUN
SIGN: BOOKS, DVDS, CDS, GAMES, COME AND SELL! / BUILDING: SELL, BUY
BOOK・OF
本
DVD CD ゲーム
おい売れよ
BOOK・OF
売れ
買え

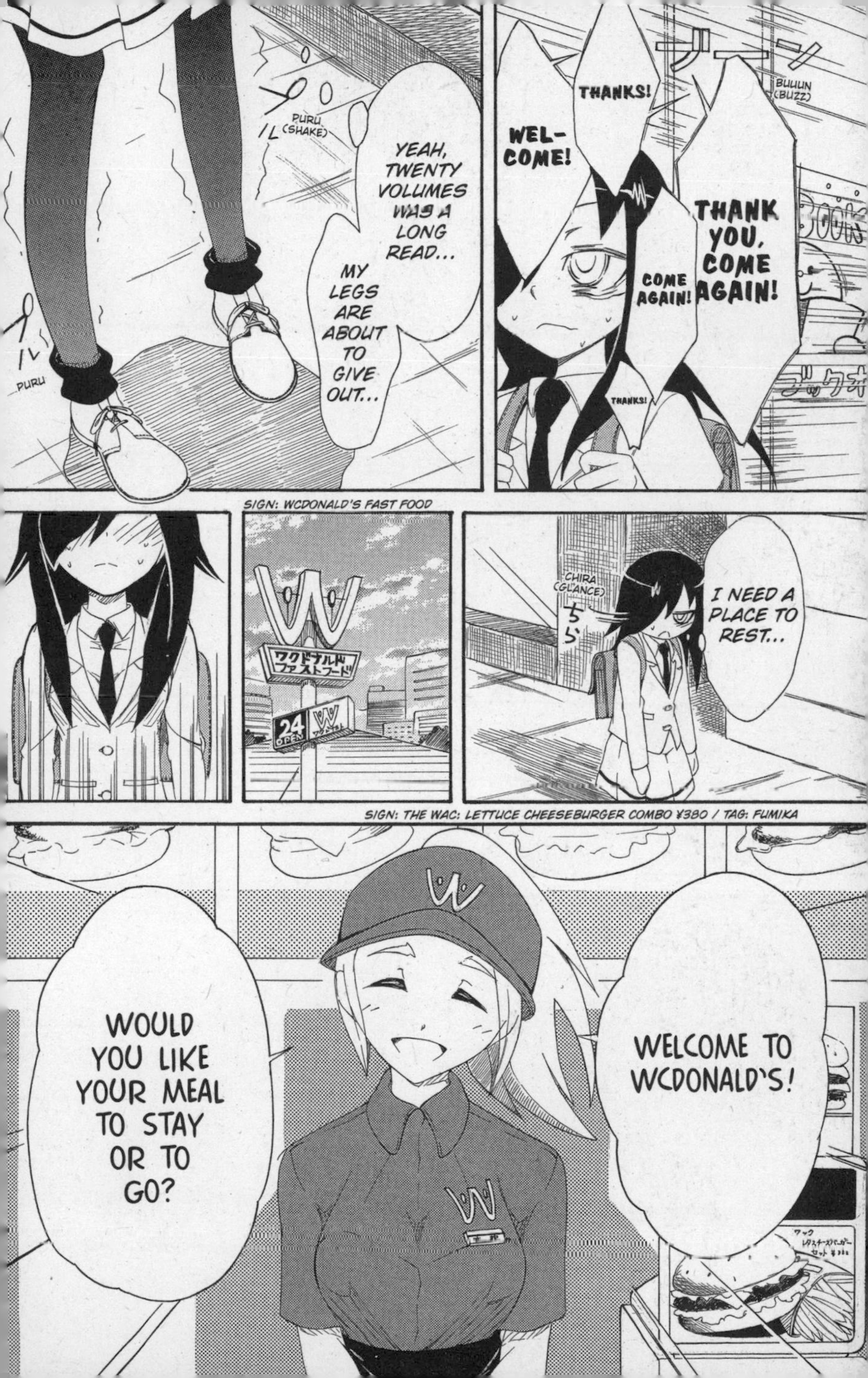
BUUUN (BUZZ)
THANKS!
WEL-COME!
THANK YOU, COME AGAIN!
COME AGAIN!
THANKS!
YEAH, TWENTY VOLUMES WAS A LONG READ...
MY LEGS ARE ABOUT TO GIVE OUT...
PURU (SHAKE)
...PURU
SIGN: WCDONALD'S FAST FOOD
CHIRA (GLANCE)
I NEED A PLACE TO REST...
ワクドナルド
ファストフード
24 OPEN
SIGN: THE WAC: LETTUCE CHEESEBURGER COMBO ¥380 / TAG: FUMIKA
WELCOME TO WCDONALD'S!
WOULD YOU LIKE YOUR MEAL TO STAY OR TO GO?

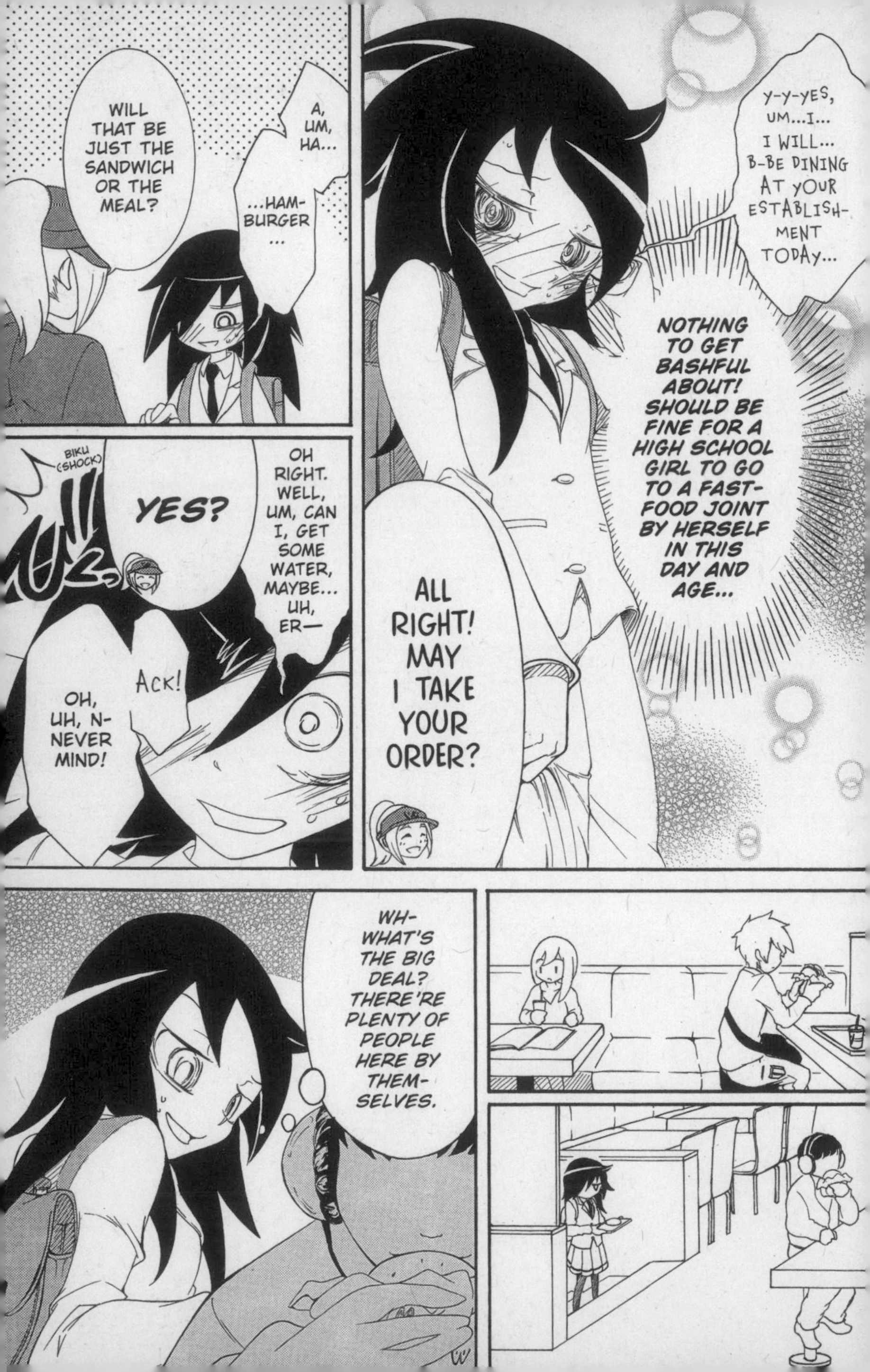
Y-Y-YES, UM...I... I WILL... B-BE DINING AT YOUR ESTABLISH-MENT TODAY...
NOTHING TO GET BASHFUL ABOUT! SHOULD BE FINE FOR A HIGH SCHOOL GIRL TO GO TO A FAST-FOOD JOINT BY HERSELF IN THIS DAY AND AGE...
ALL RIGHT! MAY I TAKE YOUR ORDER?
A, UM, HA...
...HAM-BURGER...
WILL THAT BE JUST THE SANDWICH OR THE MEAL?
OH RIGHT. WELL, UM, CAN I, GET SOME WATER, MAYBE... UH, ER—
YES?
BIKU (SHOCK)
ACK!
OH, UH, N-NEVER MIND!
WH-WHAT'S THE BIG DEAL? THERE'RE PLENTY OF PEOPLE HERE BY THEM-SELVES.

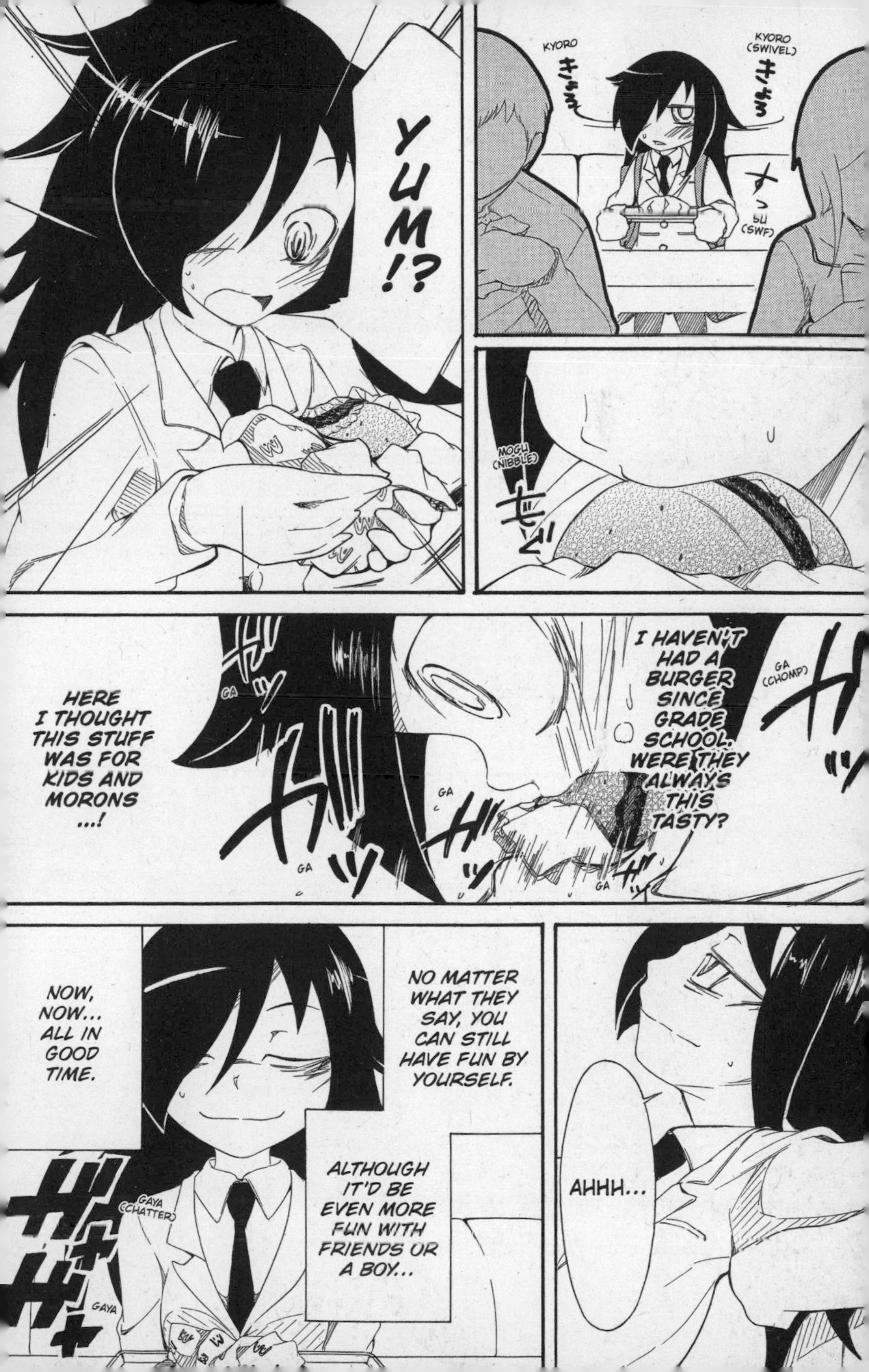
KYORO (SWIVEL)
きょろ
KYORO
きょろ
すっ
SU (SWF)
MOGU (NIBBLE)
もぐ
YUM!?
GA (CHOMP)
I HAVEN'T HAD A BURGER SINCE GRADE SCHOOL. WERE THEY ALWAYS THIS TASTY?
GA
HERE I THOUGHT THIS STUFF WAS FOR KIDS AND MORONS ...!
GA
GA
GA
AHHH...
NO MATTER WHAT THEY SAY, YOU CAN STILL HAVE FUN BY YOURSELF.
NOW, NOW... ALL IN GOOD TIME.
ALTHOUGH IT'D BE EVEN MORE FUN WITH FRIENDS OR A BOY...
GAYA (CHATTER)
GAYA

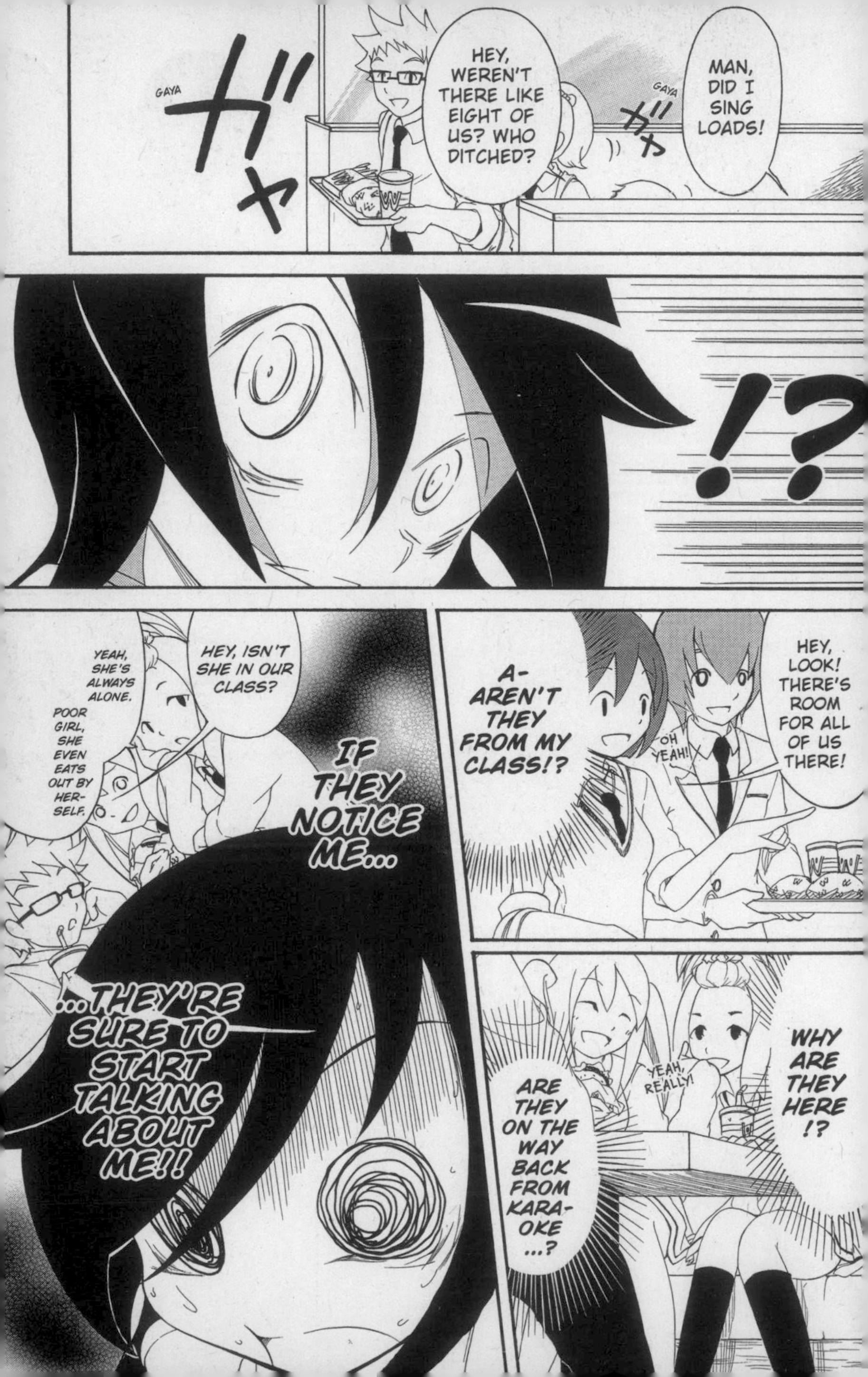
GAYA
MAN, DID I SING LOADS!
HEY, WEREN'T THERE LIKE EIGHT OF US? WHO DITCHED?
GAYA
!?
HEY, LOOK! THERE'S ROOM FOR ALL OF US THERE!
OH YEAH!
A-AREN'T THEY FROM MY CLASS!?
WHY ARE THEY HERE!?
YEAH, REALLY!
ARE THEY ON THE WAY BACK FROM KARAOKE...?
HEY, ISN'T SHE IN OUR CLASS?
YEAH, SHE'S ALWAYS ALONE.
POOR GIRL, SHE EVEN EATS OUT BY HER-SELF.
IF THEY NOTICE ME...
...THEY'RE SURE TO START TALKING ABOUT ME!!

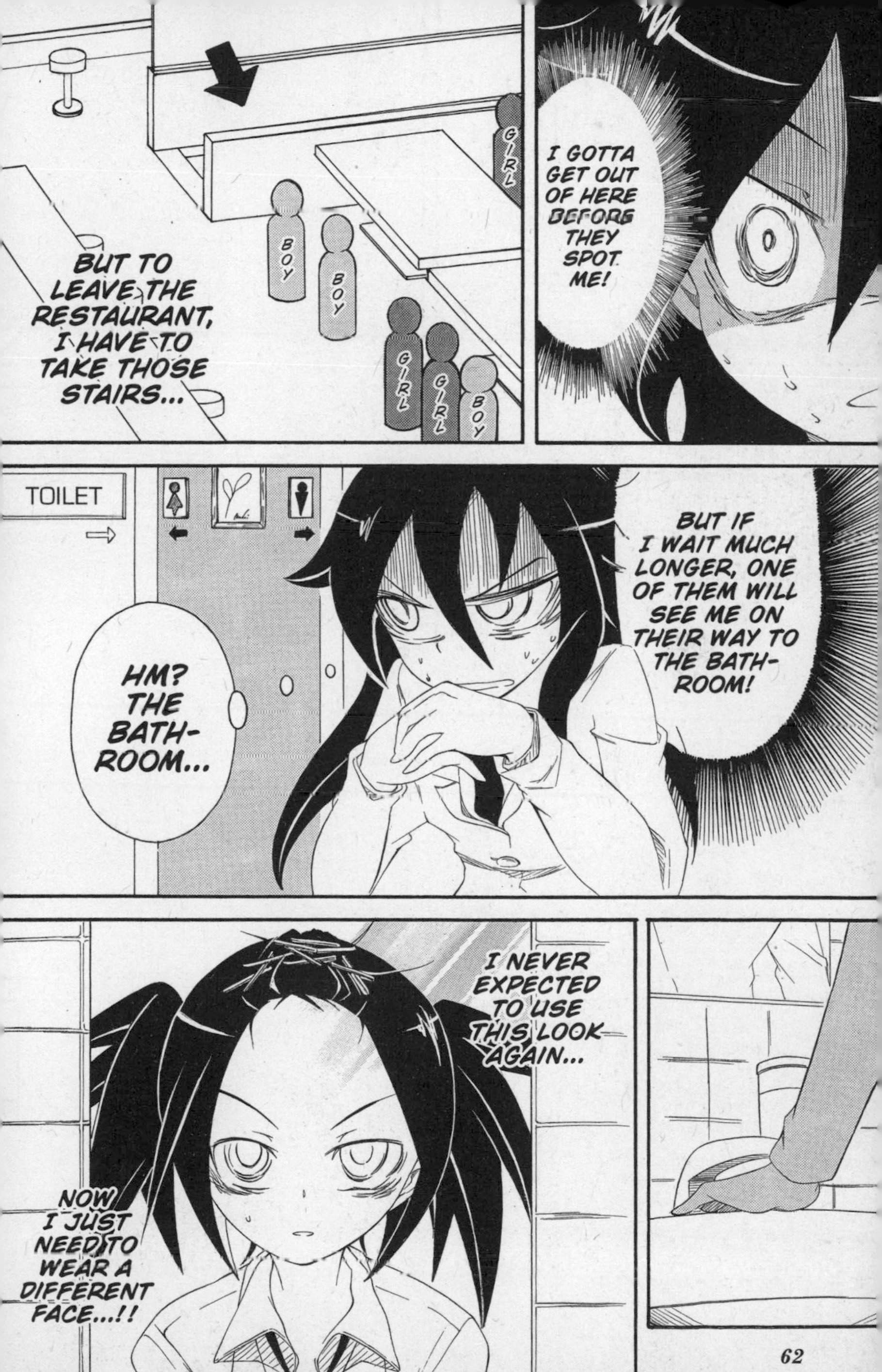
I GOTTA GET OUT OF HERE BEFORE THEY SPOT ME!
GIRL
BOY
BOY
GIRL
GIRL
BOY
BUT TO LEAVE THE RESTAURANT, I HAVE TO TAKE THOSE STAIRS...
BUT IF I WAIT MUCH LONGER, ONE OF THEM WILL SEE ME ON THEIR WAY TO THE BATH-ROOM!
TOILET
HM? THE BATH-ROOM...
I NEVER EXPECTED TO USE THIS LOOK AGAIN...
NOW I JUST NEED TO WEAR A DIFFERENT FACE...!!

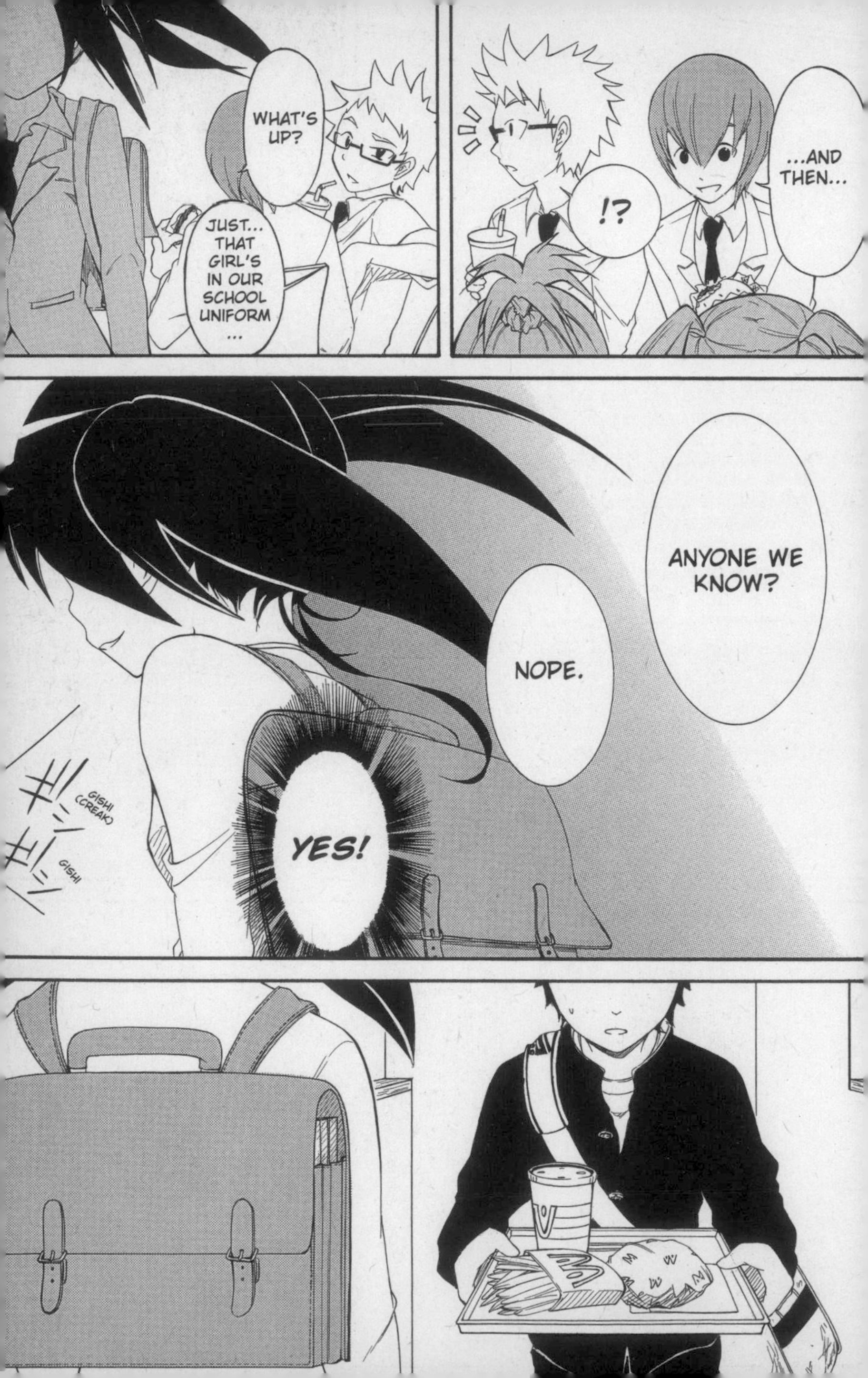
...AND THEN...
!?
WHAT'S UP?
JUST... THAT GIRL'S IN OUR SCHOOL UNIFORM ...
ANYONE WE KNOW?
NOPE.
YES!
GISHI (CREAK)
GISHI

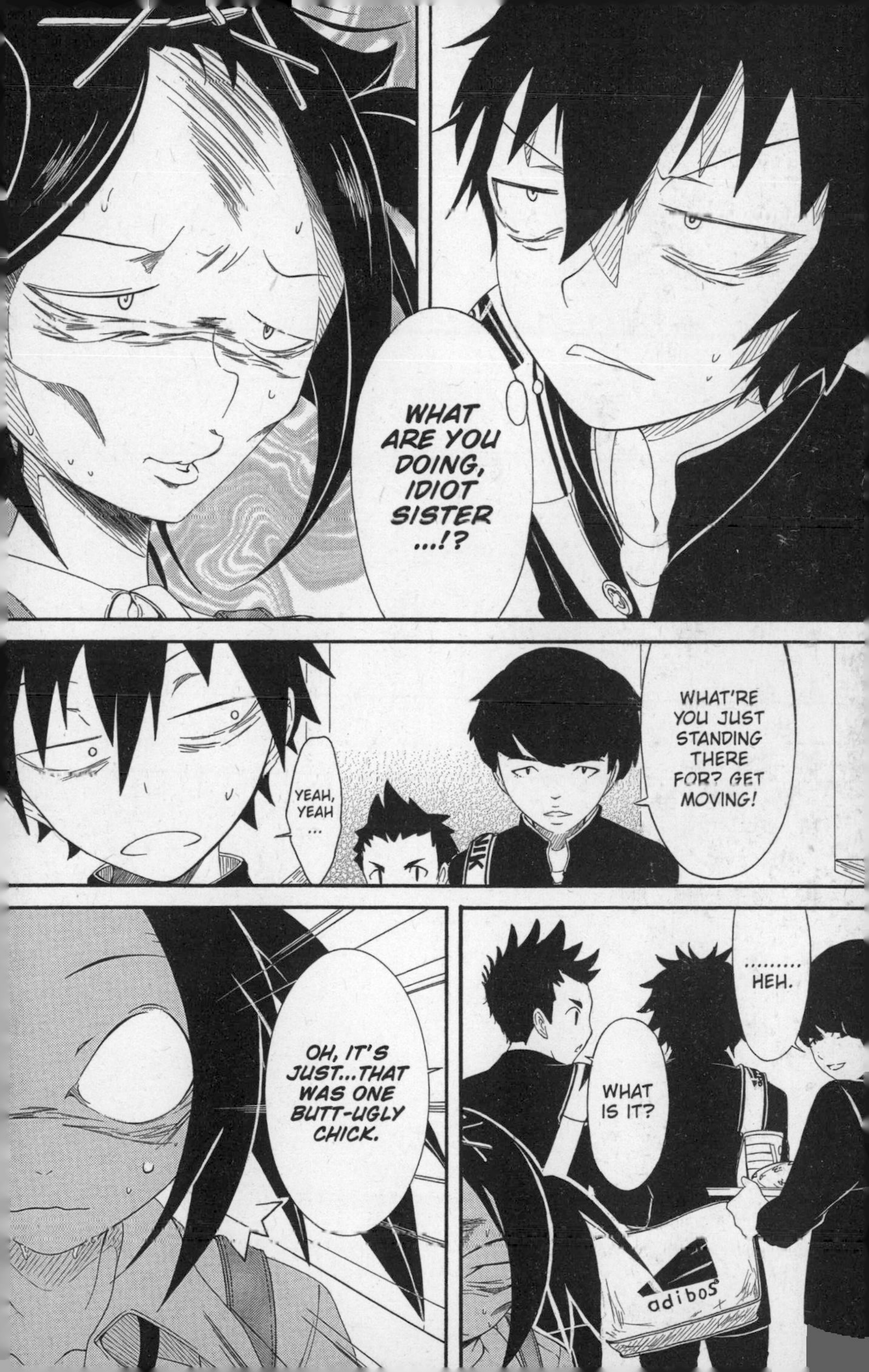
WHAT ARE YOU DOING, IDIOT SISTER ...!?
WHAT'RE YOU JUST STANDING THERE FOR? GET MOVING!
YEAH, YEAH ...
.... HEH.
WHAT IS IT?
OH, IT'S JUST...THAT WAS ONE BUTT-UGLY CHICK.
adibos

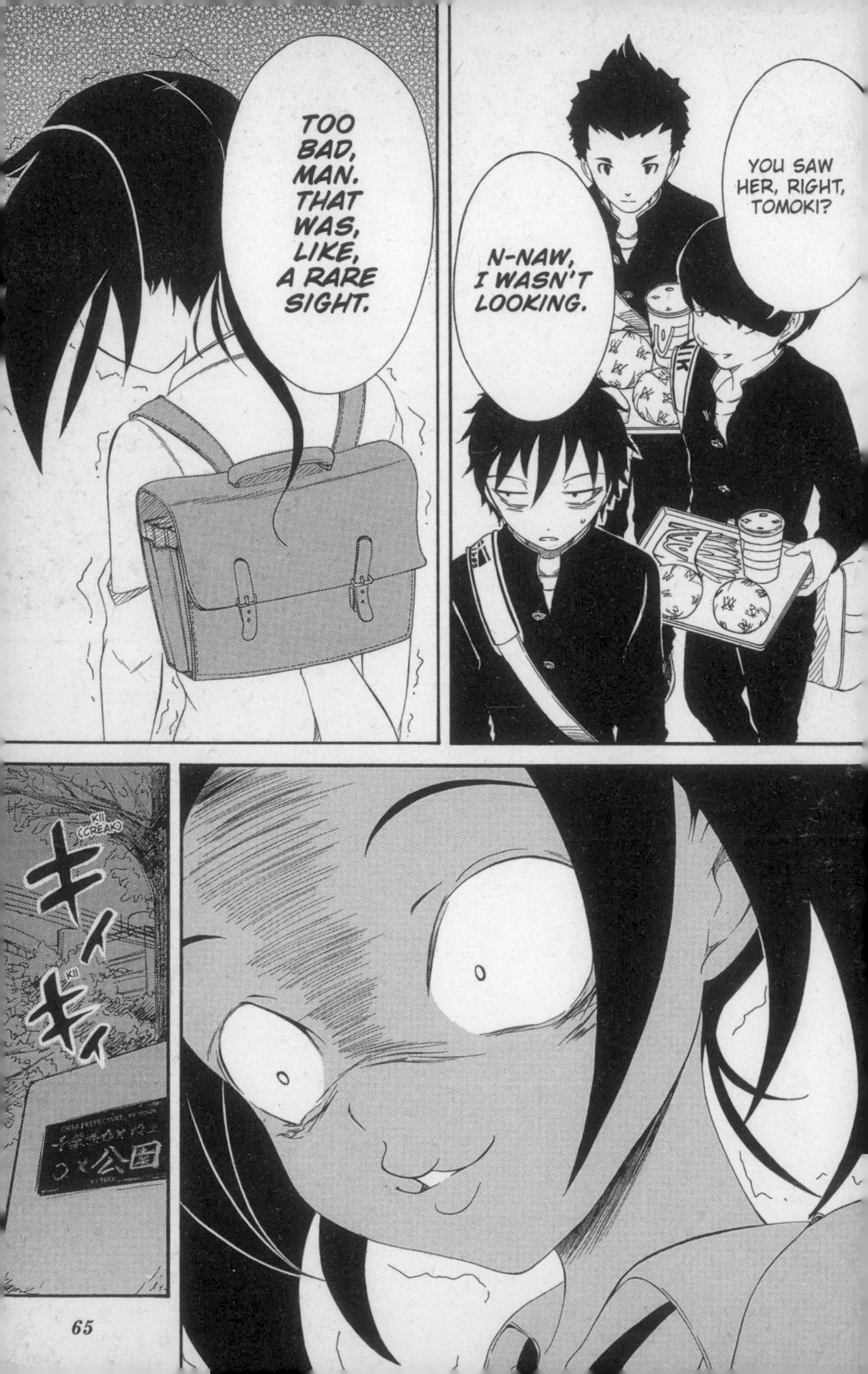
YOU SAW HER, RIGHT, TOMOKI?
N-NAW, I WASN'T LOOKING.
TOO BAD, MAN. THAT WAS, LIKE, A RARE SIGHT.
キィ
KII (CREAK)
キィ
KII
CHIBA PREFECTURE, XY TOWN
○×公園
XY PARK

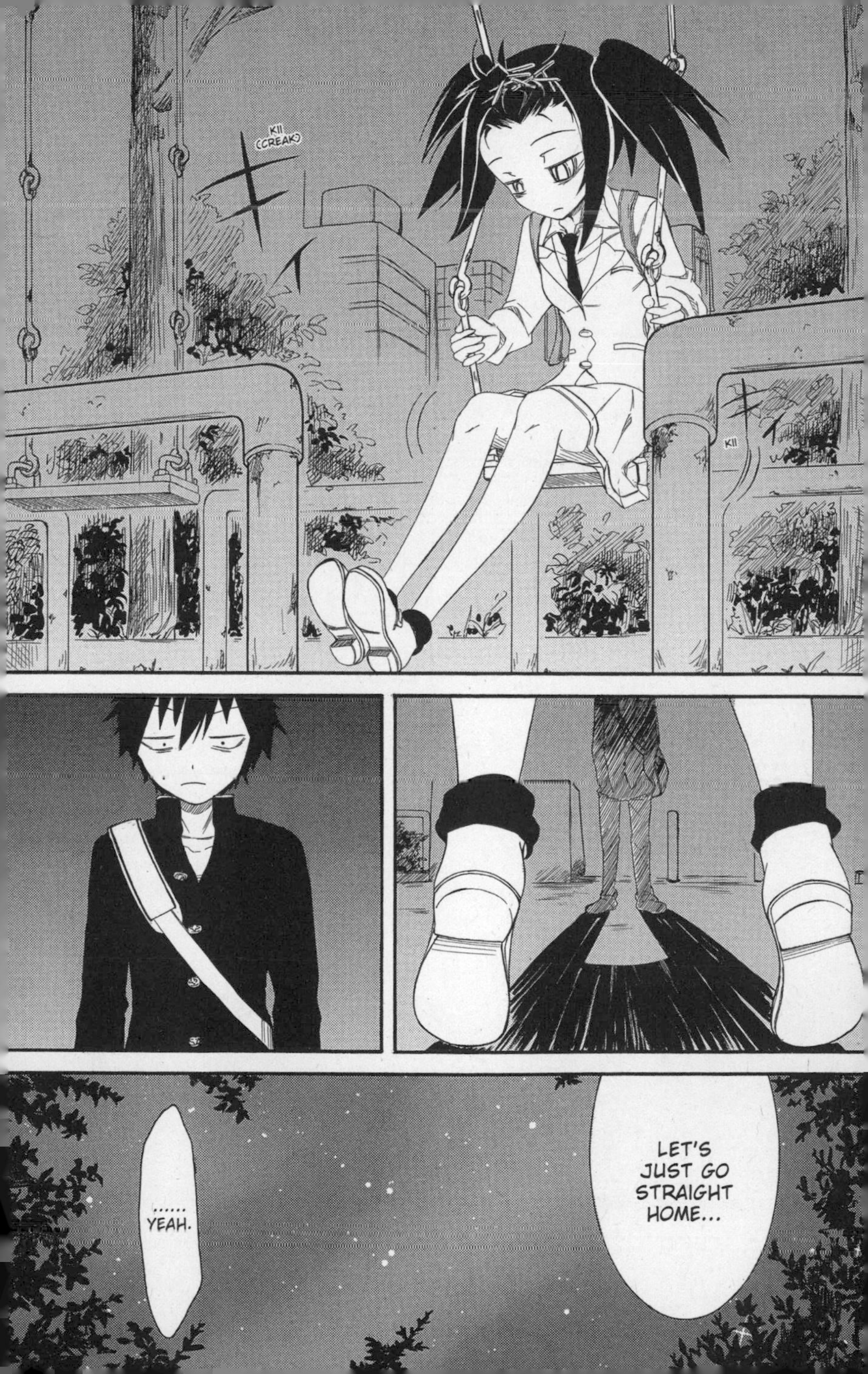
KII (CREAK)
KII
LET'S JUST GO STRAIGHT HOME...
......YEAH.

No Matter How I Look at It, It's You Guys' Fault I'm Not Popular!

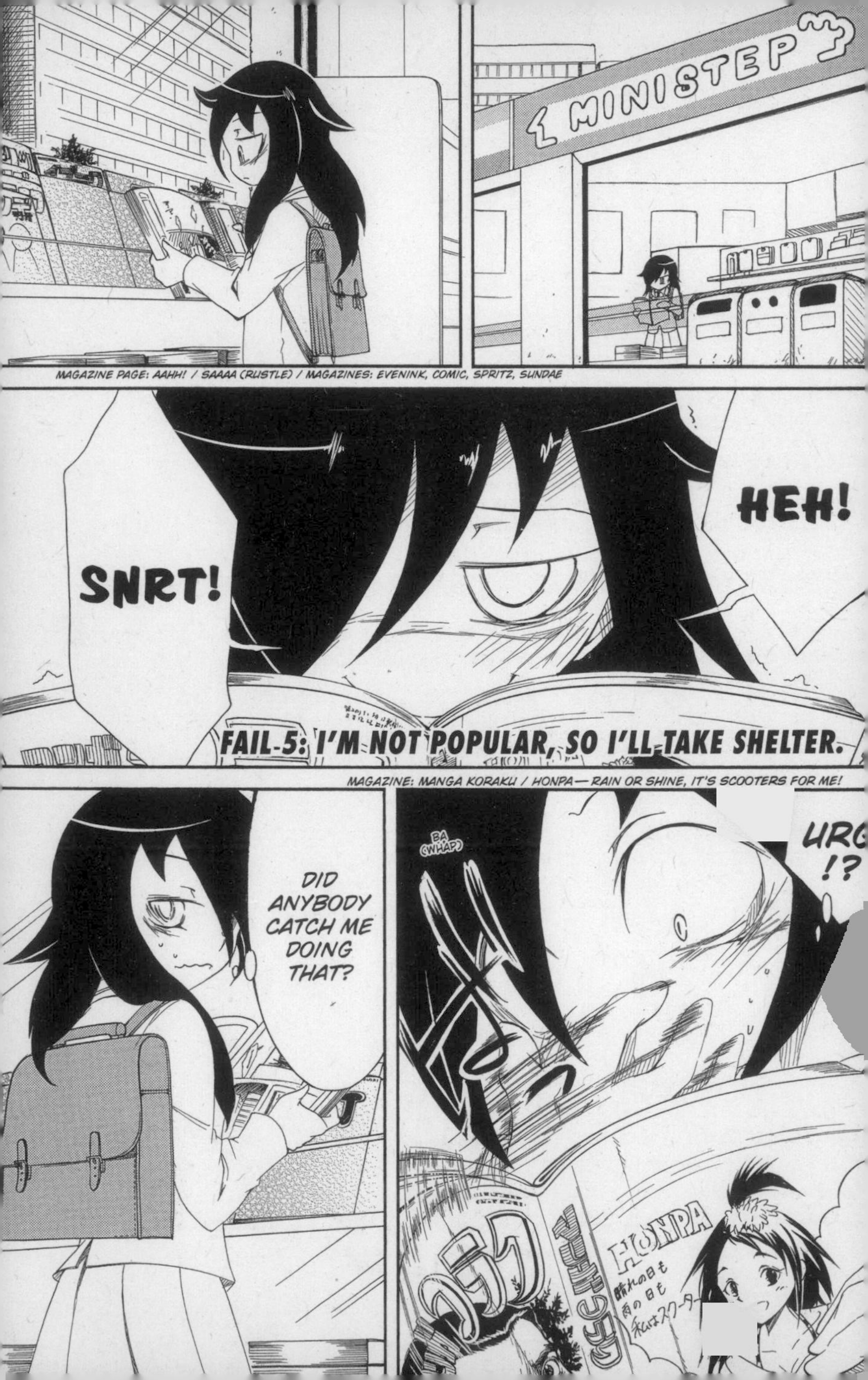
MINISTEP
MAGAZINE PAGE: AAHH! / SAAAA (RUSTLE) / MAGAZINES: EVENINK, COMIC, SPRITZ, SUNDAE
HEH!
SNRT!
FAIL 5: I'M NOT POPULAR, SO I'LL TAKE SHELTER.
MAGAZINE: MANGA KORAKU / HONPA— RAIN OR SHINE, IT'S SCOOTERS FOR ME!
URG !?
BA (WHAP)
HONPA
晴れの日も
雨の日も
私はスクーター
DID ANYBODY CATCH ME DOING THAT?

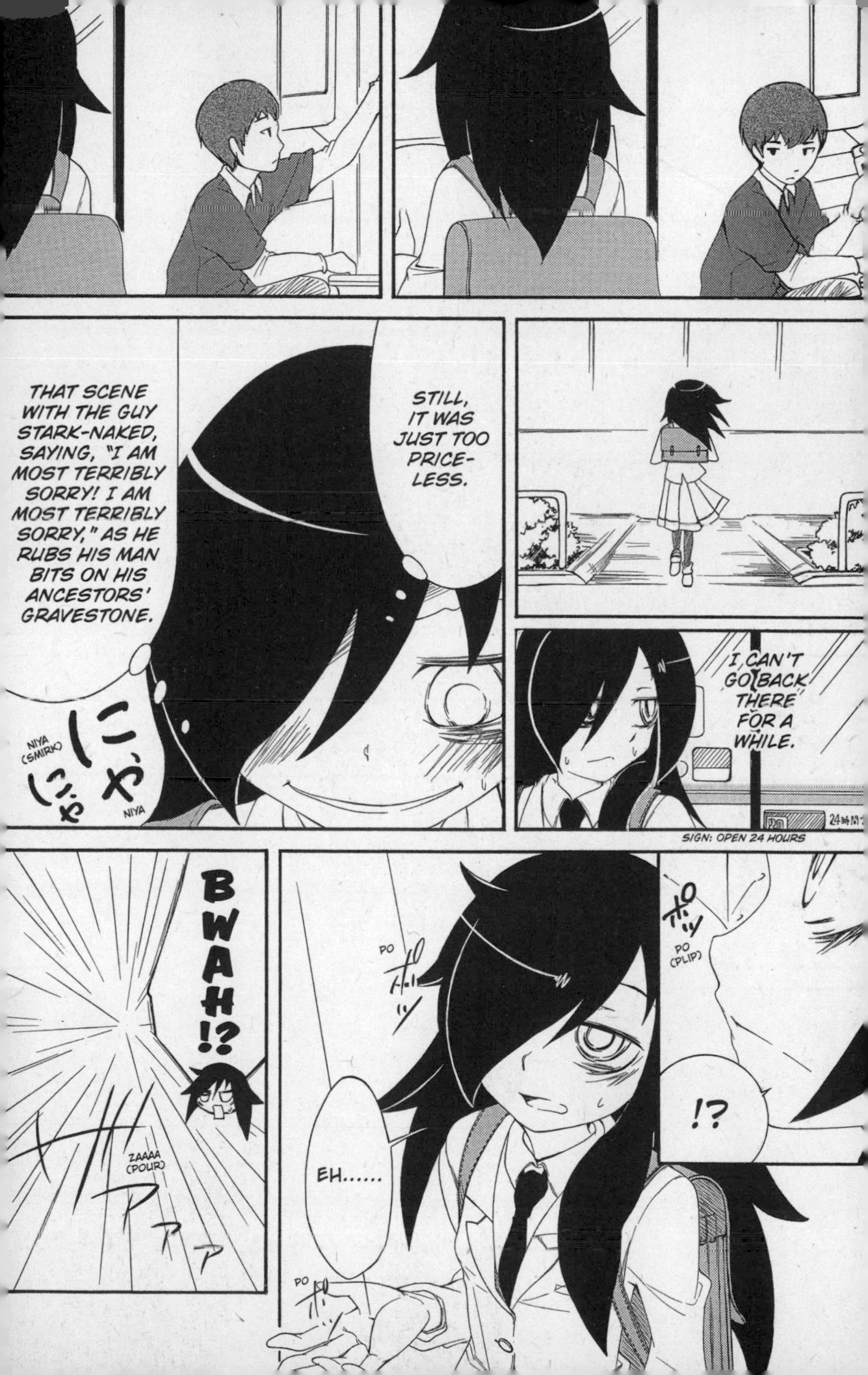

I CAN'T GO BACK THERE FOR A WHILE.
SIGN: OPEN 24 HOURS
STILL, IT WAS JUST TOO PRICELESS.
THAT SCENE WITH THE GUY STARK-NAKED, SAYING, "I AM MOST TERRIBLY SORRY! I AM MOST TERRIBLY SORRY," AS HE RUBS HIS MAN BITS ON HIS ANCESTORS' GRAVESTONE.
NIYA (SMIRK)
NIYA
!?
PO (PLIP)
PO
EH......
PO
BWAH!?
ZAAAA (POUR)

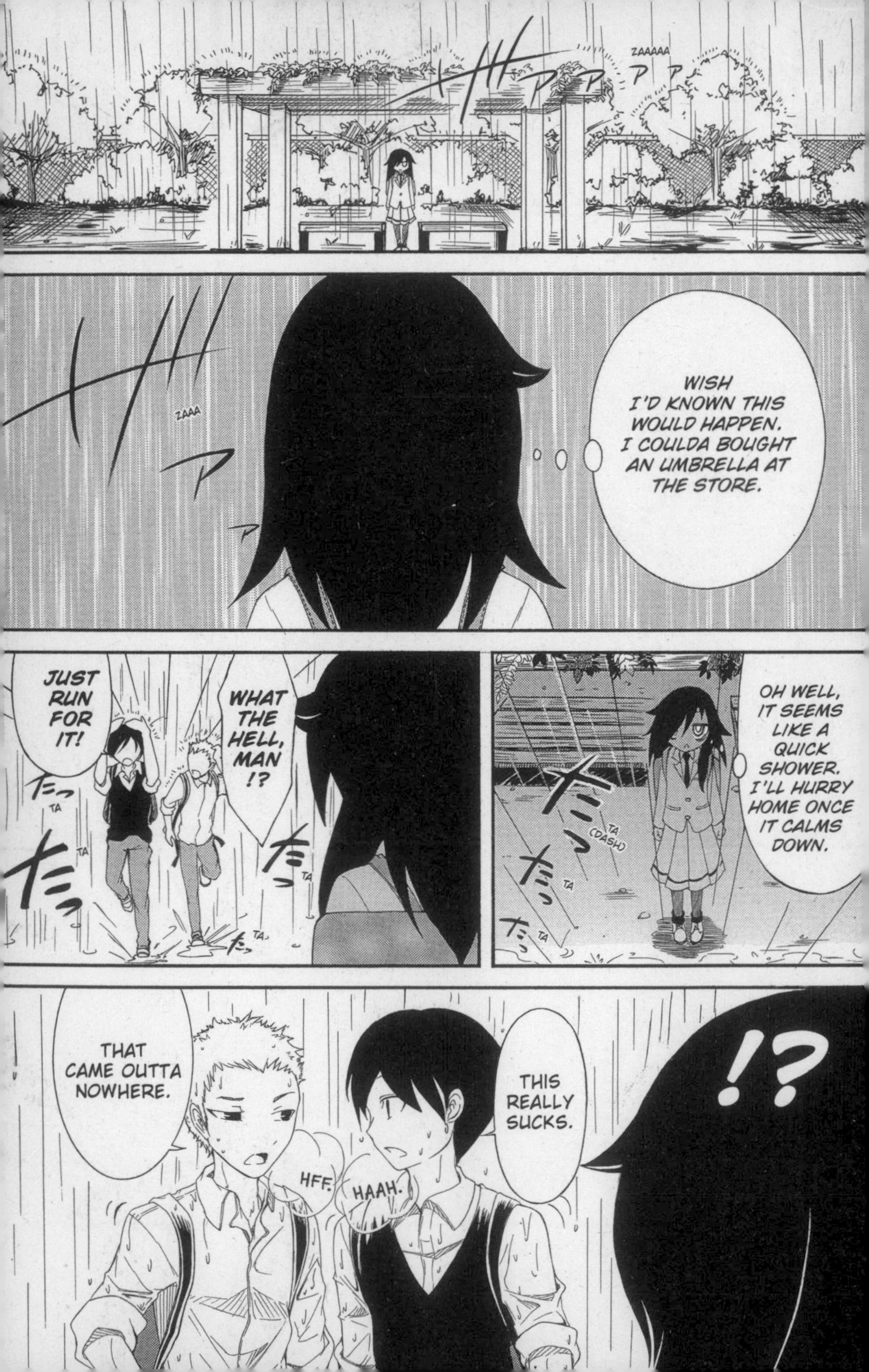
ZAAAAA
ZAAA
WISH I'D KNOWN THIS WOULD HAPPEN. I COULDA BOUGHT AN UMBRELLA AT THE STORE.
OH WELL, IT SEEMS LIKE A QUICK SHOWER. I'LL HURRY HOME ONCE IT CALMS DOWN.
TA (DASH)
TA
TA
WHAT THE HELL, MAN!?
JUST RUN FOR IT!
TA
TA
TA
TA
!?
THIS REALLY SUCKS.
HAAH.
HFF.
THAT CAME OUTTA NOWHERE.

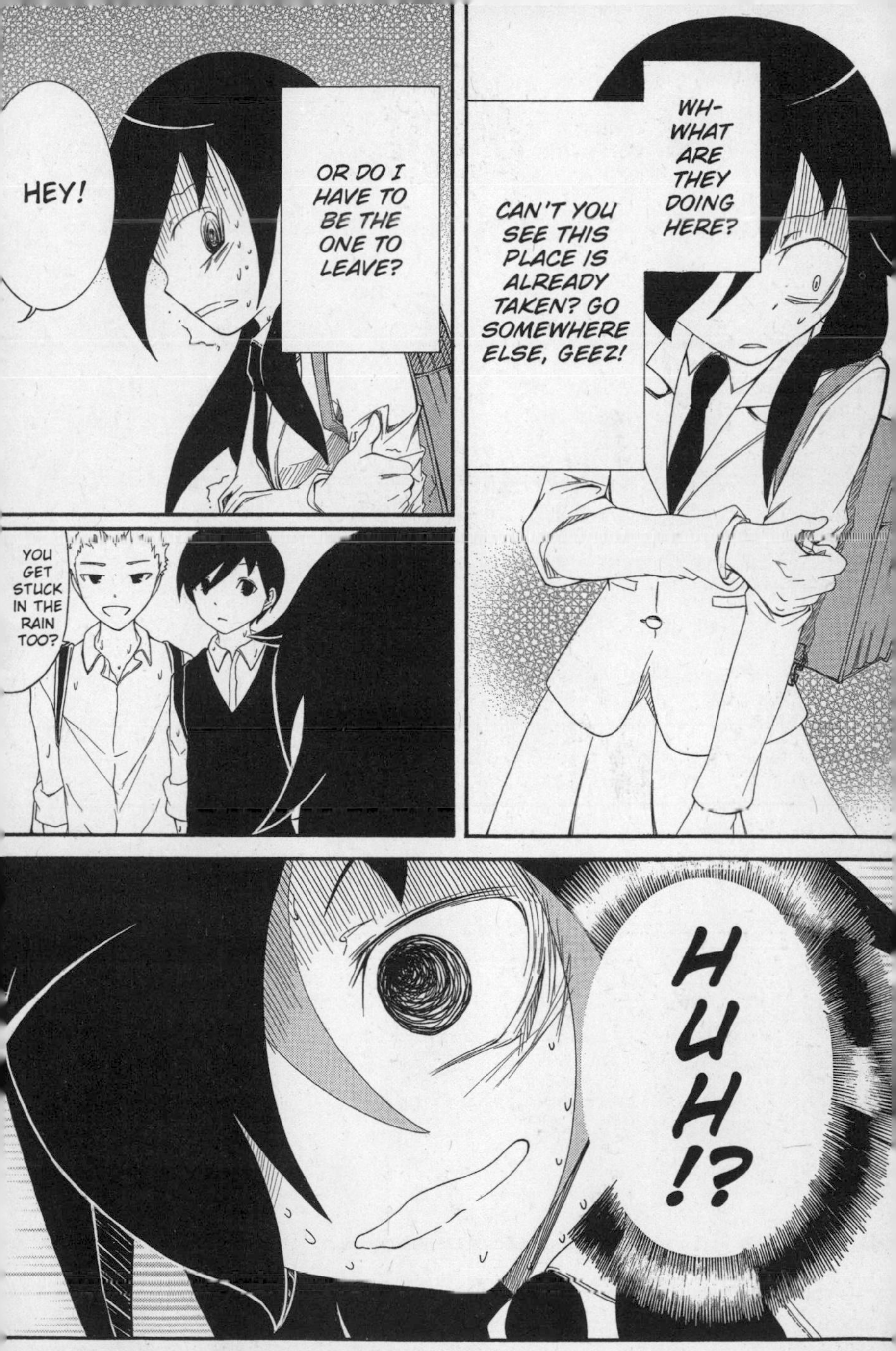
WH- WHAT ARE THEY DOING HERE?
CAN'T YOU SEE THIS PLACE IS ALREADY TAKEN? GO SOMEWHERE ELSE, GEEZ!
OR DO I HAVE TO BE THE ONE TO LEAVE?
HEY!
YOU GET STUCK IN THE RAIN TOO?
HUH!?

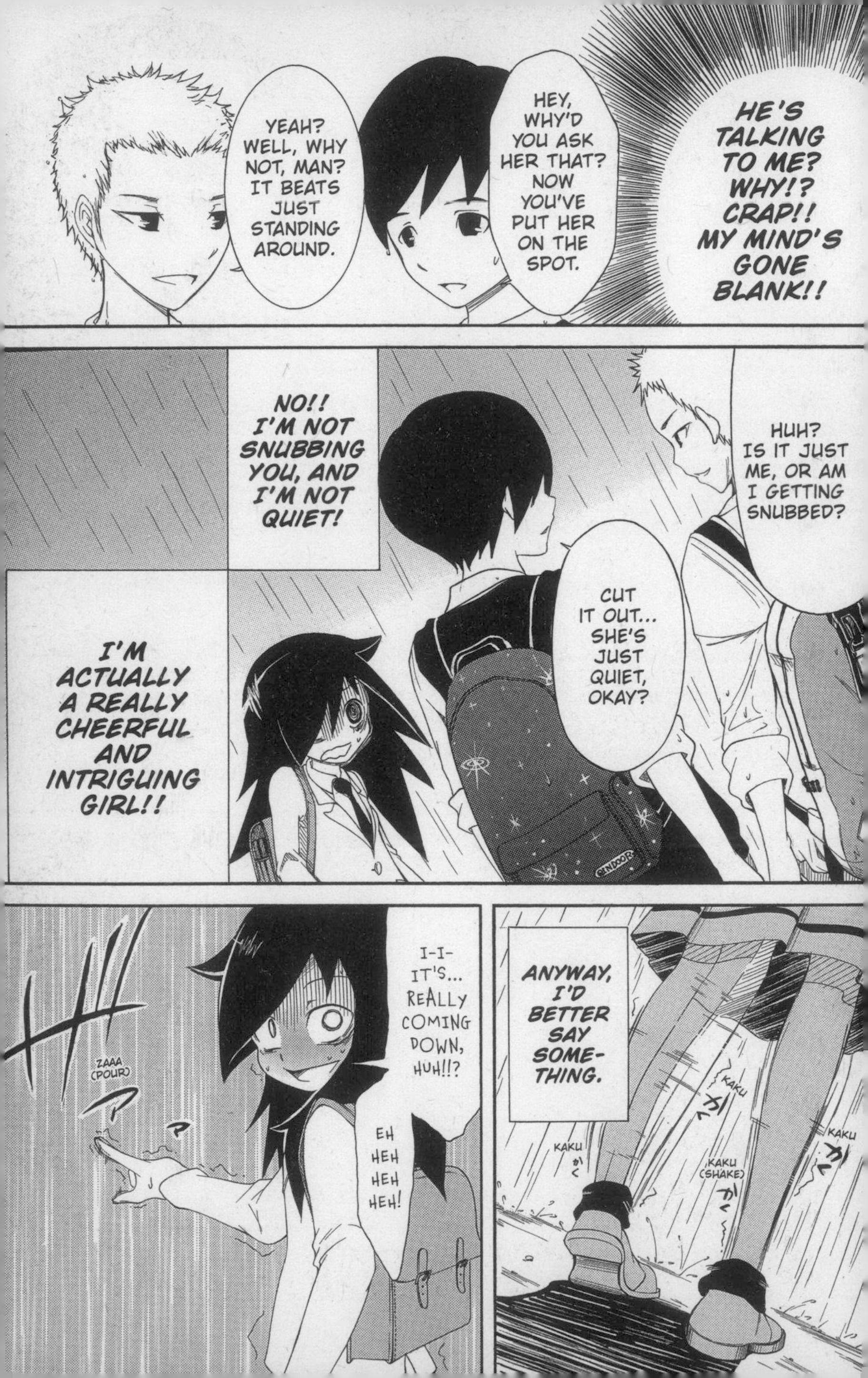

HE'S TALKING TO ME? WHY!? CRAP!! MY MIND'S GONE BLANK!!
HEY, WHY'D YOU ASK HER THAT? NOW YOU'VE PUT HER ON THE SPOT.
YEAH? WELL, WHY NOT, MAN? IT BEATS JUST STANDING AROUND.
HUH? IS IT JUST ME, OR AM I GETTING SNUBBED?
CUT IT OUT... SHE'S JUST QUIET, OKAY?
SINDOOR
NO!! I'M NOT SNUBBING YOU, AND I'M NOT QUIET!
I'M ACTUALLY A REALLY CHEERFUL AND INTRIGUING GIRL!!
ANYWAY, I'D BETTER SAY SOME-THING.
KAKU
KAKU
KAKU
KAKU (SHAKE)
I-I-IT'S... REALLY COMING DOWN, HUH!!?
EH HEH HEH HEH!
ZAAA (POUR)

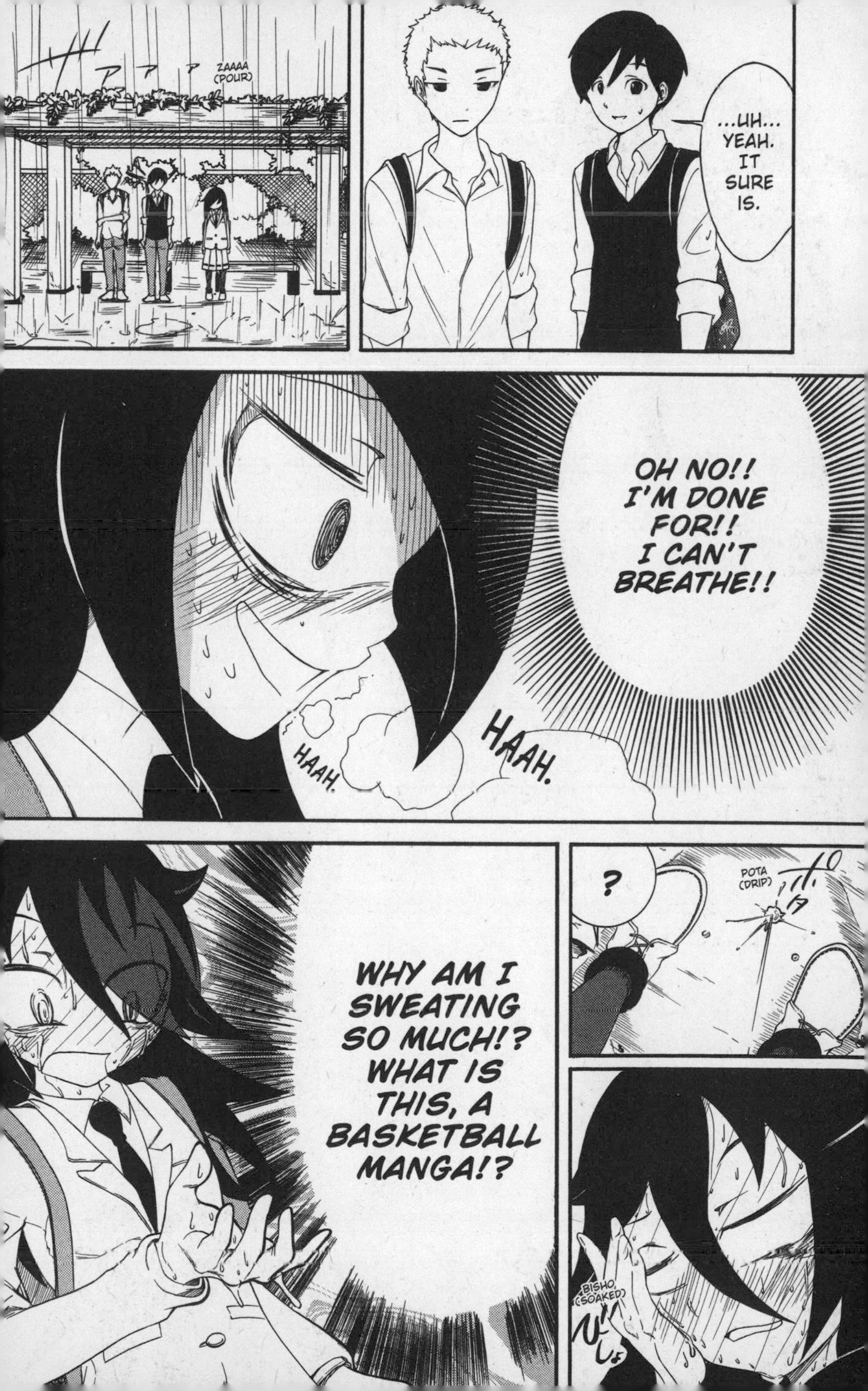
...UH... YEAH. IT SURE IS.
ZAAAA (POUR)
OH NO!! I'M DONE FOR!! I CAN'T BREATHE!!
HAAAH.
HAAAH.
?
POTA (DRIP)
BISHO (SOAKED)
WHY AM I SWEATING SO MUCH!? WHAT IS THIS, A BASKETBALL MANGA!?

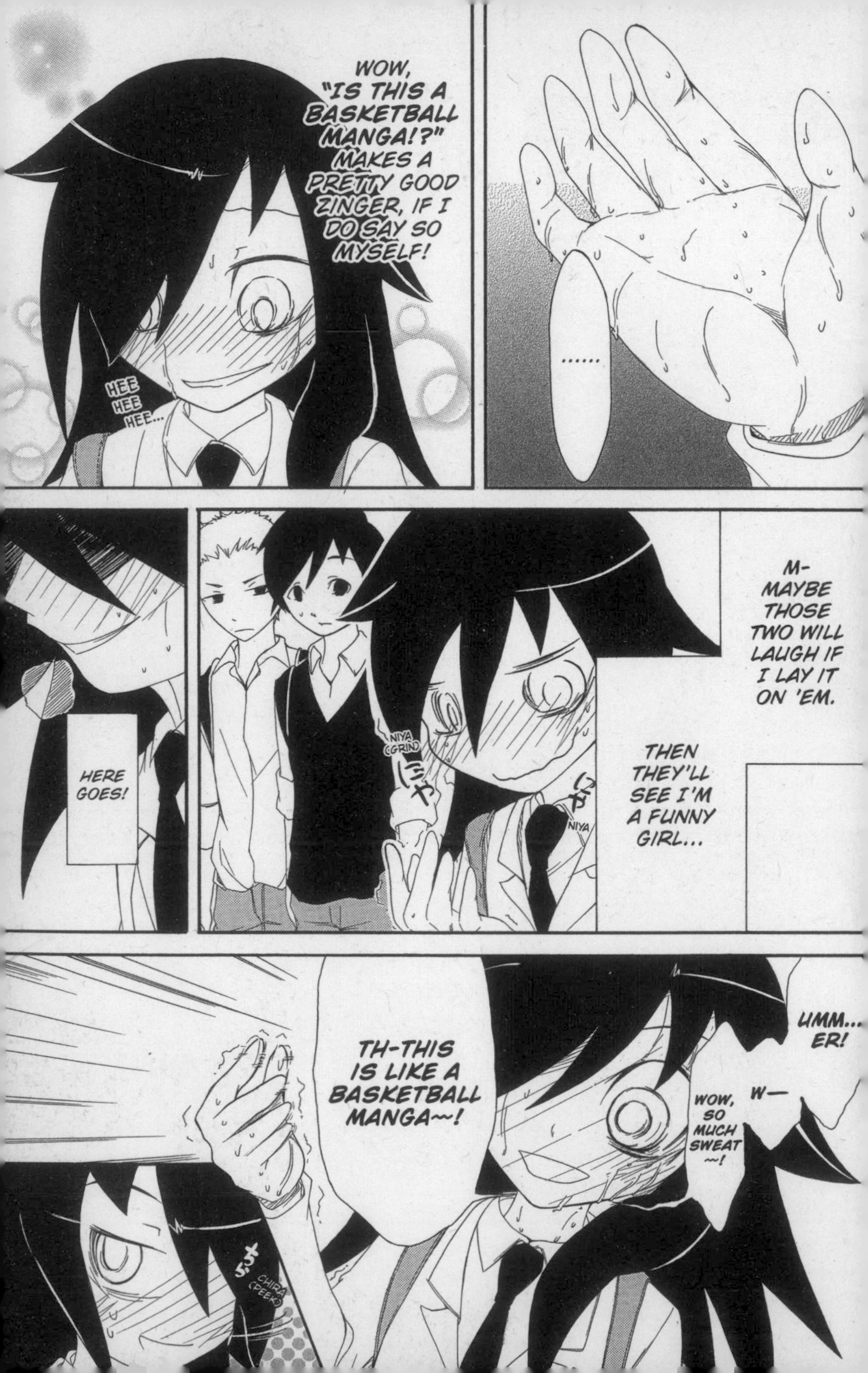
......
WOW, "IS THIS A BASKETBALL MANGA!?" MAKES A PRETTY GOOD ZINGER, IF I DO SAY SO MYSELF!
HEE HEE HEE...
M-MAYBE THOSE TWO WILL LAUGH IF I LAY IT ON 'EM.
THEN THEY'LL SEE I'M A FUNNY GIRL...
NIYA
NIYA (GRIN)
HERE GOES!
UMM... ER!
W—
WOW, SO MUCH SWEAT ~~!
TH-THIS IS LIKE A BASKETBALL MANGA~~!
CHIRA (PEEK)

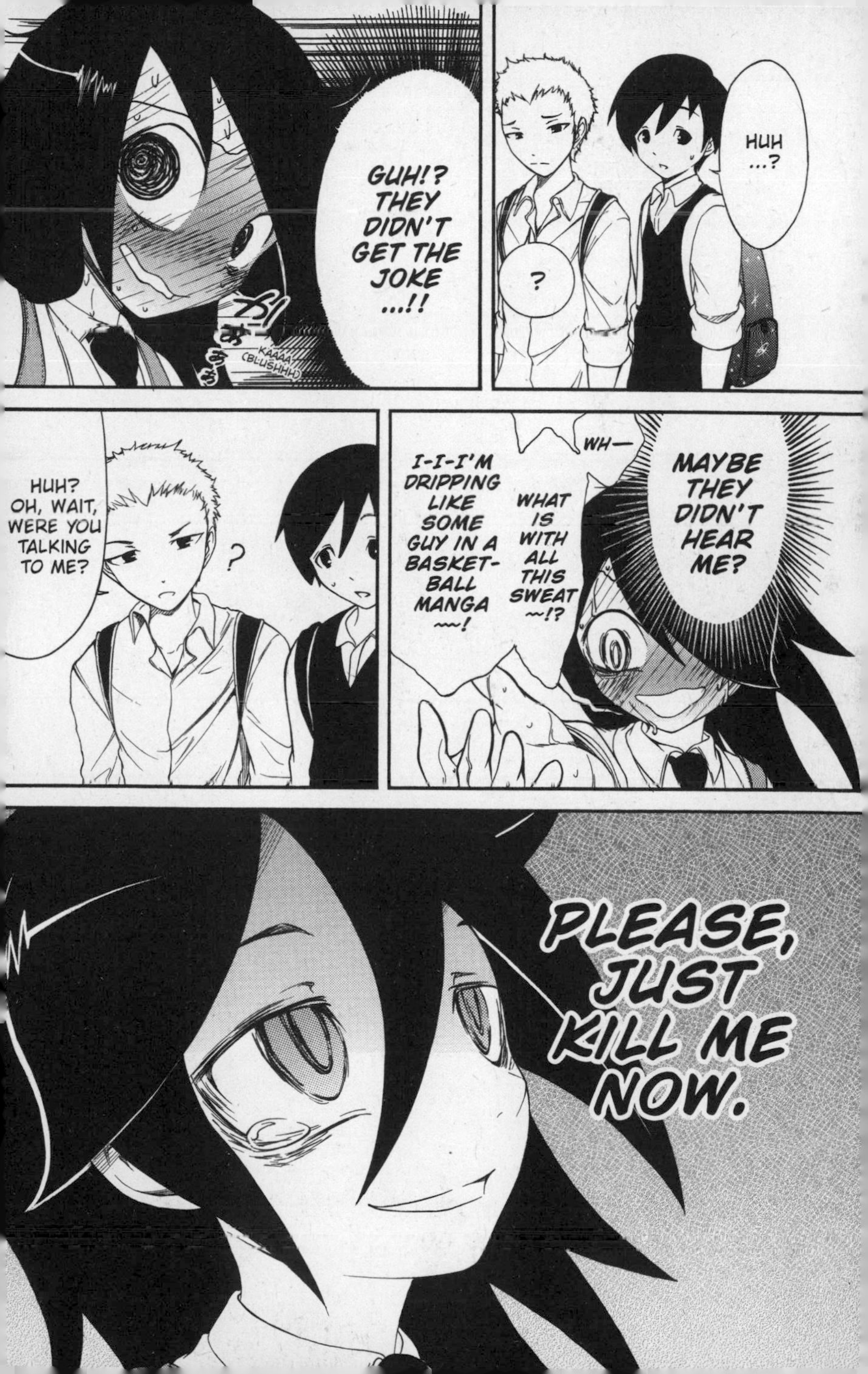
HUH ...?
?
GUH!? THEY DIDN'T GET THE JOKE ...!!
KAAAA (BLUSHHH)
MAYBE THEY DIDN'T HEAR ME?
WH—
WHAT IS WITH ALL THIS SWEAT ~!?
I-I-I'M DRIPPING LIKE SOME GUY IN A BASKET-BALL MANGA ~~!
?
HUH? OH, WAIT, WERE YOU TALKING TO ME?
PLEASE, JUST KILL ME NOW.

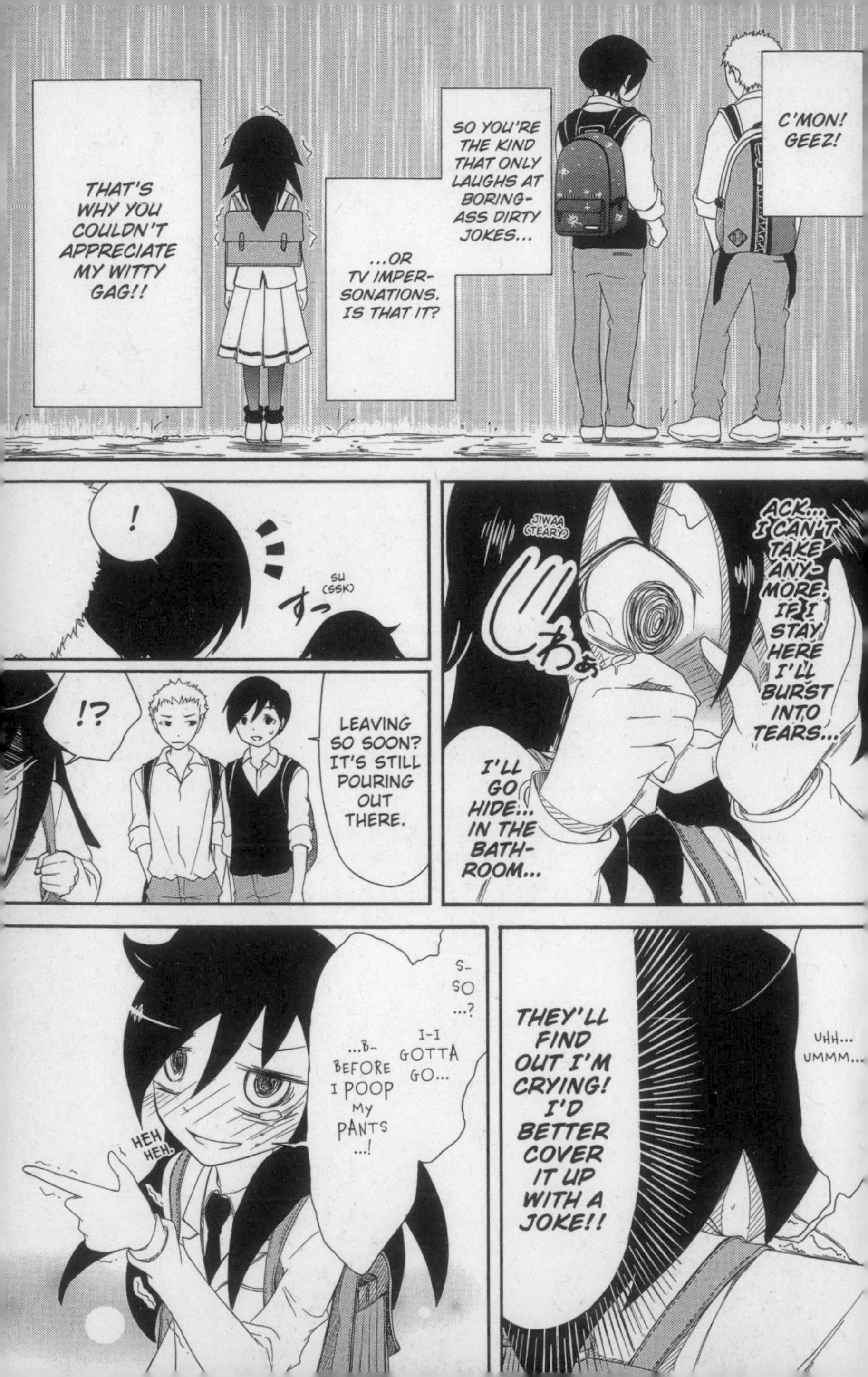
C'MON! GEEZ!
SO YOU'RE THE KIND THAT ONLY LAUGHS AT BORING-ASS DIRTY JOKES...
...OR TV IMPERSONATIONS. IS THAT IT?
THAT'S WHY YOU COULDN'T APPRECIATE MY WITTY GAG!!
JIWAA (TEARY)
ACK... I CAN'T TAKE ANYMORE. IF I STAY HERE I'LL BURST INTO TEARS...
I'LL GO HIDE... IN THE BATHROOM...
!
SU (SSK)
!?
LEAVING SO SOON? IT'S STILL POURING OUT THERE.
THEY'LL FIND OUT I'M CRYING! I'D BETTER COVER IT UP WITH A JOKE!!
UHH... UMMM...
S-SO ...?
I-I GOTTA GO...
...B-BEFORE I POOP MY PANTS ...!
HEH HEH.

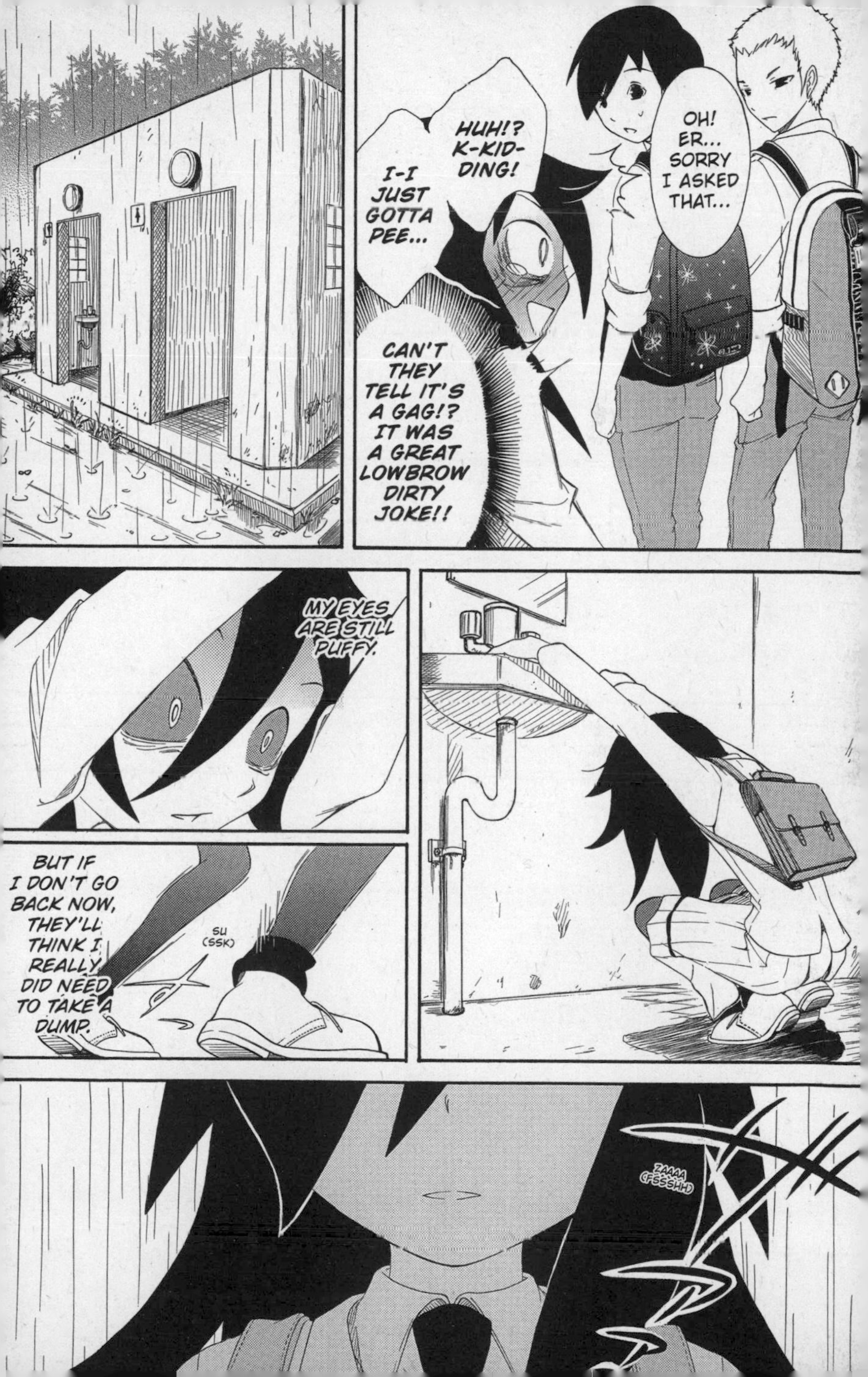
OH! ER... SORRY I ASKED THAT...
HUH!? K-KID-DING!
I-I JUST GOTTA PEE...
CAN'T THEY TELL IT'S A GAG!? IT WAS A GREAT LOWBROW DIRTY JOKE!!
MY EYES ARE STILL PUFFY.
BUT IF I DON'T GO BACK NOW, THEY'LL THINK I REALLY DID NEED TO TAKE A DUMP.
SU (SSK)
ZAAAA (FSSSHH)

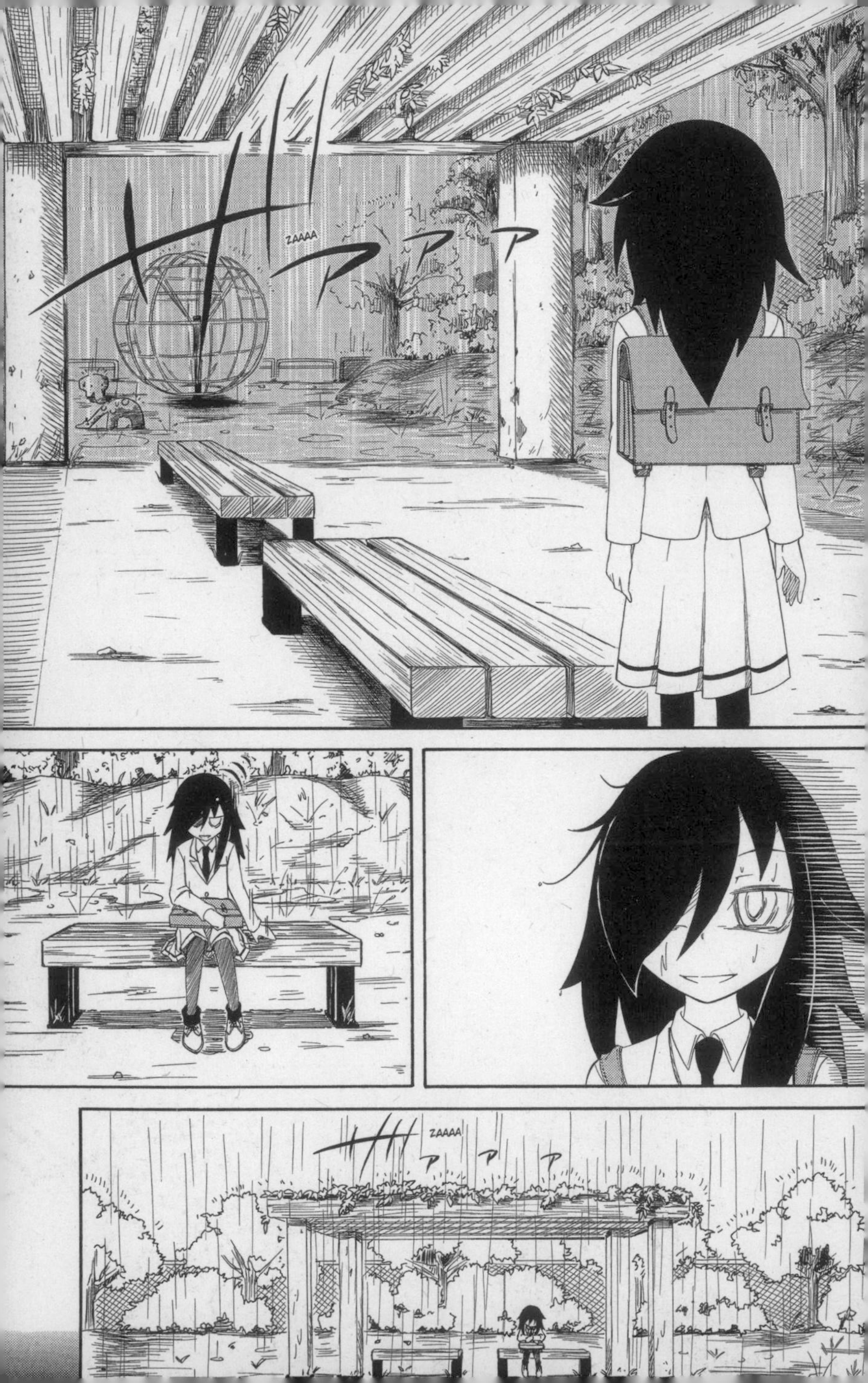
ZAAAA
ZAAAA

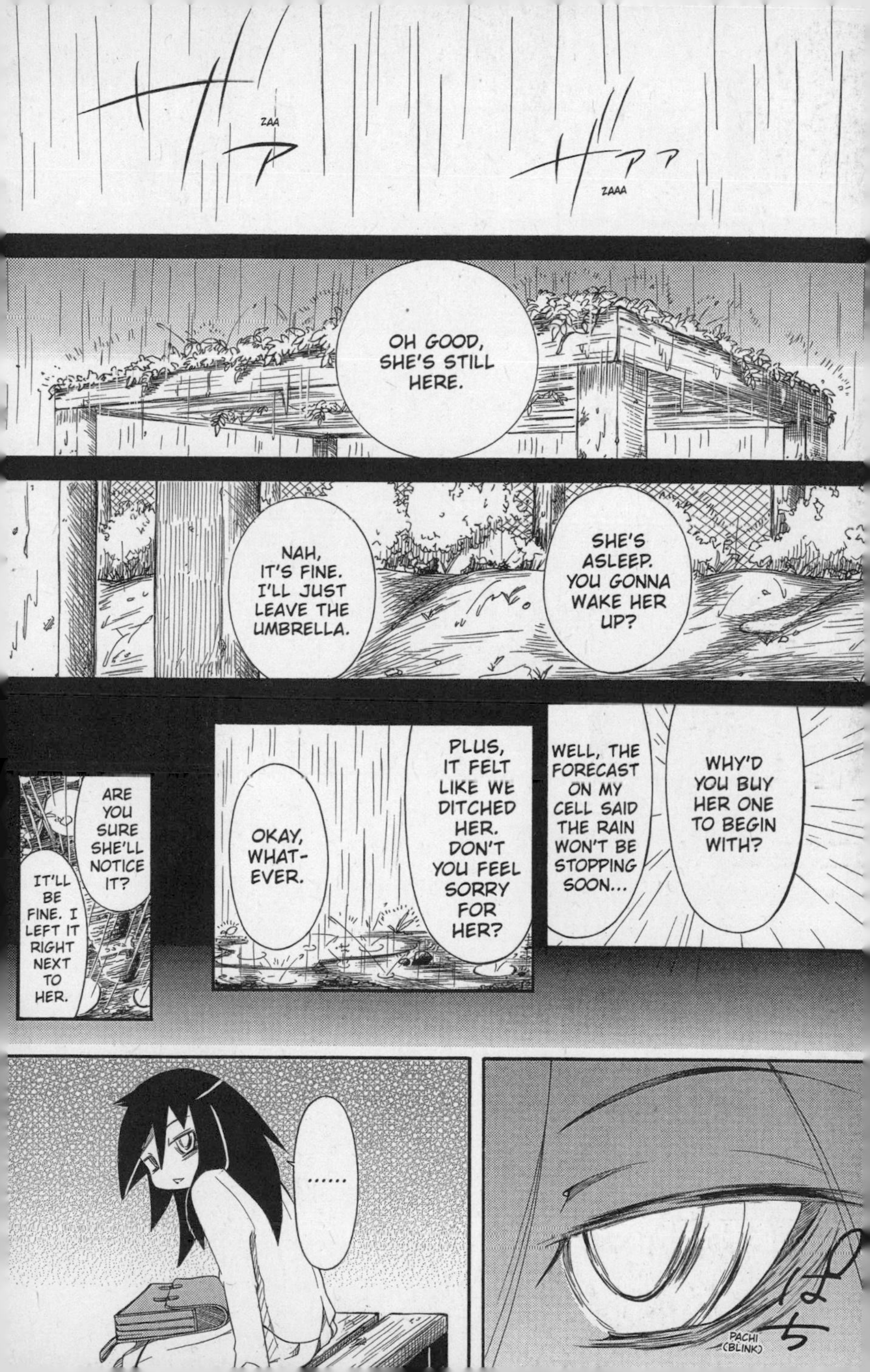
ZAAA
ZAA
OH GOOD, SHE'S STILL HERE.
SHE'S ASLEEP. YOU GONNA WAKE HER UP?
NAH, IT'S FINE. I'LL JUST LEAVE THE UMBRELLA.
WHY'D YOU BUY HER ONE TO BEGIN WITH?
WELL, THE FORECAST ON MY CELL SAID THE RAIN WON'T BE STOPPING SOON...
PLUS, IT FELT LIKE WE DITCHED HER. DON'T YOU FEEL SORRY FOR HER?
OKAY, WHAT-EVER.
ARE YOU SURE SHE'LL NOTICE IT?
IT'LL BE FINE. I LEFT IT RIGHT NEXT TO HER.
PACHI (BLINK)
......

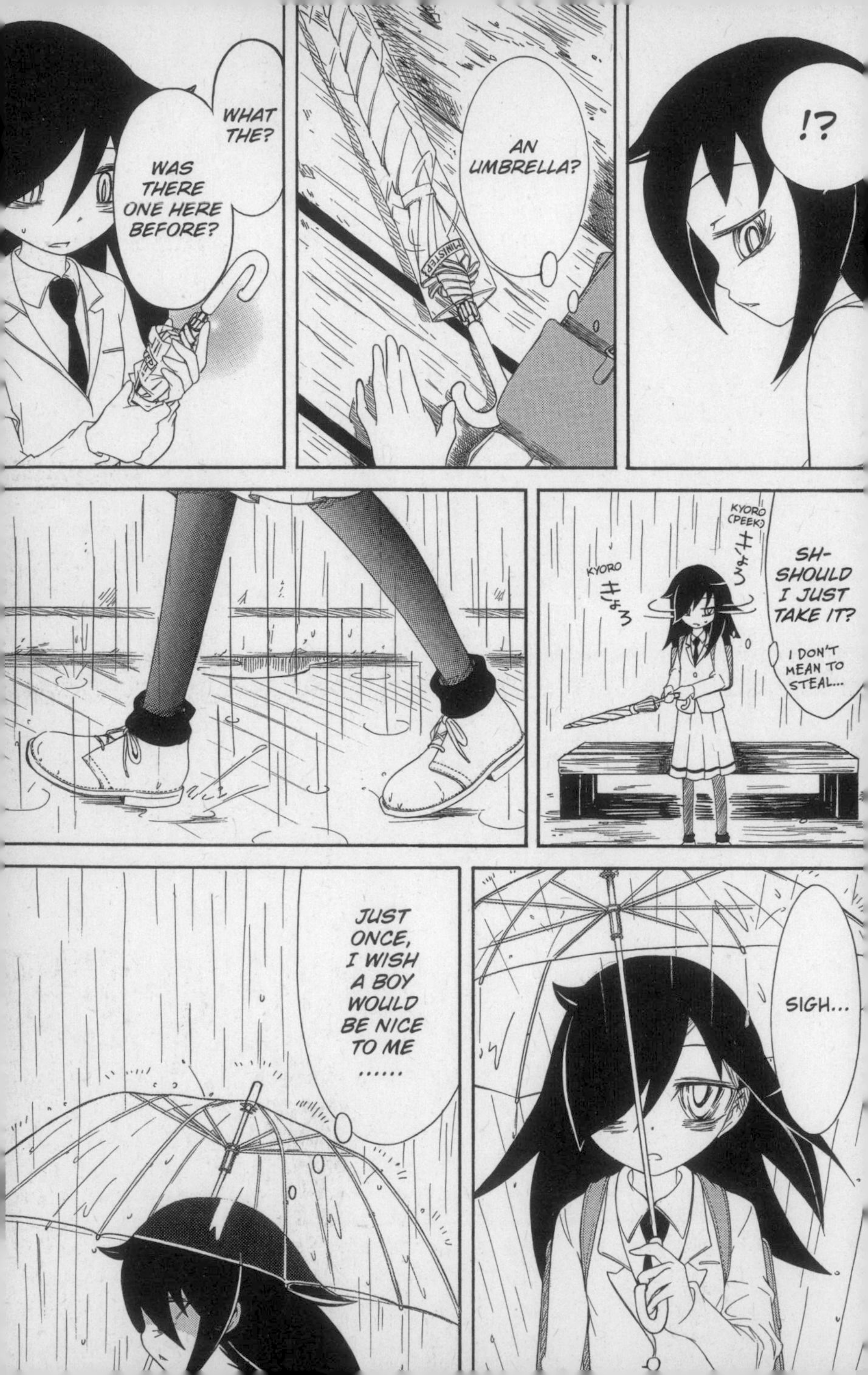
!?
AN UMBRELLA?
WHAT THE?
WAS THERE ONE HERE BEFORE?
KYORO (PEEK)
きょろ
KYORO
きょろ
SH-SHOULD I JUST TAKE IT?
I DON'T MEAN TO STEAL...
SIGH...
JUST ONCE, I WISH A BOY WOULD BE NICE TO ME ......

No Matter How I Look at It, It's You Guys' Fault I'm Not Popular!

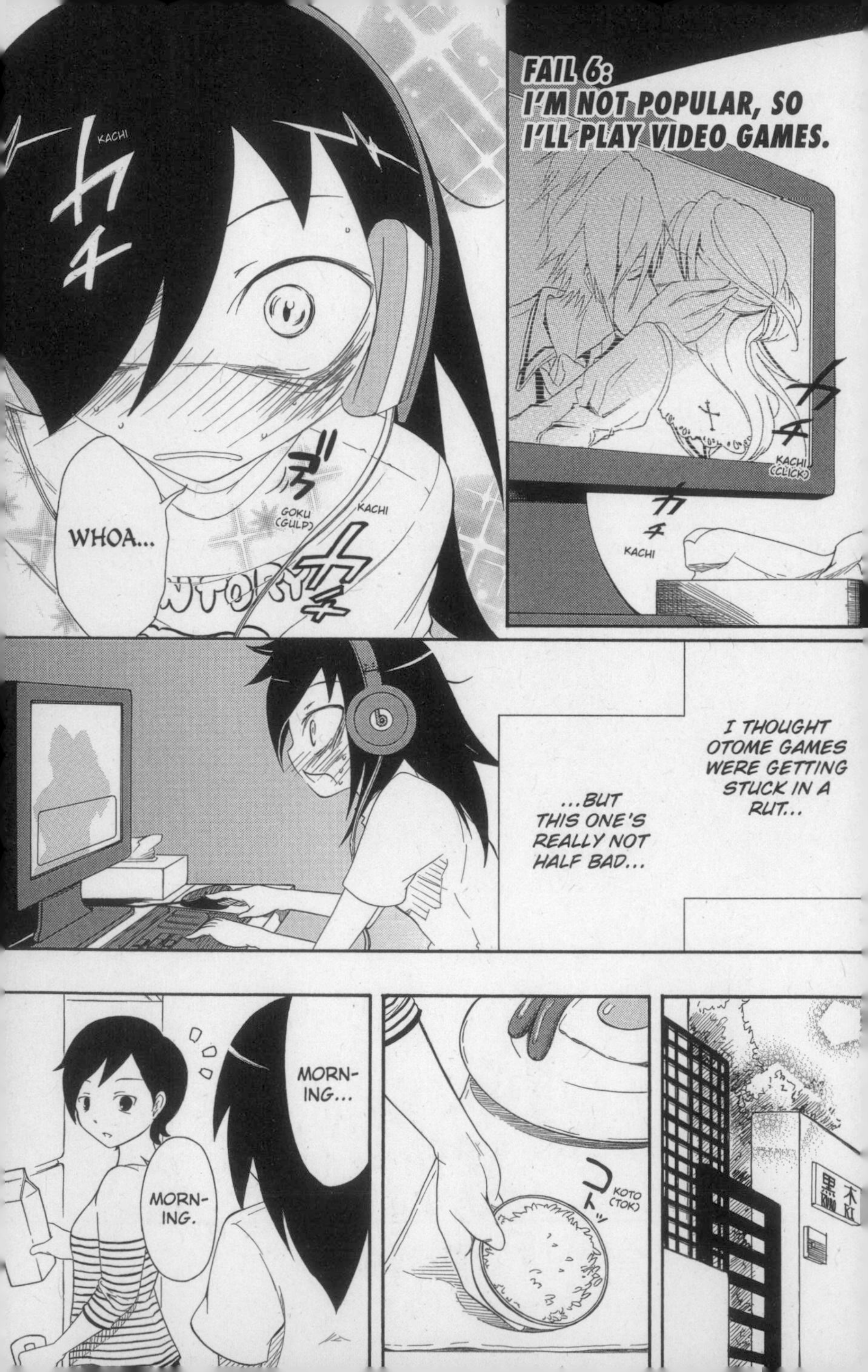
FAIL 6:
I'M NOT POPULAR, SO I'LL PLAY VIDEO GAMES.
KACHI (CLICK)
KACHI
KACHI
GOKU (GULP)
KACHI
WHOA...
I THOUGHT OTOME GAMES WERE GETTING STUCK IN A RUT...
...BUT THIS ONE'S REALLY NOT HALF BAD...
黒 KURO 木 KI
KOTO (TOK)
MORN-ING...
MORN-ING.

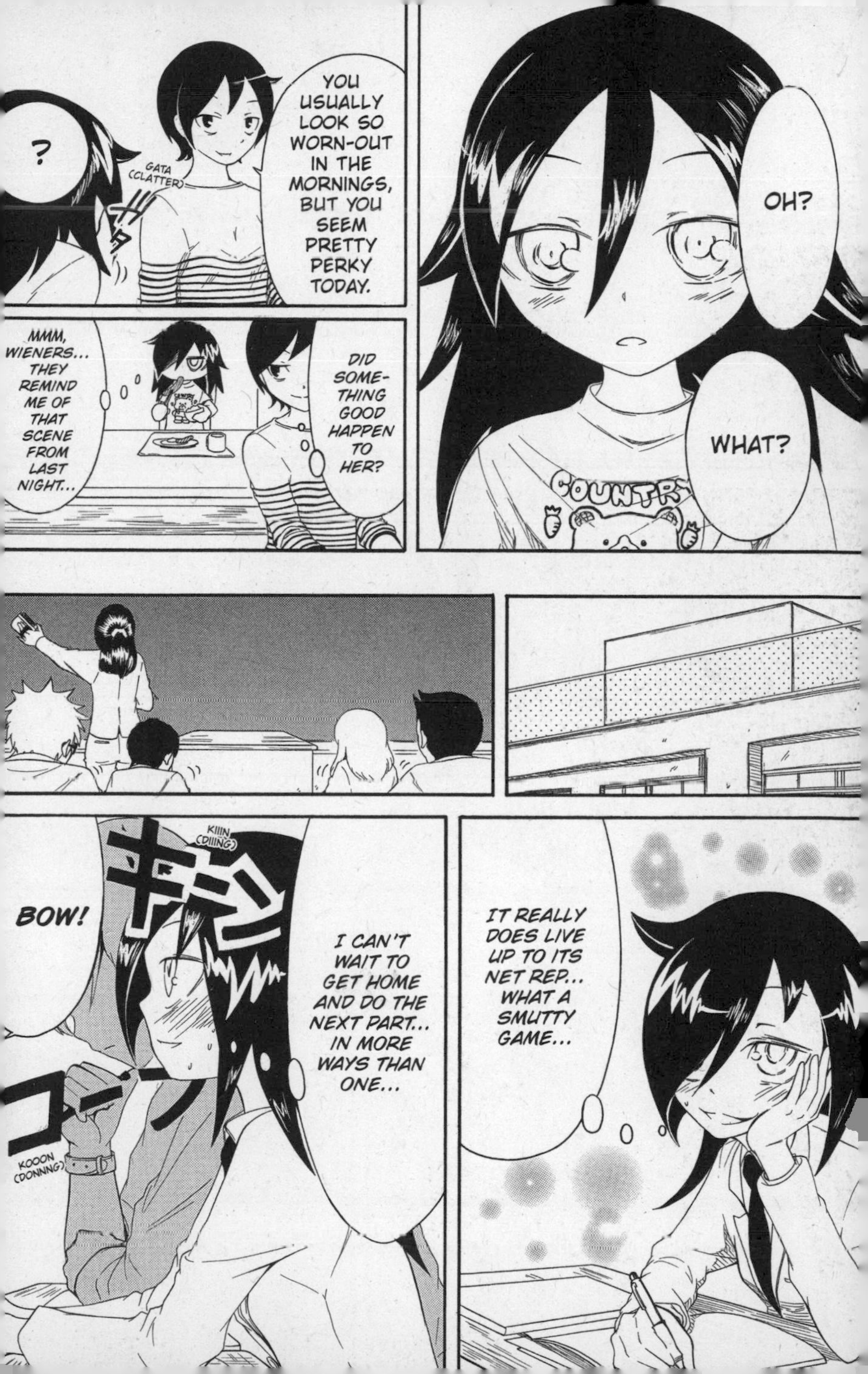
OH?
WHAT?
YOU USUALLY LOOK SO WORN-OUT IN THE MORNINGS, BUT YOU SEEM PRETTY PERKY TODAY.
GATA (CLATTER)
?
DID SOME-THING GOOD HAPPEN TO HER?
MMM, WIENERS... THEY REMIND ME OF THAT SCENE FROM LAST NIGHT...
IT REALLY DOES LIVE UP TO ITS NET REP... WHAT A SMUTTY GAME...
I CAN'T WAIT TO GET HOME AND DO THE NEXT PART... IN MORE WAYS THAN ONE...
KIIN (DIIING)
BOW!
KOOON (DONNNG)

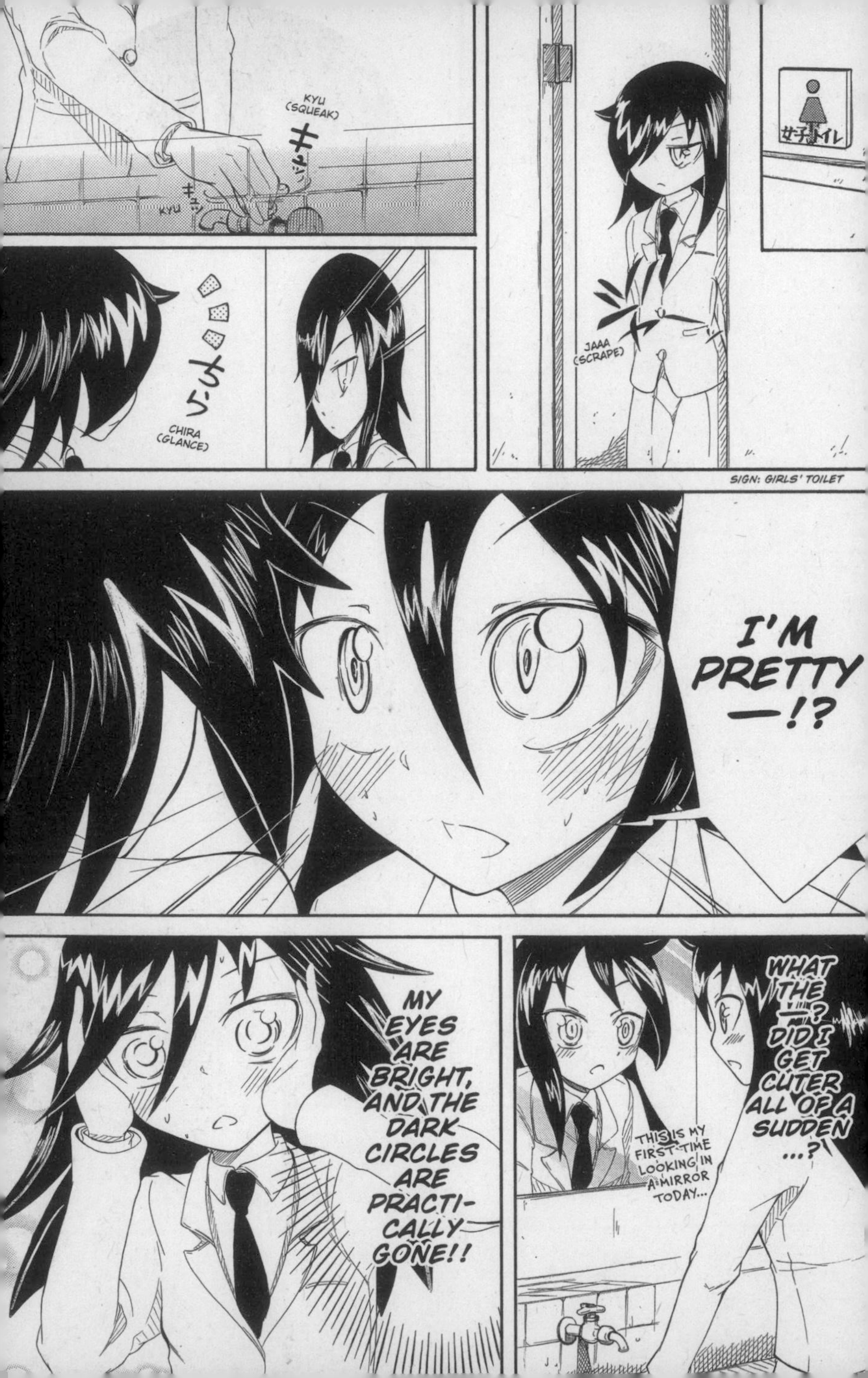
女子トイレ
JAAA (SCRAPE)
SIGN: GIRLS' TOILET
キュッ
KYU (SQUEAK)
キュッ
KYU
ちら
CHIRA (GLANCE)
I'M PRETTY—!?
WHAT THE—? DID I GET CUTER ALL OF A SUDDEN...?
THIS IS MY FIRST TIME LOOKING IN A MIRROR TODAY...
MY EYES ARE BRIGHT, AND THE DARK CIRCLES ARE PRACTICALLY GONE!!

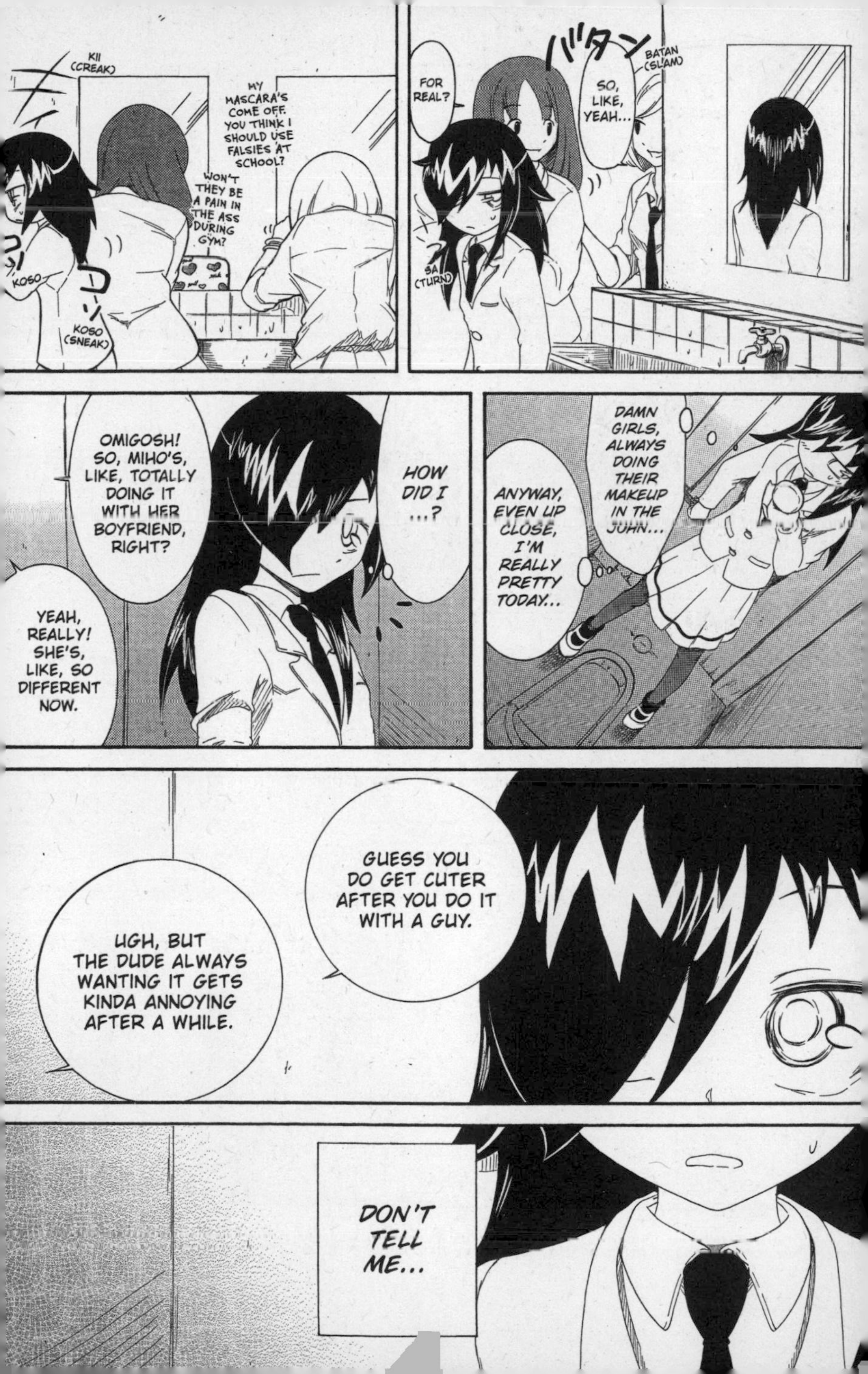

バタン
BATAN (SLAM)
SO, LIKE, YEAH...
FOR REAL?
SA (TURN)
MY MASCARA'S COME OFF. YOU THINK I SHOULD USE FALSIES AT SCHOOL?
WON'T THEY BE A PAIN IN THE ASS DURING GYM?
KII (CREAK)
KOSO
KOSO (SNEAK)
DAMN GIRLS, ALWAYS DOING THEIR MAKEUP IN THE JOHN...
ANYWAY, EVEN UP CLOSE, I'M REALLY PRETTY TODAY...
HOW DID I ...?
OMIGOSH! SO, MIHO'S, LIKE, TOTALLY DOING IT WITH HER BOYFRIEND, RIGHT?
YEAH, REALLY! SHE'S, LIKE, SO DIFFERENT NOW.
GUESS YOU DO GET CUTER AFTER YOU DO IT WITH A GUY.
UGH, BUT THE DUDE ALWAYS WANTING IT GETS KINDA ANNOYING AFTER A WHILE.
DON'T TELL ME...

WHAT'S UP PEOPLE? 10 THINGS THEY WON'T TELL YOU

GIRLS' REAL-LIFE SURVEYS

SHOCKING XXXXX

WOMEN TURN PRETTY WHEN IN LOVE!

FEATURE

LET YOUR BODY GLOW WITH S#X!

400

UNITED CLOSE SATIN POUCH

PARA

PARA (FLIP)

!

THIS LOOKS LIKE A MAG MADE FOR SUPER-BRAIN-LESS BIMBOS ......

...AND ACTS ON THE BUST AND HIPS...

...TO PRODUCE A MORE WOMANLY FIGURE.

WOMEN WHO ARE IN LOVE SECRETE ESTROGEN, A FEMALE HORMONE THAT HAS A BEAUTIFYING EFFECT.

LET YOUR BODY GLOW WITH S#X!

ESTROGEN HELPS TO MOISTURIZE YOUR SKIN...

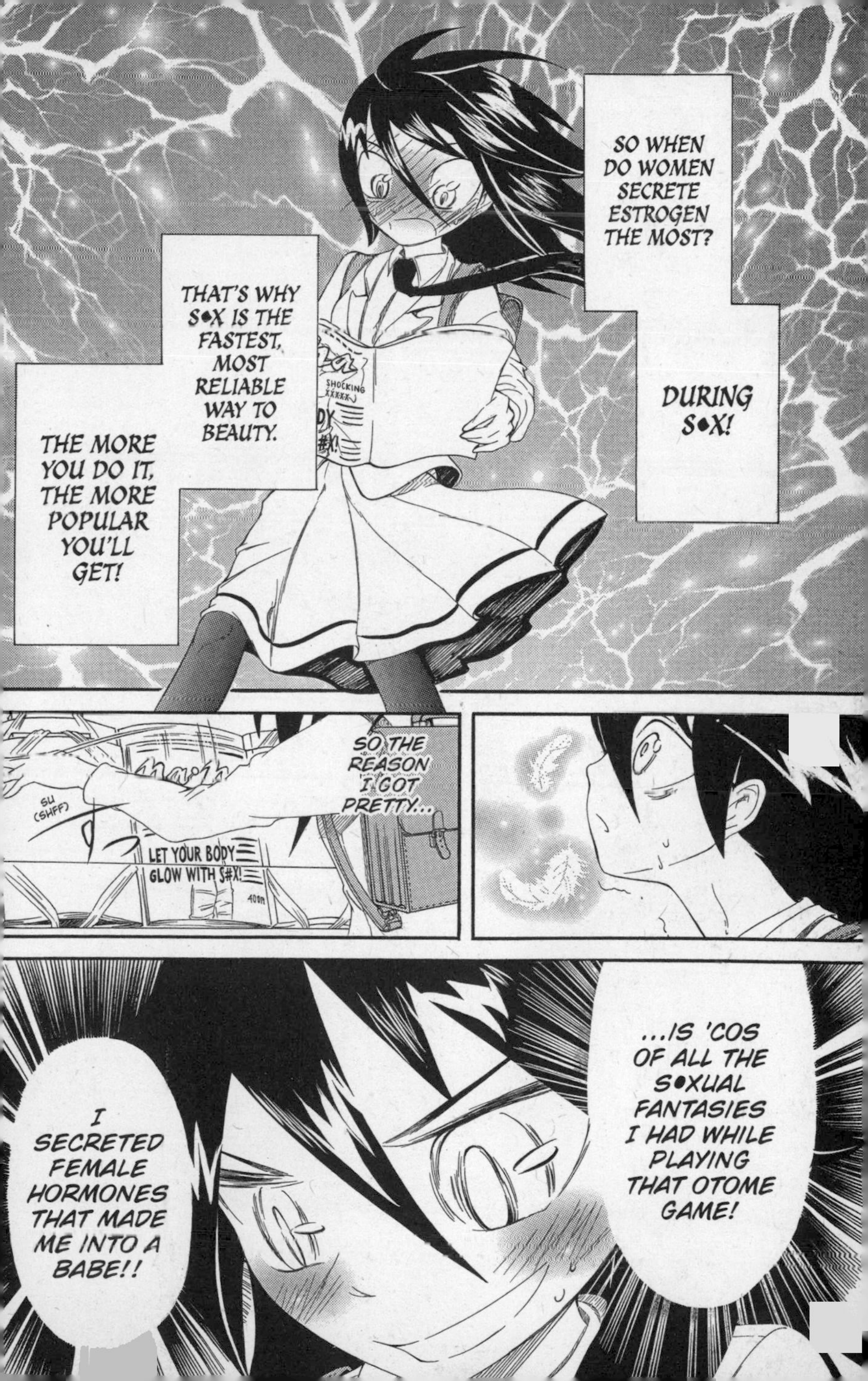
SO WHEN DO WOMEN SECRETE ESTROGEN THE MOST?
DURING S♦X!
THAT'S WHY S♦X IS THE FASTEST, MOST RELIABLE WAY TO BEAUTY.
THE MORE YOU DO IT, THE MORE POPULAR YOU'LL GET!
SHOCKING XXXXX
SO THE REASON I GOT PRETTY...
SU (SHFF)
LET YOUR BODY GLOW WITH S#X!
...IS 'COS OF ALL THE S♦XUAL FANTASIES I HAD WHILE PLAYING THAT OTOME GAME!
I SECRETED FEMALE HORMONES THAT MADE ME INTO A BABE!!

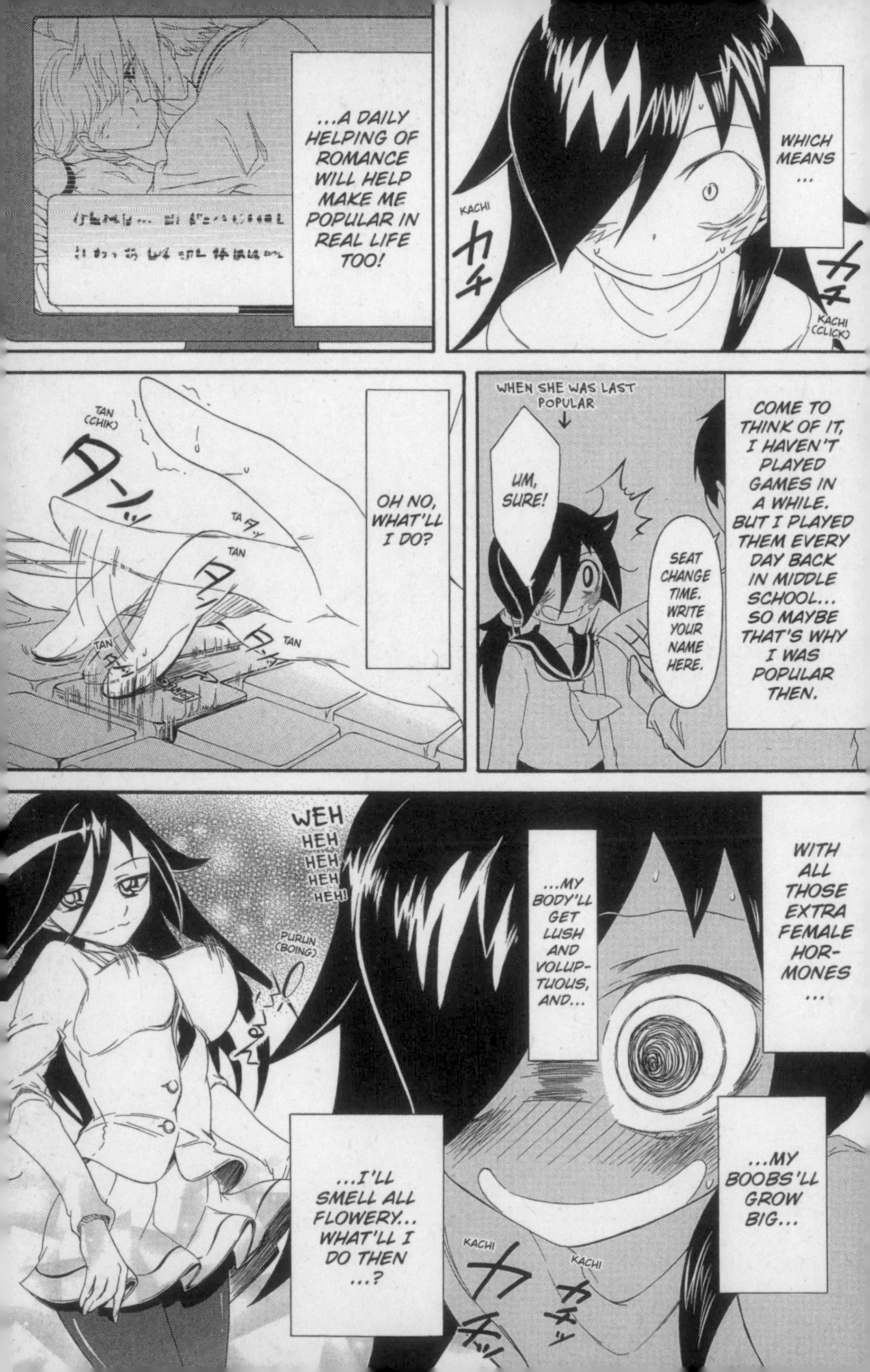
WHICH MEANS ...
KACHI
KACHI (CLICK)
...A DAILY HELPING OF ROMANCE WILL HELP MAKE ME POPULAR IN REAL LIFE TOO!
COME TO THINK OF IT, I HAVEN'T PLAYED GAMES IN A WHILE. BUT I PLAYED THEM EVERY DAY BACK IN MIDDLE SCHOOL... SO MAYBE THAT'S WHY I WAS POPULAR THEN.
WHEN SHE WAS LAST POPULAR
SEAT CHANGE TIME. WRITE YOUR NAME HERE.
UM, SURE!
OH NO, WHAT'LL I DO?
TAN (CHIK)
TA
TAN
TAN
TAN
WITH ALL THOSE EXTRA FEMALE HOR-MONES ...
...MY BODY'LL GET LUSH AND VOLUP-TUOUS, AND...
...MY BOOBS'LL GROW BIG...
KACHI
KACHI
...I'LL SMELL ALL FLOWERY... WHAT'LL I DO THEN ...?
WEH HEH HEH HEH HEH!
PURUN (BOING)

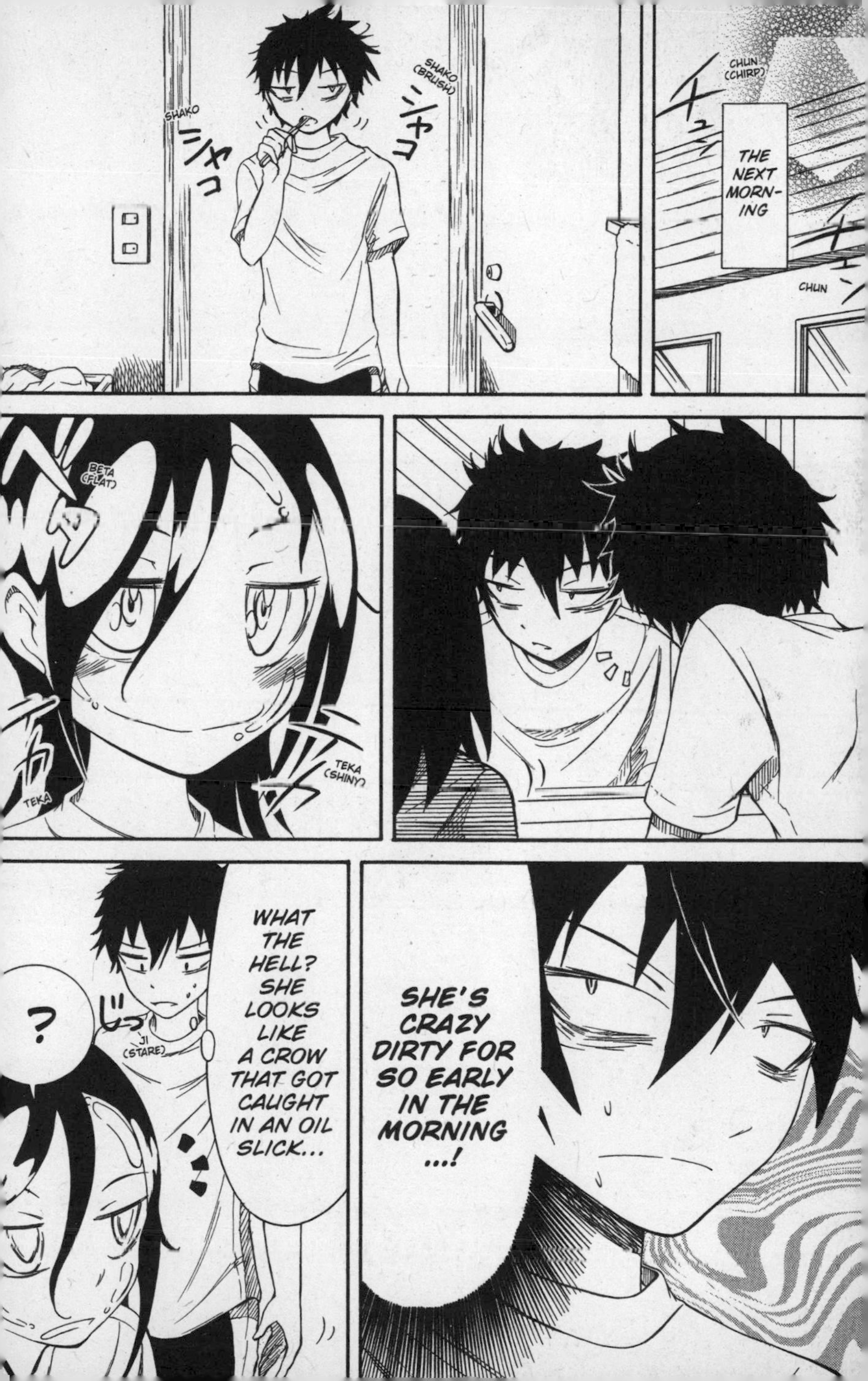
CHUN (CHIRP)
THE NEXT MORN-ING
CHUN
SHAKO (BRUSH)
シャコ
SHAKO
シャコ
BETA (FLAT)
TEKA (SHINY)
TEKA
SHE'S CRAZY DIRTY FOR SO EARLY IN THE MORNING ...!
WHAT THE HELL? SHE LOOKS LIKE A CROW THAT GOT CAUGHT IN AN OIL SLICK...
?
JI (STARE)

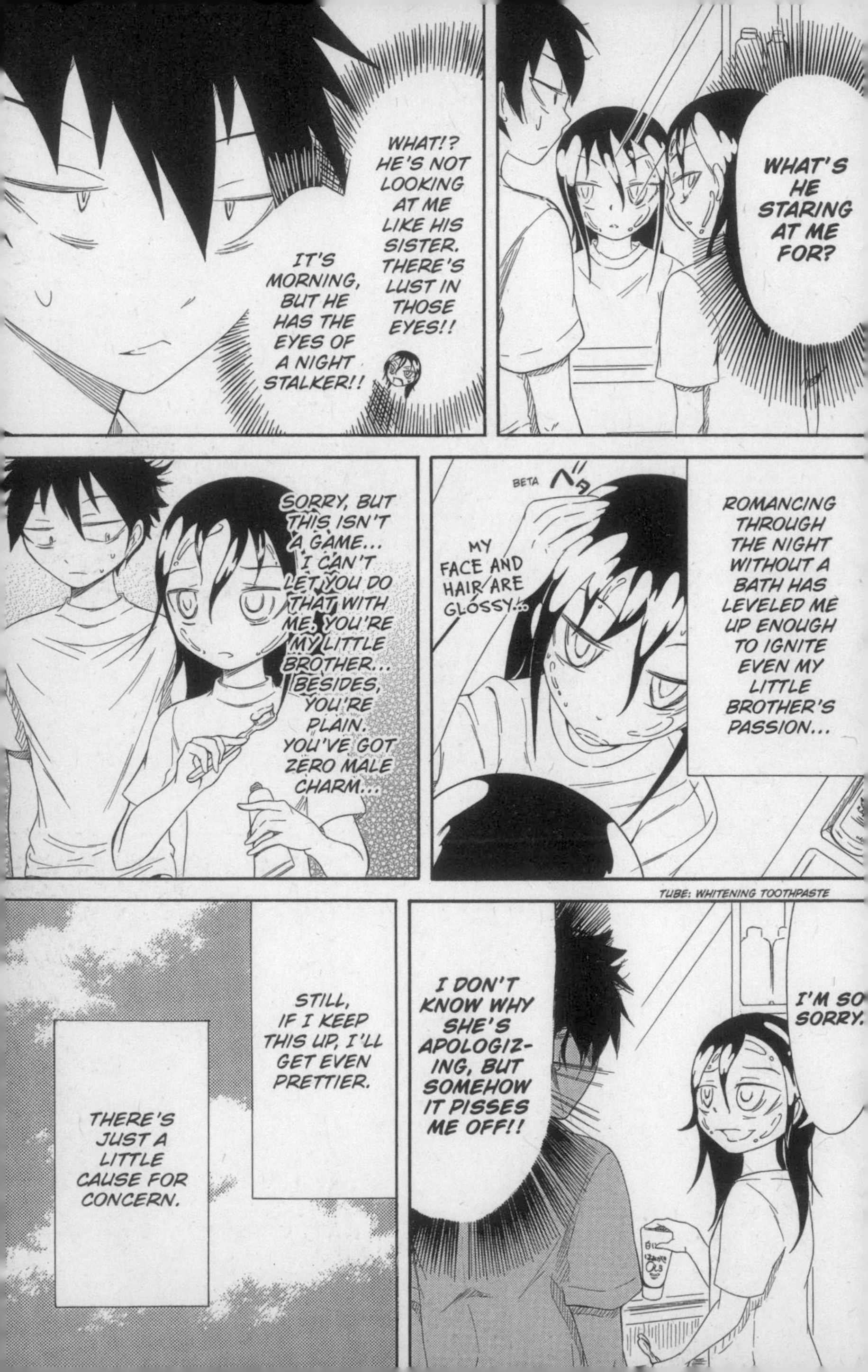
WHAT'S HE STARING AT ME FOR?
WHAT!? HE'S NOT LOOKING AT ME LIKE HIS SISTER. THERE'S LUST IN THOSE EYES!!
IT'S MORNING, BUT HE HAS THE EYES OF A NIGHT STALKER!!
ROMANCING THROUGH THE NIGHT WITHOUT A BATH HAS LEVELED ME UP ENOUGH TO IGNITE EVEN MY LITTLE BROTHER'S PASSION...
BETA
MY FACE AND HAIR ARE GLOSSY...
SORRY, BUT THIS ISN'T A GAME... I CAN'T LET YOU DO THAT WITH ME. YOU'RE MY LITTLE BROTHER... BESIDES, YOU'RE PLAIN. YOU'VE GOT ZERO MALE CHARM...
TUBE: WHITENING TOOTHPASTE
I'M SO SORRY.
I DON'T KNOW WHY SHE'S APOLOGIZ-ING, BUT SOMEHOW IT PISSES ME OFF!!
STILL, IF I KEEP THIS UP, I'LL GET EVEN PRETTIER.
THERE'S JUST A LITTLE CAUSE FOR CONCERN.

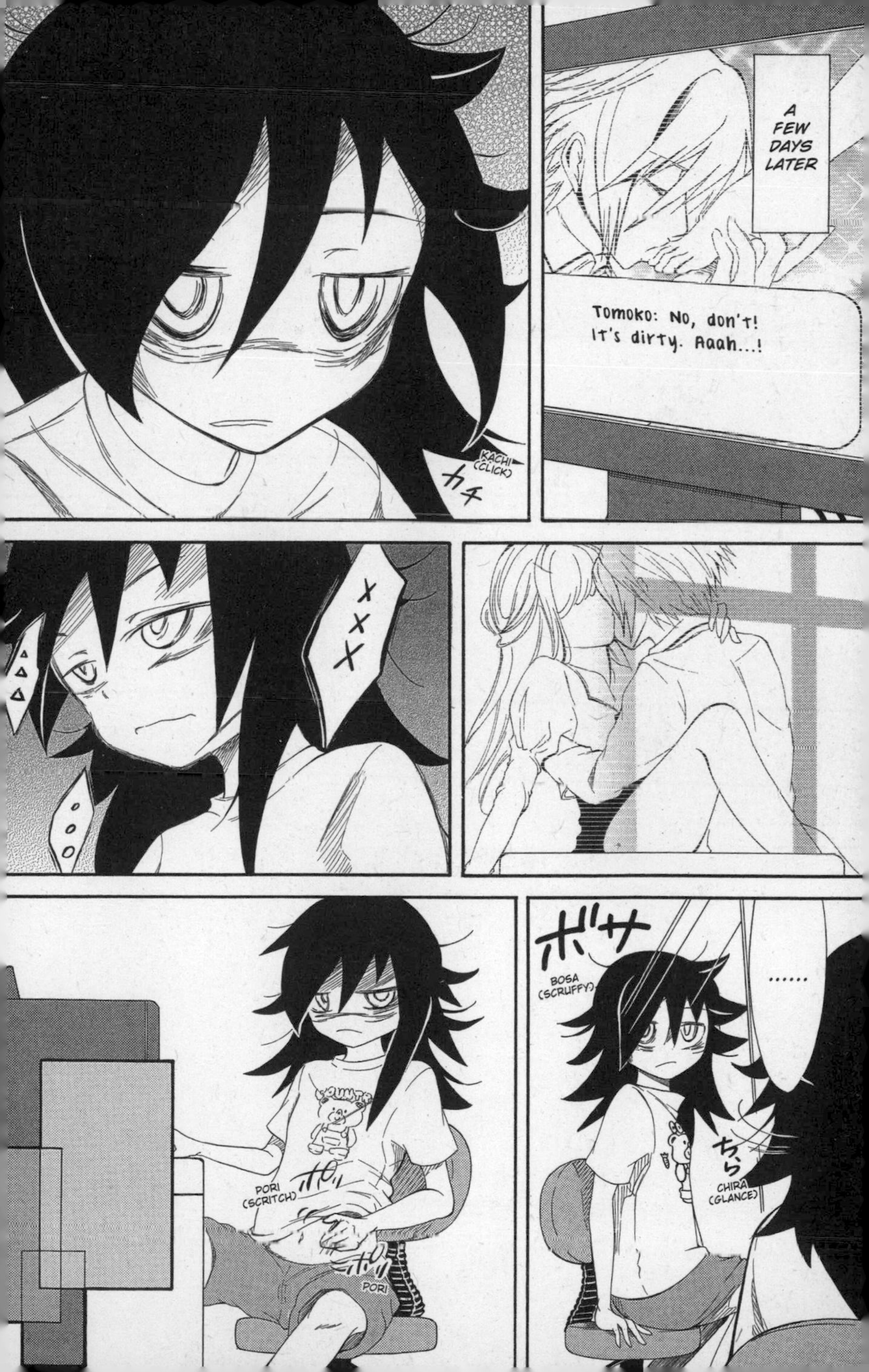
A FEW DAYS LATER
Tomoko: No, don't! It's dirty. Aaah...!
カチ
KACHI (CLICK)
ボサ
BOSA (SCRUFFY)
......
ちら
CHIRA (GLANCE)
ポリ
PORI (SCRITCH)
ポリ
PORI

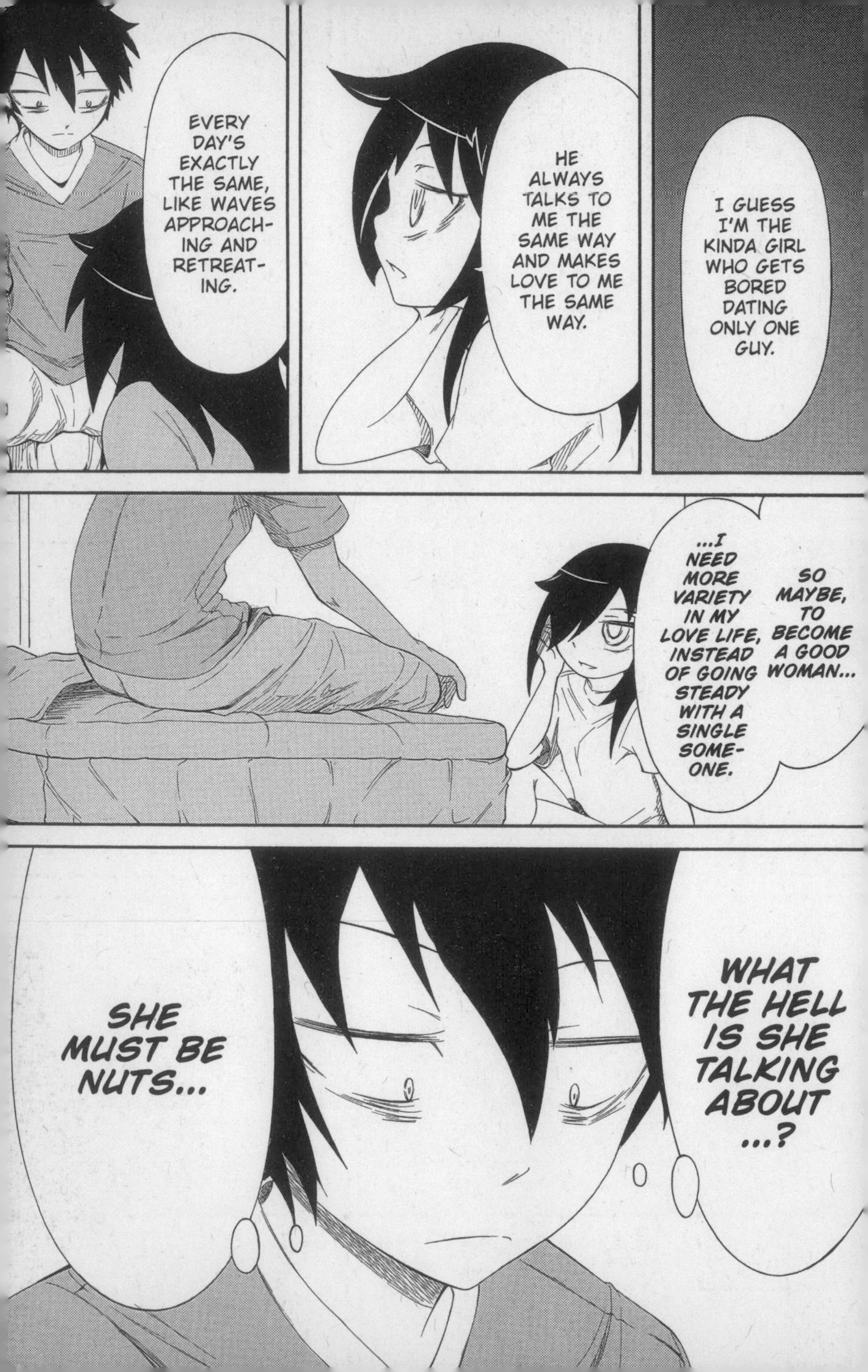
I GUESS I'M THE KINDA GIRL WHO GETS BORED DATING ONLY ONE GUY.
HE ALWAYS TALKS TO ME THE SAME WAY AND MAKES LOVE TO ME THE SAME WAY.
EVERY DAY'S EXACTLY THE SAME, LIKE WAVES APPROACH-ING AND RETREAT-ING.
SO MAYBE, TO BECOME A GOOD WOMAN...
...I NEED MORE VARIETY IN MY LOVE LIFE, INSTEAD OF GOING STEADY WITH A SINGLE SOME-ONE.
WHAT THE HELL IS SHE TALKING ABOUT ...?
SHE MUST BE NUTS...

No Matter How I Look at It, It's You Guys' Fault I'm Not Popular!

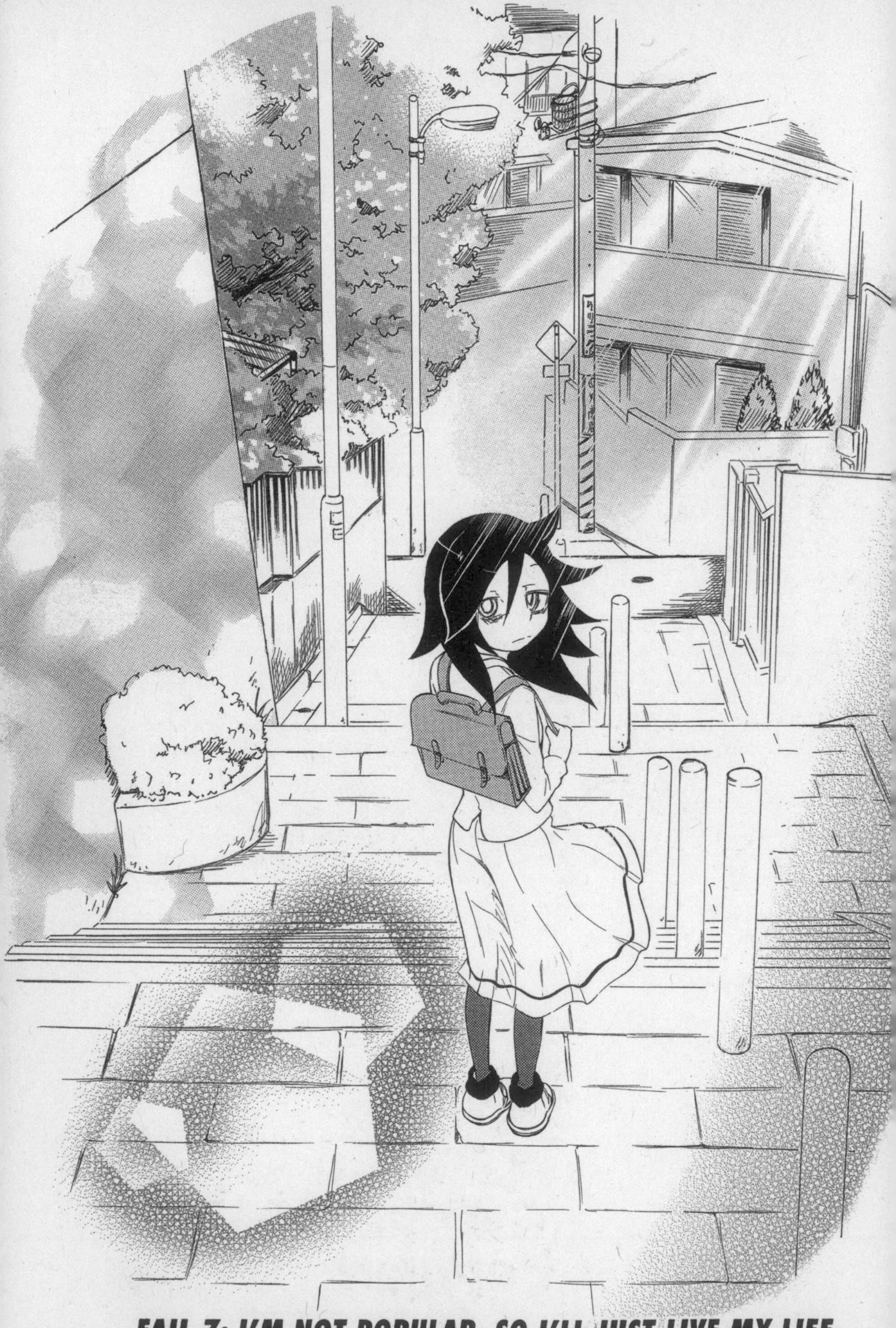

FAIL 7: I'M NOT POPULAR, SO I'LL JUST LIVE MY LIFE.

GOING TO SCHOOL

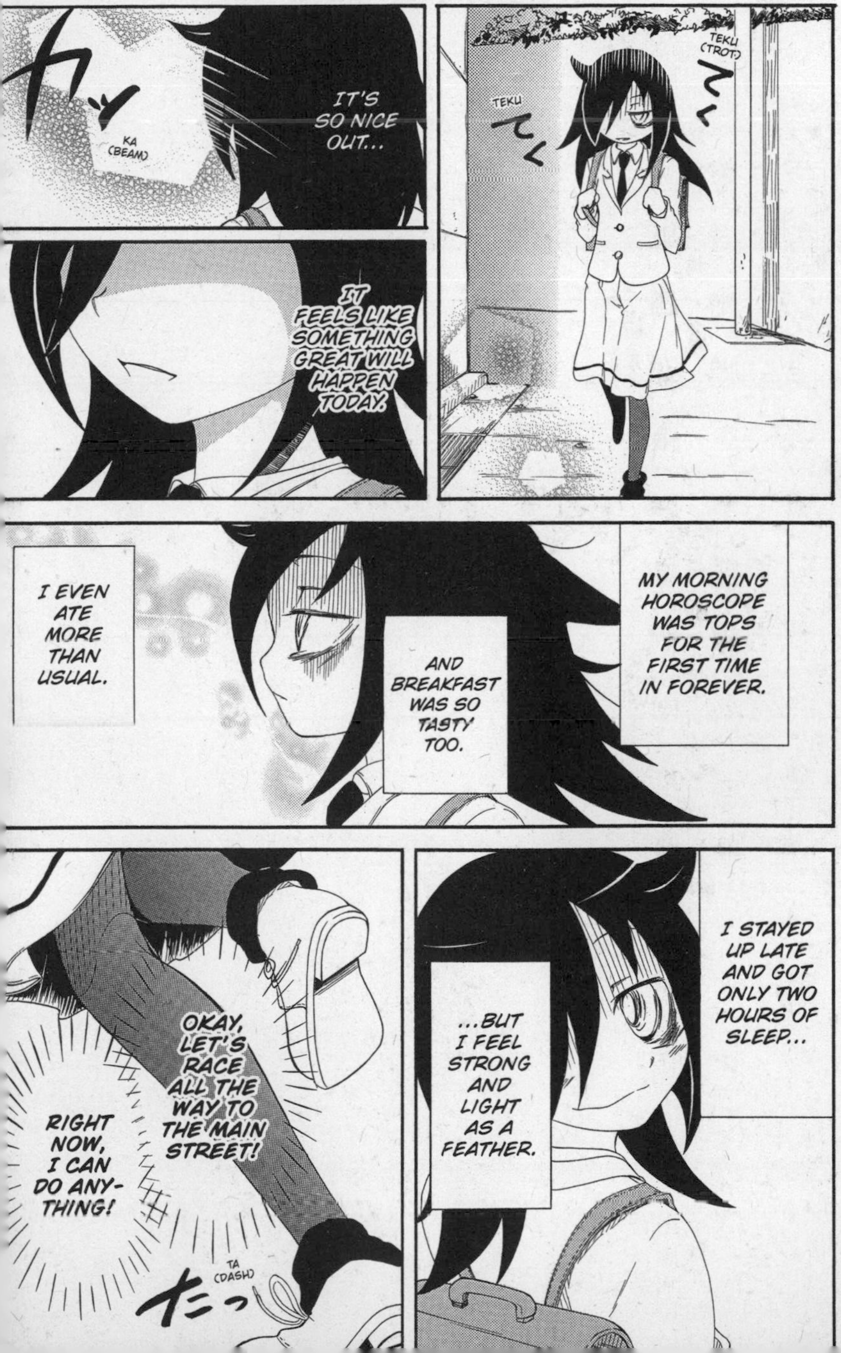
TEKU (TROT)
TEKU
KA (BEAM)
IT'S SO NICE OUT...
IT FEELS LIKE SOMETHING GREAT WILL HAPPEN TODAY.
MY MORNING HOROSCOPE WAS TOPS FOR THE FIRST TIME IN FOREVER.
AND BREAKFAST WAS SO TASTY TOO.
I EVEN ATE MORE THAN USUAL.
I STAYED UP LATE AND GOT ONLY TWO HOURS OF SLEEP...
...BUT I FEEL STRONG AND LIGHT AS A FEATHER.
OKAY, LET'S RACE ALL THE WAY TO THE MAIN STREET!
RIGHT NOW, I CAN DO ANY-THING!
TA (DASH)

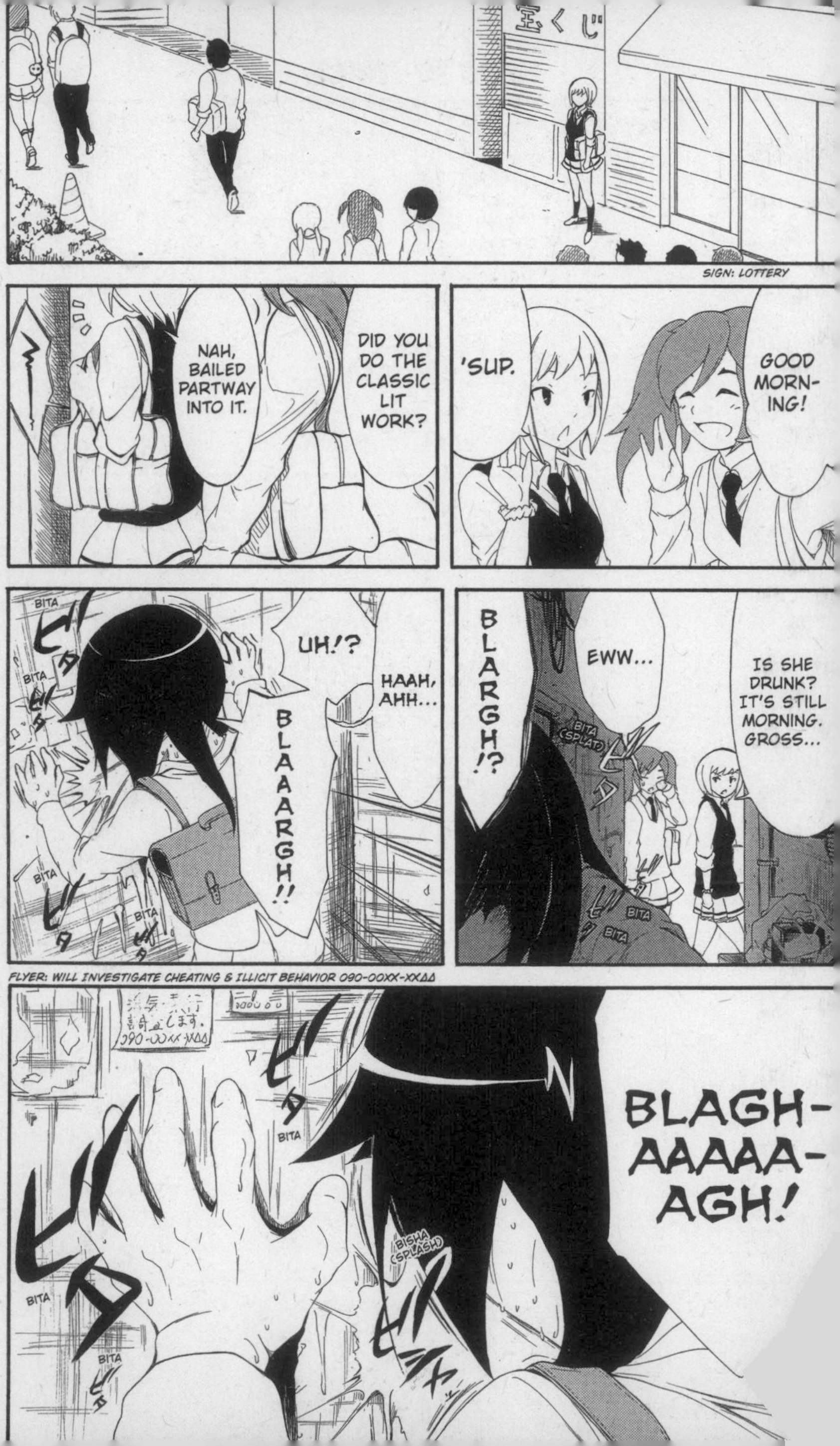
宝くじ
GOOD MORNING!
'SUP.
DID YOU DO THE CLASSIC LIT WORK?
NAH, BAILED PARTWAY INTO IT.
IS SHE DRUNK? IT'S STILL MORNING. GROSS...
EWW...
BLARGH!?
BITA (SPLAT)
BITA
BITA
HAAH, AHH...
UH!?
BLAAAARGH!!
BITA
BITA
BITA
BITA
BLAGH-AAAAA-AGH!
BISHA (SPLASH)
BITA
BITA
BITA
090-00XX-XXΔΔ

SIGN: LOTTERY

FLYER: WILL INVESTIGATE CHEATING & ILLICIT BEHAVIOR 090-00XX-XXΔΔ

AN EARLY LUNCH

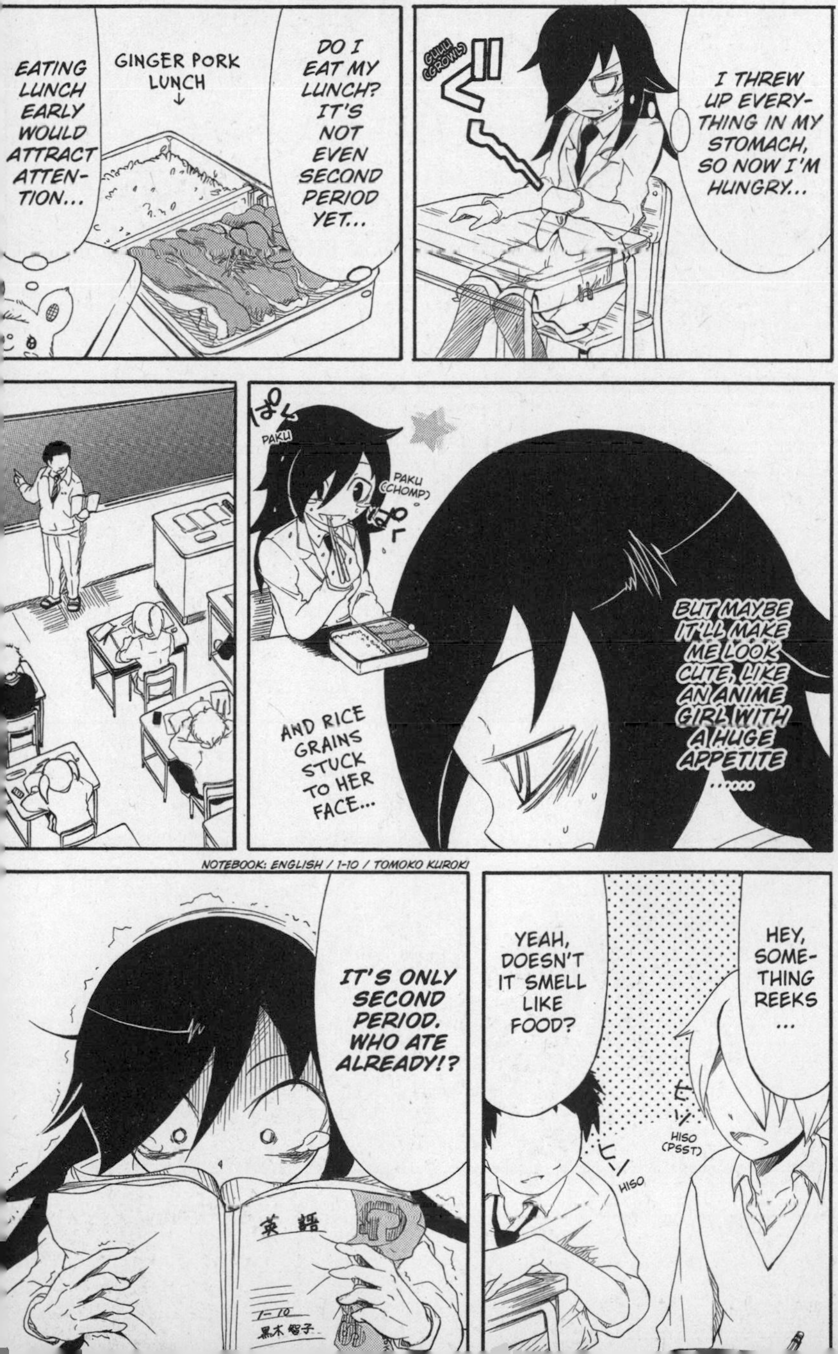
GUUU (GROWL)
I THREW UP EVERYTHING IN MY STOMACH, SO NOW I'M HUNGRY...
DO I EAT MY LUNCH? IT'S NOT EVEN SECOND PERIOD YET...
GINGER PORK LUNCH
EATING LUNCH EARLY WOULD ATTRACT ATTENTION...
PAKU
PAKU (CHOMP)
BUT MAYBE IT'LL MAKE ME LOOK CUTE, LIKE AN ANIME GIRL WITH A HUGE APPETITE ......
AND RICE GRAINS STUCK TO HER FACE...
NOTEBOOK: ENGLISH / 1-10 / TOMOKO KUROKI
HEY, SOMETHING REEKS ...
YEAH, DOESN'T IT SMELL LIKE FOOD?
HISO (PSST)
HISO
IT'S ONLY SECOND PERIOD. WHO ATE ALREADY!?
英語
1-10
黒木智子

SNOOZING

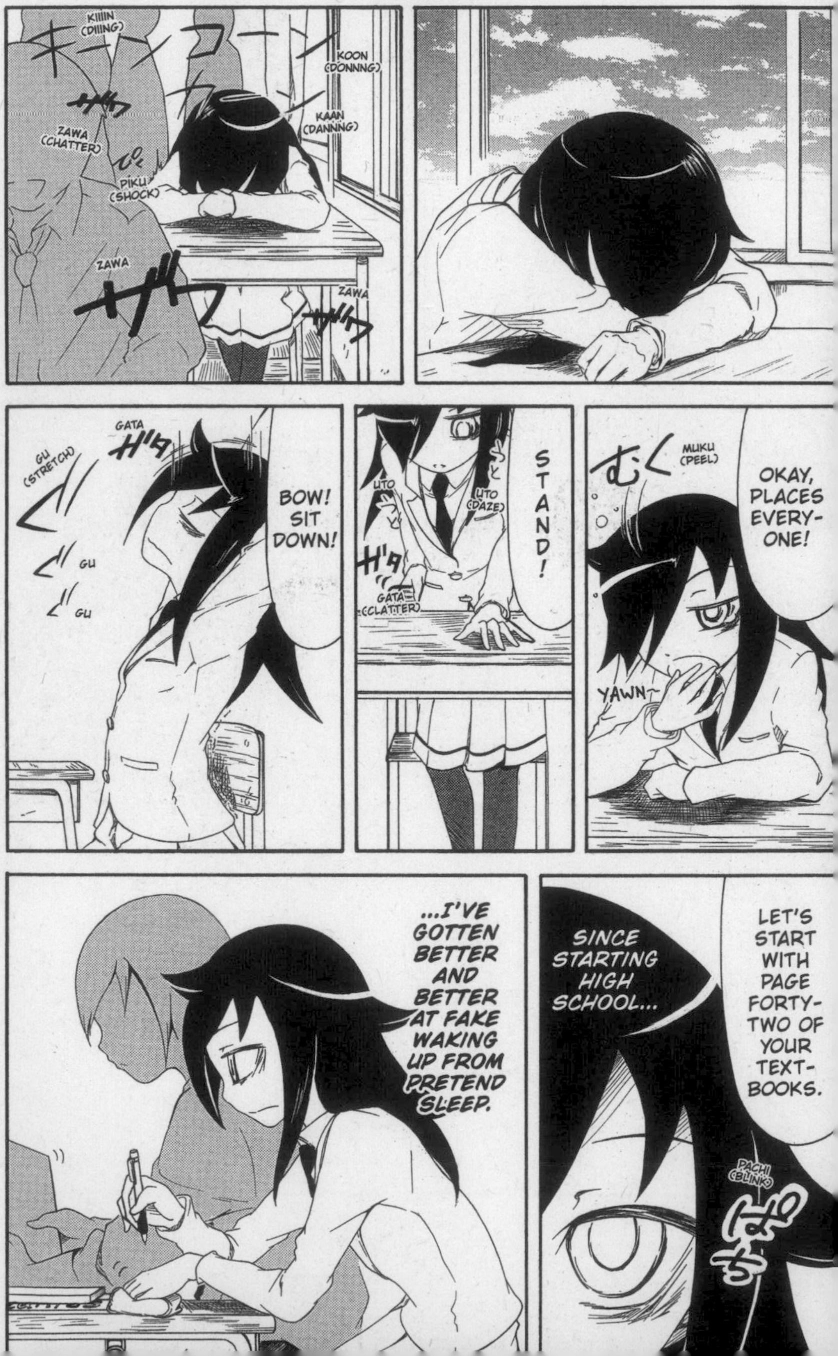
KIIIN (DIIING)
KOON (DONNNG)
KAAN (DANNNG)
ZAWA (CHATTER)
PIKU (SHOCK)
ZAWA
ZAWA
MUKU (PEEL)
OKAY, PLACES EVERY-ONE!
YAWN~
STAND!
UTO
UTO (DAZE)
GATA (CLATTER)
BOW! SIT DOWN!
GATA
GU (STRETCH)
GU
GU
LET'S START WITH PAGE FORTY-TWO OF YOUR TEXT-BOOKS.
SINCE STARTING HIGH SCHOOL...
PACHI (BLINK)
...I'VE GOTTEN BETTER AND BETTER AT FAKE WAKING UP FROM PRETEND SLEEP.

THE MOST INFURIATING TYPE

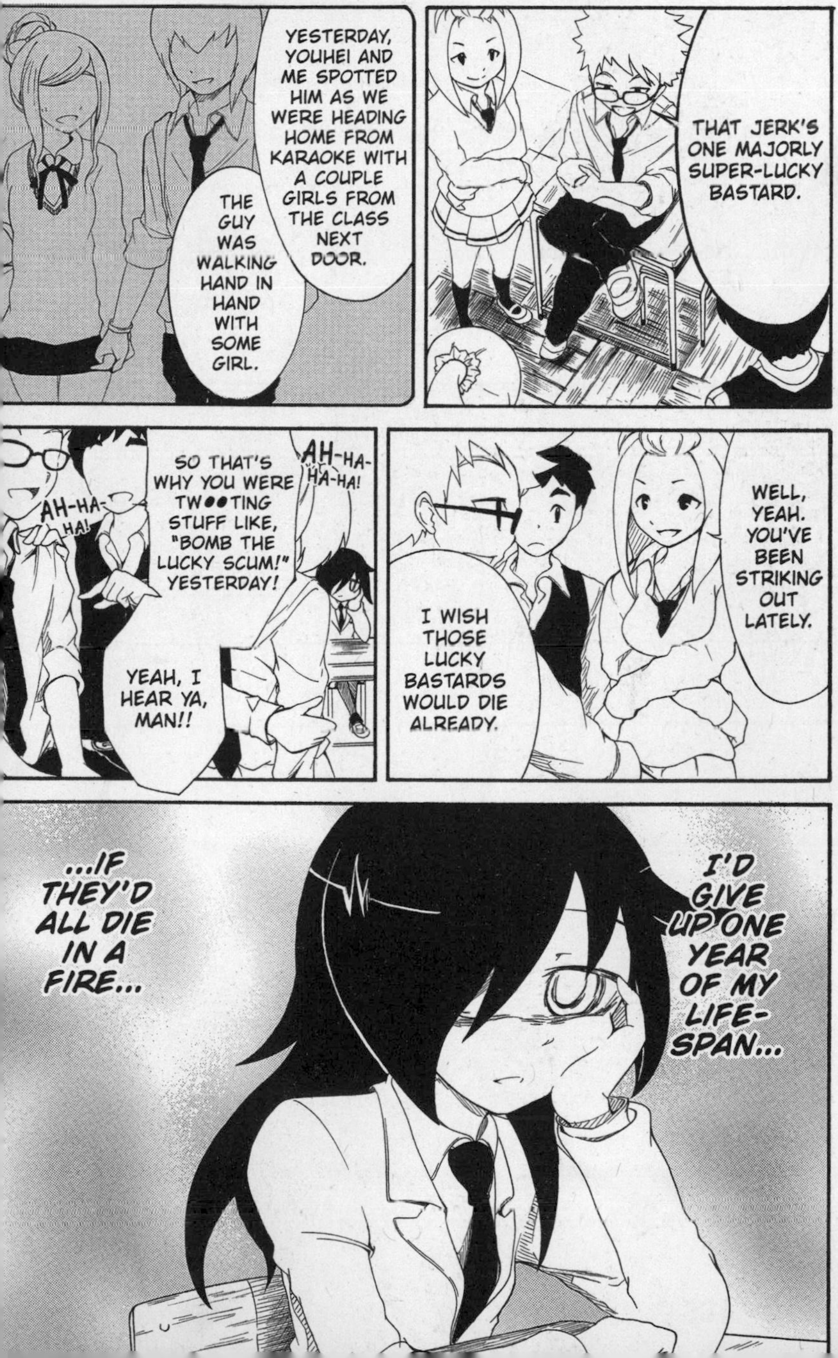
THAT JERK'S ONE MAJORLY SUPER-LUCKY BASTARD.
YESTERDAY, YOUHEI AND ME SPOTTED HIM AS WE WERE HEADING HOME FROM KARAOKE WITH A COUPLE GIRLS FROM THE CLASS NEXT DOOR.
THE GUY WAS WALKING HAND IN HAND WITH SOME GIRL.
WELL, YEAH. YOU'VE BEEN STRIKING OUT LATELY.
I WISH THOSE LUCKY BASTARDS WOULD DIE ALREADY.
AH-HA-HA-HA!
SO THAT'S WHY YOU WERE TWOOTING STUFF LIKE, "BOMB THE LUCKY SCUM!" YESTERDAY!
AH-HA-HA!
YEAH, I HEAR YA, MAN!!
I'D GIVE UP ONE YEAR OF MY LIFE-SPAN...
...IF THEY'D ALL DIE IN A FIRE...

TOO FRIGHTENING TO IMAGINE

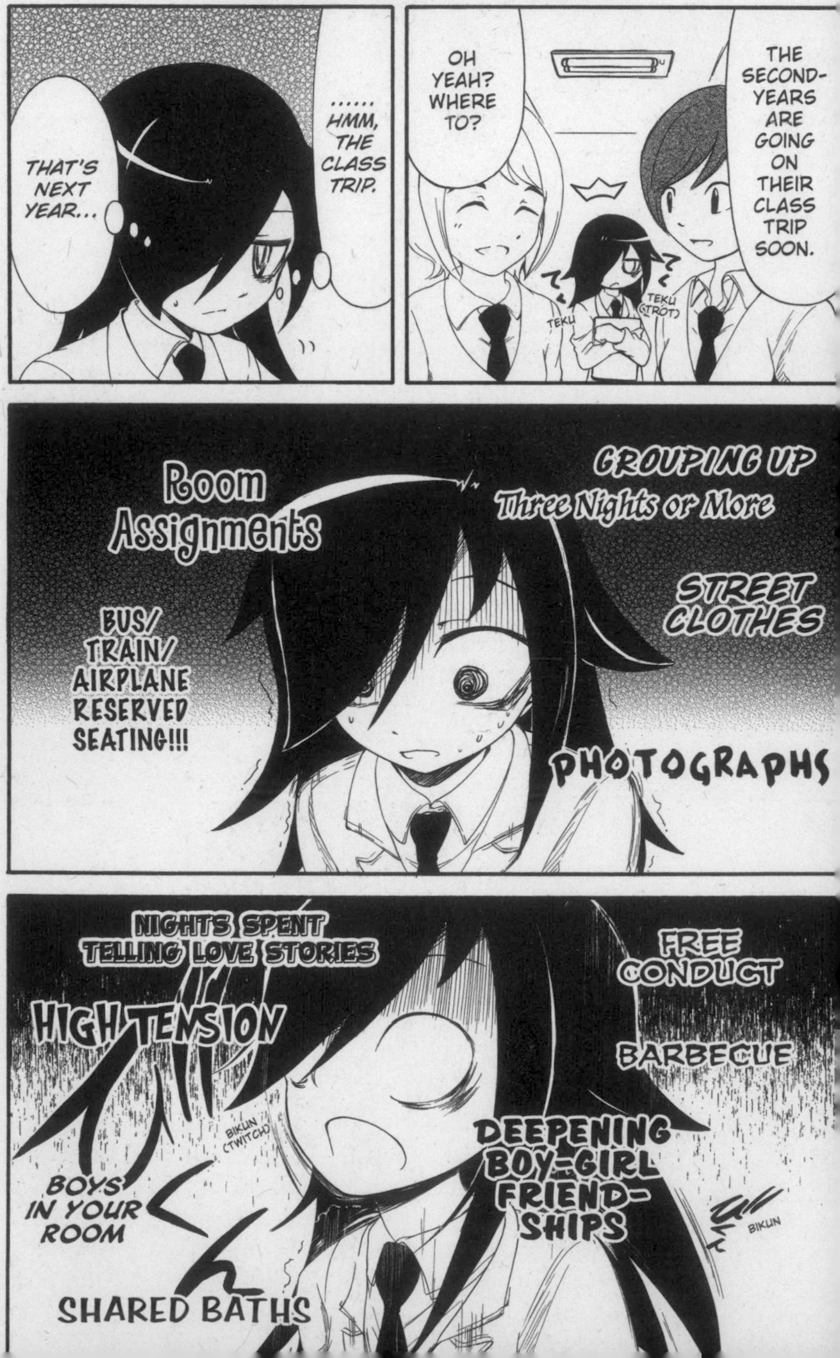

THE SECOND-YEARS ARE GOING ON THEIR CLASS TRIP SOON.
OH YEAH? WHERE TO?
TEKU (TROT)
TEKU
......HMM, THE CLASS TRIP.
THAT'S NEXT YEAR...
GROUPING UP
Three Nights or More
Room Assignments
STREET CLOTHES
BUS/ TRAIN/ AIRPLANE RESERVED SEATING!!!
PHOTOGRAPHS
FREE CONDUCT
NIGHTS SPENT TELLING LOVE STORIES
HIGH TENSION
BARBECUE
BIKUN
DEEPENING BOY-GIRL FRIEND-SHIPS
BIKUN (TWITCH)
BOYS IN YOUR ROOM
SHARED BATHS

EVASION

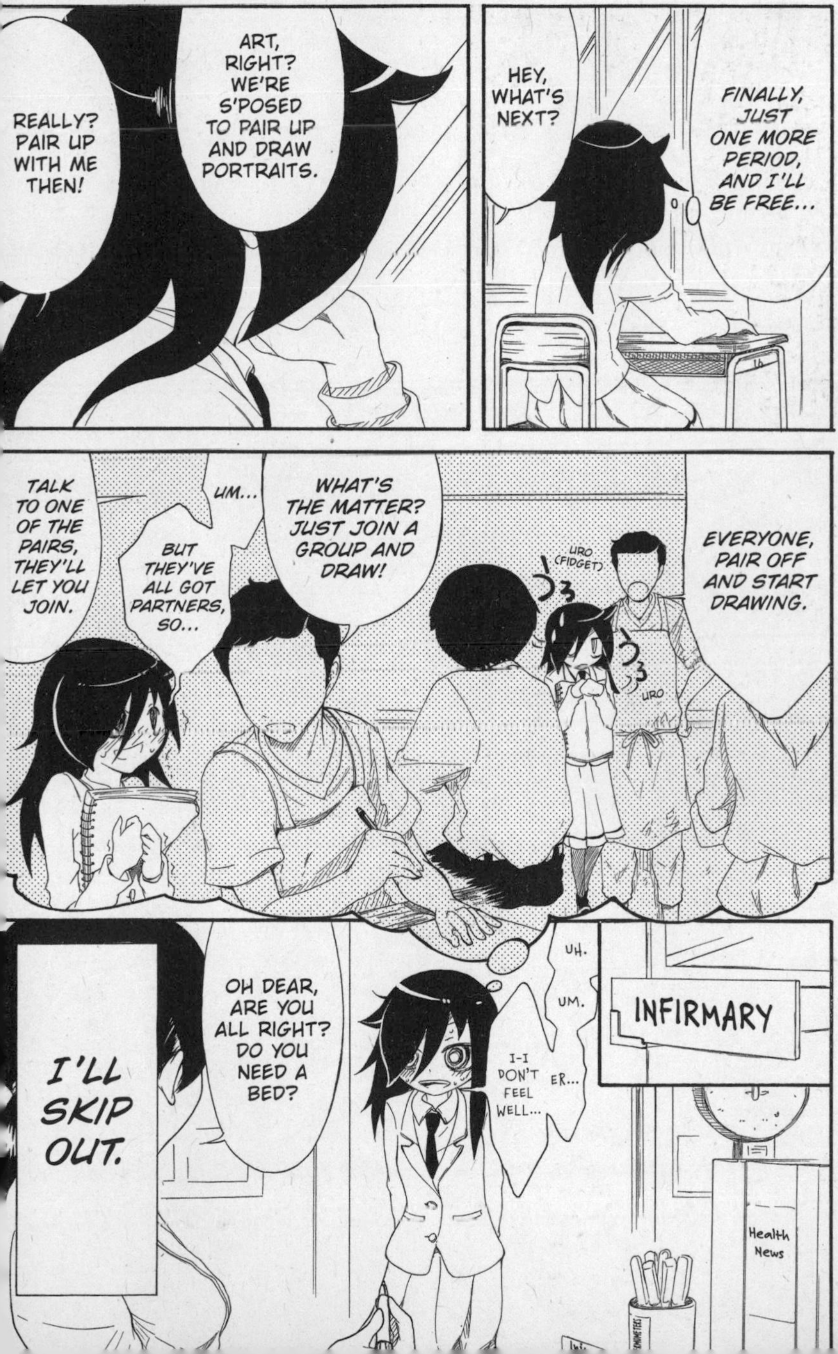
FINALLY, JUST ONE MORE PERIOD, AND I'LL BE FREE...
HEY, WHAT'S NEXT?
ART, RIGHT? WE'RE S'POSED TO PAIR UP AND DRAW PORTRAITS.
REALLY? PAIR UP WITH ME THEN!
EVERYONE, PAIR OFF AND START DRAWING.
URO (FIDGET)
URO
WHAT'S THE MATTER? JUST JOIN A GROUP AND DRAW!
UM...
BUT THEY'VE ALL GOT PARTNERS, SO...
TALK TO ONE OF THE PAIRS, THEY'LL LET YOU JOIN.
INFIRMARY
Health News
UH.
UM.
ER...
I-I DON'T FEEL WELL...
OH DEAR, ARE YOU ALL RIGHT? DO YOU NEED A BED?
I'LL SKIP OUT.

INFIRMARY

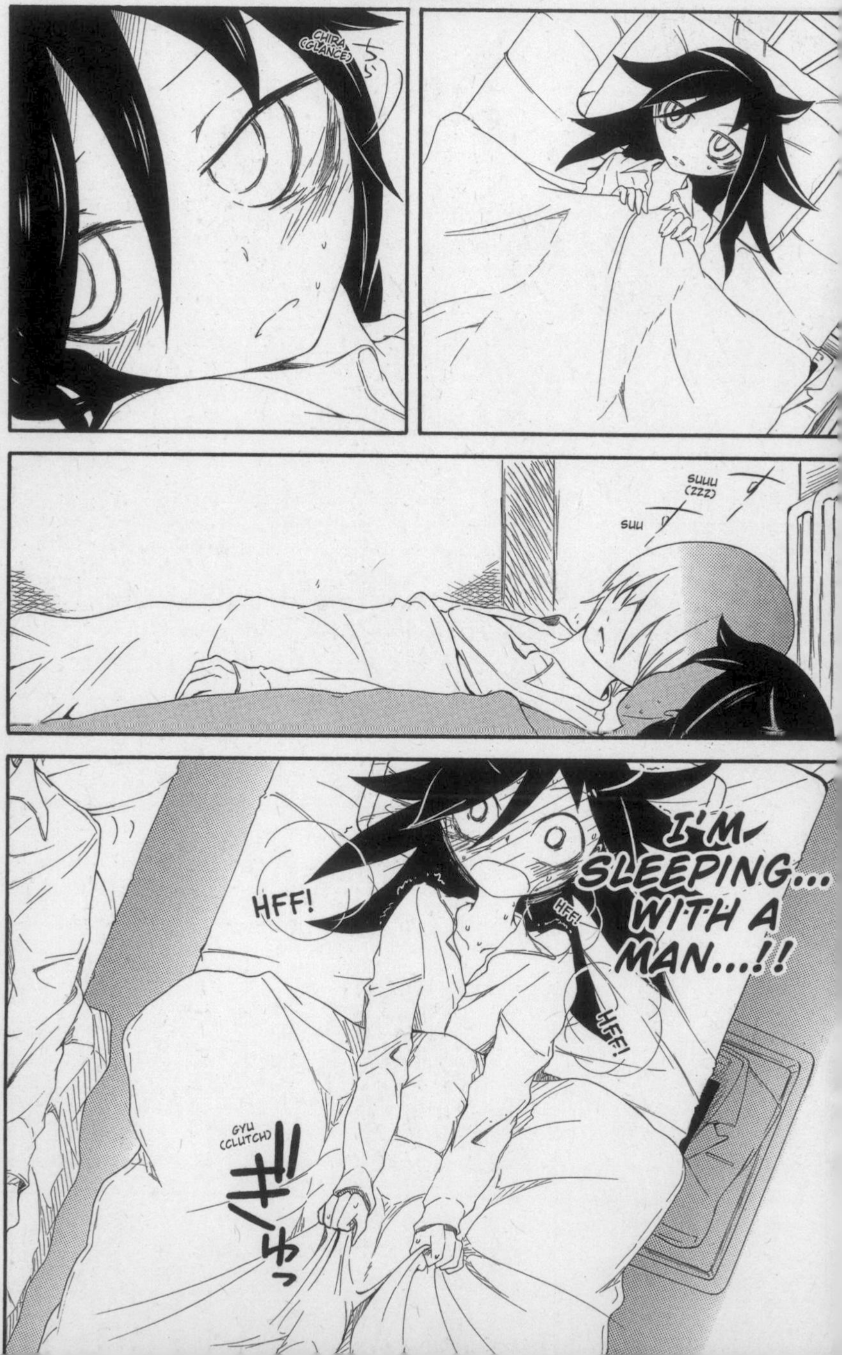
CHIRA (GLANCE)
SUUU (ZZZ)
SUU
I'M SLEEPING... WITH A MAN...!!
HFF!
HFF!
HFF!
GYU (CLUTCH)

LEAVING SCHOOL 1

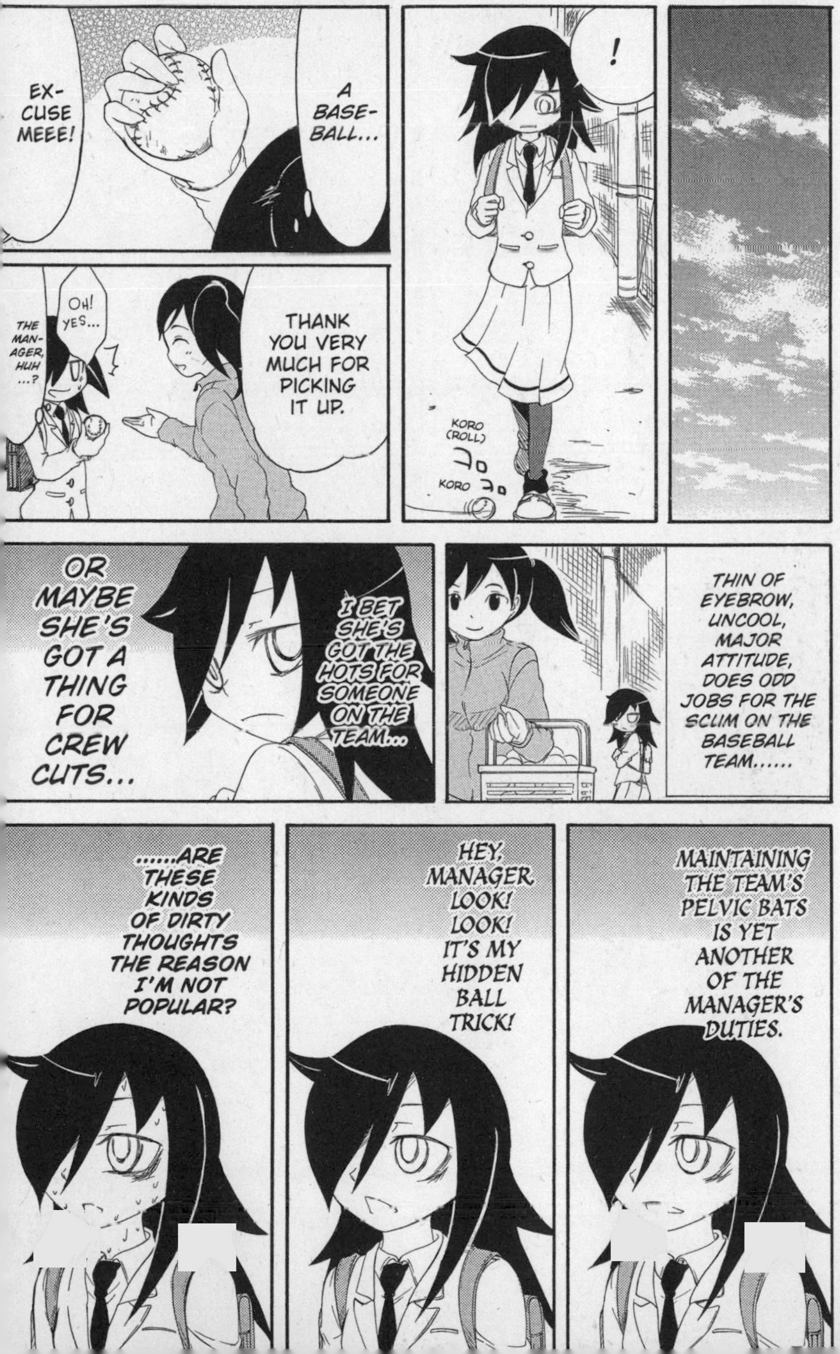
!
KORO (ROLL)
KORO
A BASE-BALL...
EX-CUSE MEEE!
THANK YOU VERY MUCH FOR PICKING IT UP.
OH! YES...
THE MAN-AGER, HUH ...?
THIN OF EYEBROW, UNCOOL, MAJOR ATTITUDE, DOES ODD JOBS FOR THE SCUM ON THE BASEBALL TEAM......
I BET SHE'S GOT THE HOTS FOR SOMEONE ON THE TEAM...
OR MAYBE SHE'S GOT A THING FOR CREW CUTS...
MAINTAINING THE TEAM'S PELVIC BATS IS YET ANOTHER OF THE MANAGER'S DUTIES.
HEY, MANAGER. LOOK! LOOK! IT'S MY HIDDEN BALL TRICK!
......ARE THESE KINDS OF DIRTY THOUGHTS THE REASON I'M NOT POPULAR?

LEAVING SCHOOL 2

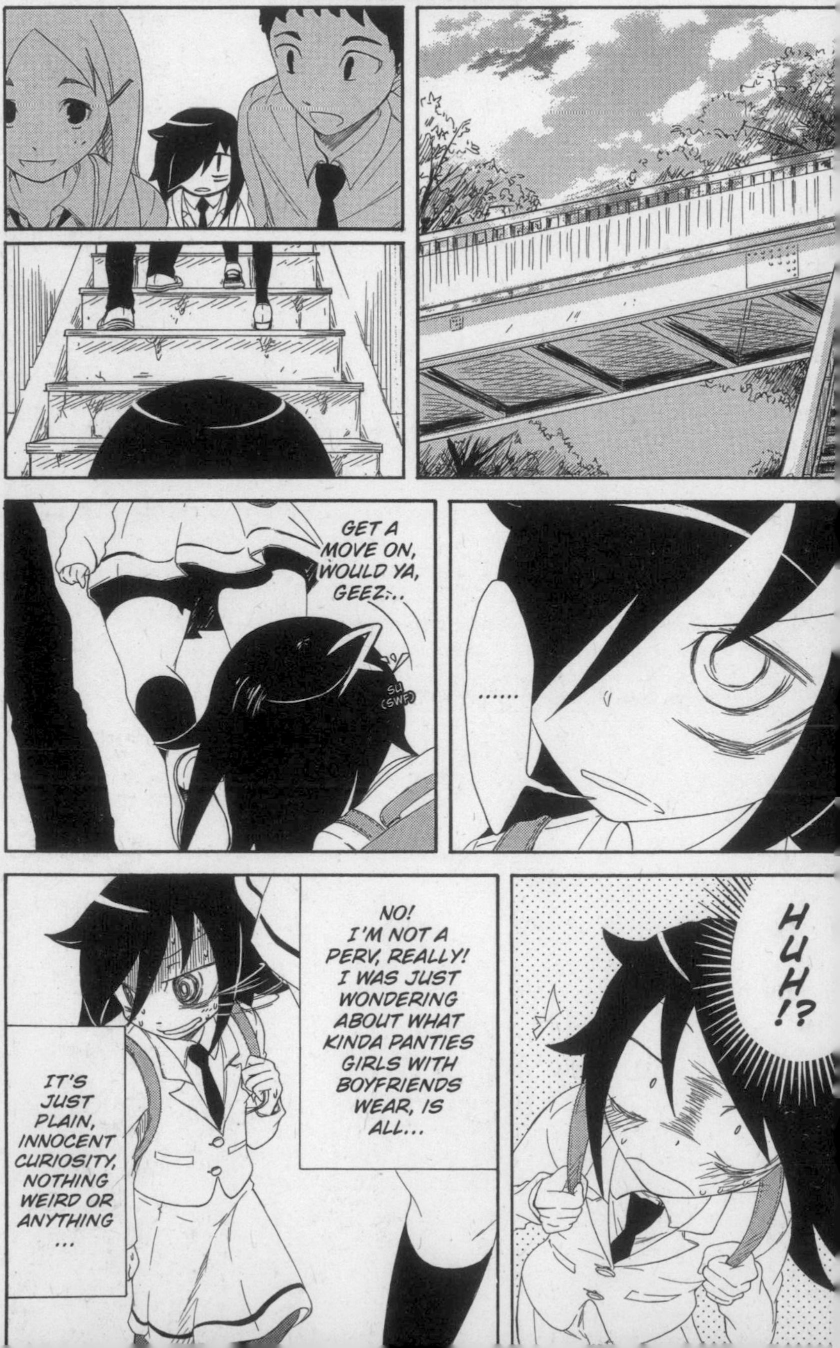
......
GET A MOVE ON, WOULD YA, GEEZ...
SLI (SWF)
HUH!?
NO! I'M NOT A PERV, REALLY! I WAS JUST WONDERING ABOUT WHAT KINDA PANTIES GIRLS WITH BOYFRIENDS WEAR, IS ALL...
IT'S JUST PLAIN, INNOCENT CURIOSITY, NOTHING WEIRD OR ANYTHING ...

LOOKING BACK

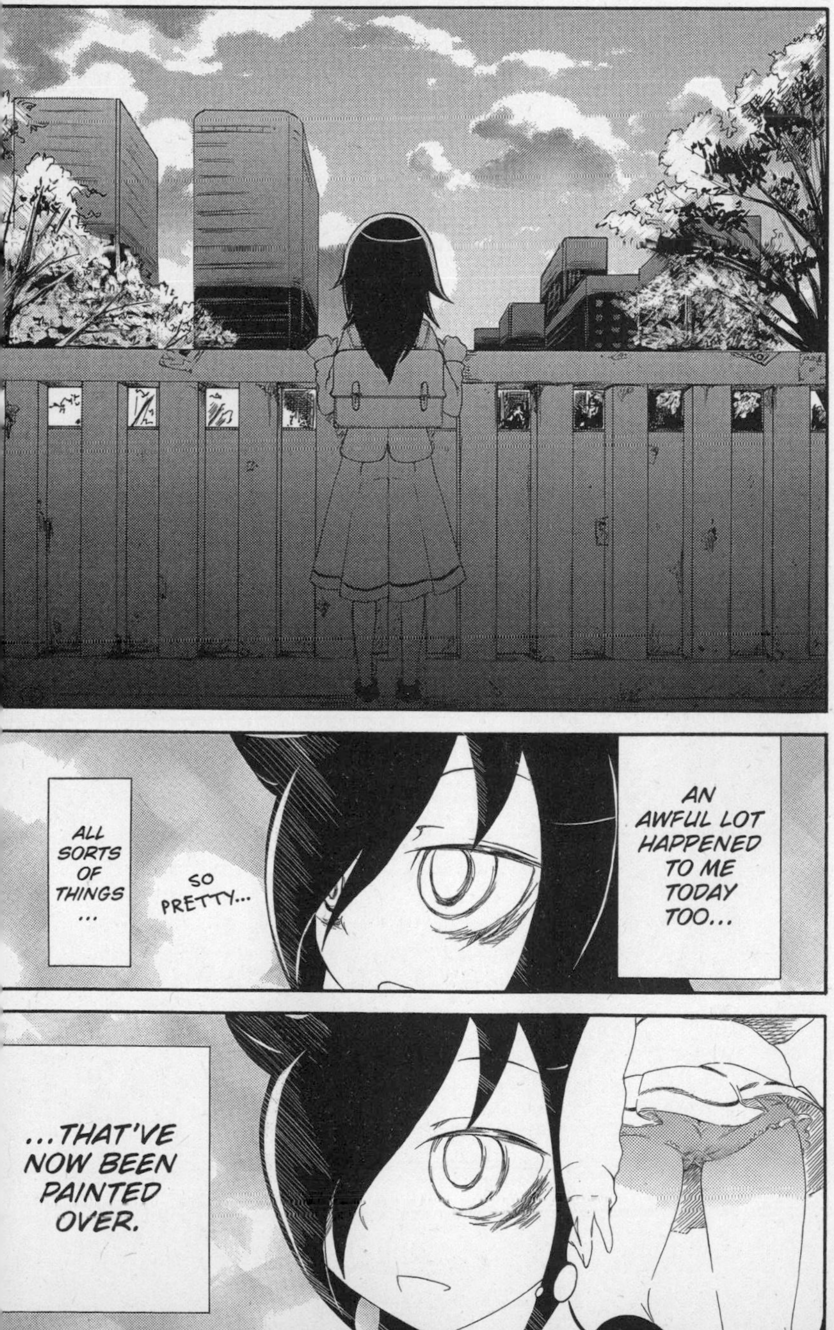
AN AWFUL LOT HAPPENED TO ME TODAY TOO...
SO PRETTY...
ALL SORTS OF THINGS ...
...THAT'VE NOW BEEN PAINTED OVER.

No Matter How I Look at It, It's You Guys' Fault I'm Not Popular!

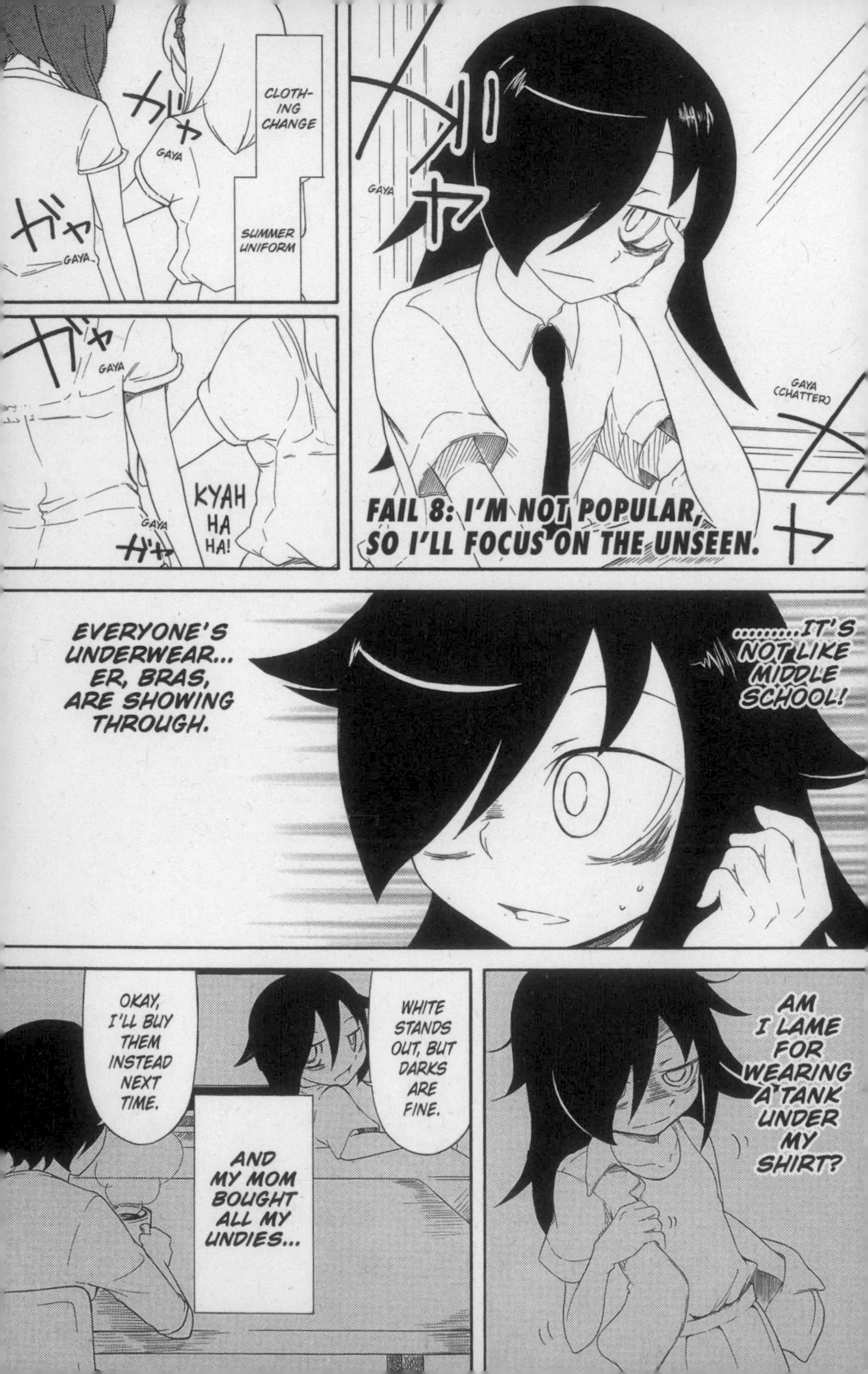
GAYA (CHATTER)
GAYA
FAIL 8: I'M NOT POPULAR, SO I'LL FOCUS ON THE UNSEEN.
CLOTHING CHANGE
SUMMER UNIFORM
GAYA
GAYA
GAYA
KYAH HA HA!
GAYA
..........IT'S NOT LIKE MIDDLE SCHOOL!
EVERYONE'S UNDERWEAR... ER, BRAS, ARE SHOWING THROUGH.
AM I LAME FOR WEARING A TANK UNDER MY SHIRT?
WHITE STANDS OUT, BUT DARKS ARE FINE.
OKAY, I'LL BUY THEM INSTEAD NEXT TIME.
AND MY MOM BOUGHT ALL MY UNDIES...

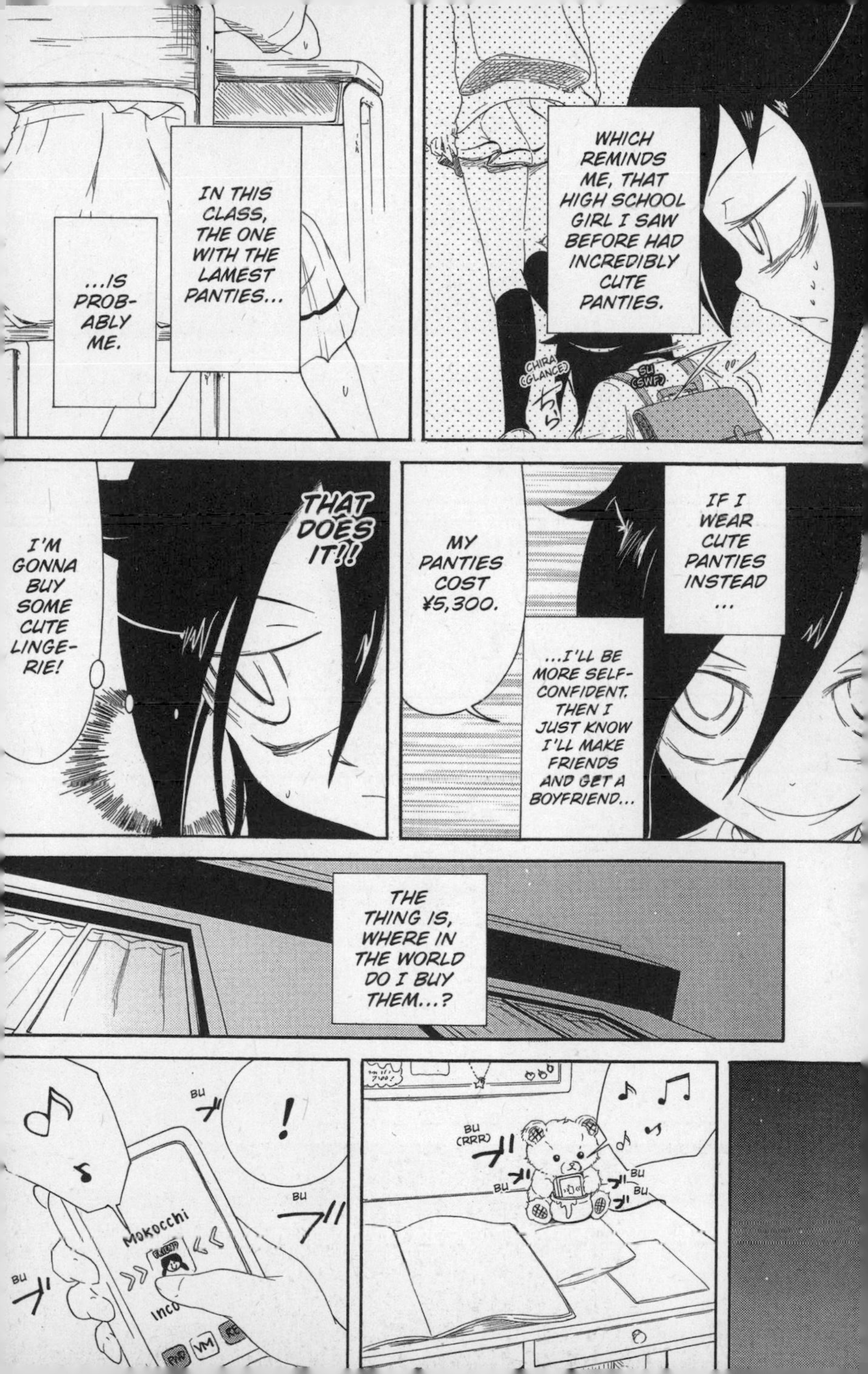
WHICH REMINDS ME, THAT HIGH SCHOOL GIRL I SAW BEFORE HAD INCREDIBLY CUTE PANTIES.
SU (SWF)
CHIRA (GLANCE)
IN THIS CLASS, THE ONE WITH THE LAMEST PANTIES...
...IS PROBABLY ME.
IF I WEAR CUTE PANTIES INSTEAD...
...I'LL BE MORE SELF-CONFIDENT. THEN I JUST KNOW I'LL MAKE FRIENDS AND GET A BOYFRIEND...
MY PANTIES COST ¥5,300.
THAT DOES IT!!
I'M GONNA BUY SOME CUTE LINGERIE!
THE THING IS, WHERE IN THE WORLD DO I BUY THEM...?
BU (RRR)
BU
BU
BU
BU
!
BU
Mokocchi
BU

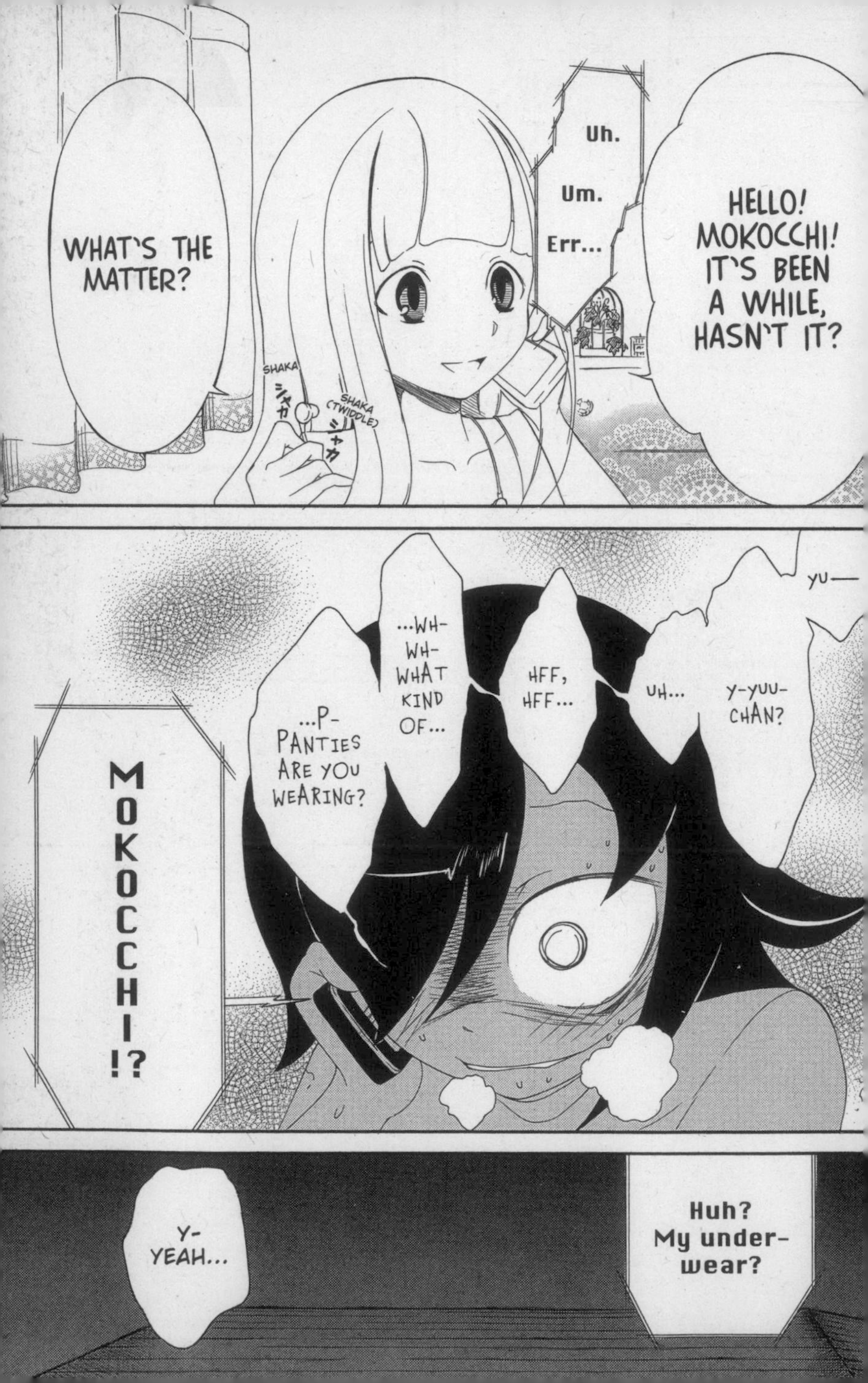
HELLO! MOKOCCHI! IT'S BEEN A WHILE, HASN'T IT?
Uh.
Um.
Err...
SHAKA シャカ
SHAKA (TWIDDLE) シャカ
WHAT'S THE MATTER?
YU—
Y-YUU-CHAN?
UH...
HFF, HFF...
...WH-WH-WHAT KIND OF...
...P-PANTIES ARE YOU WEARING?
MOKOCCHI!?
Huh? My under-wear?
Y-YEAH...

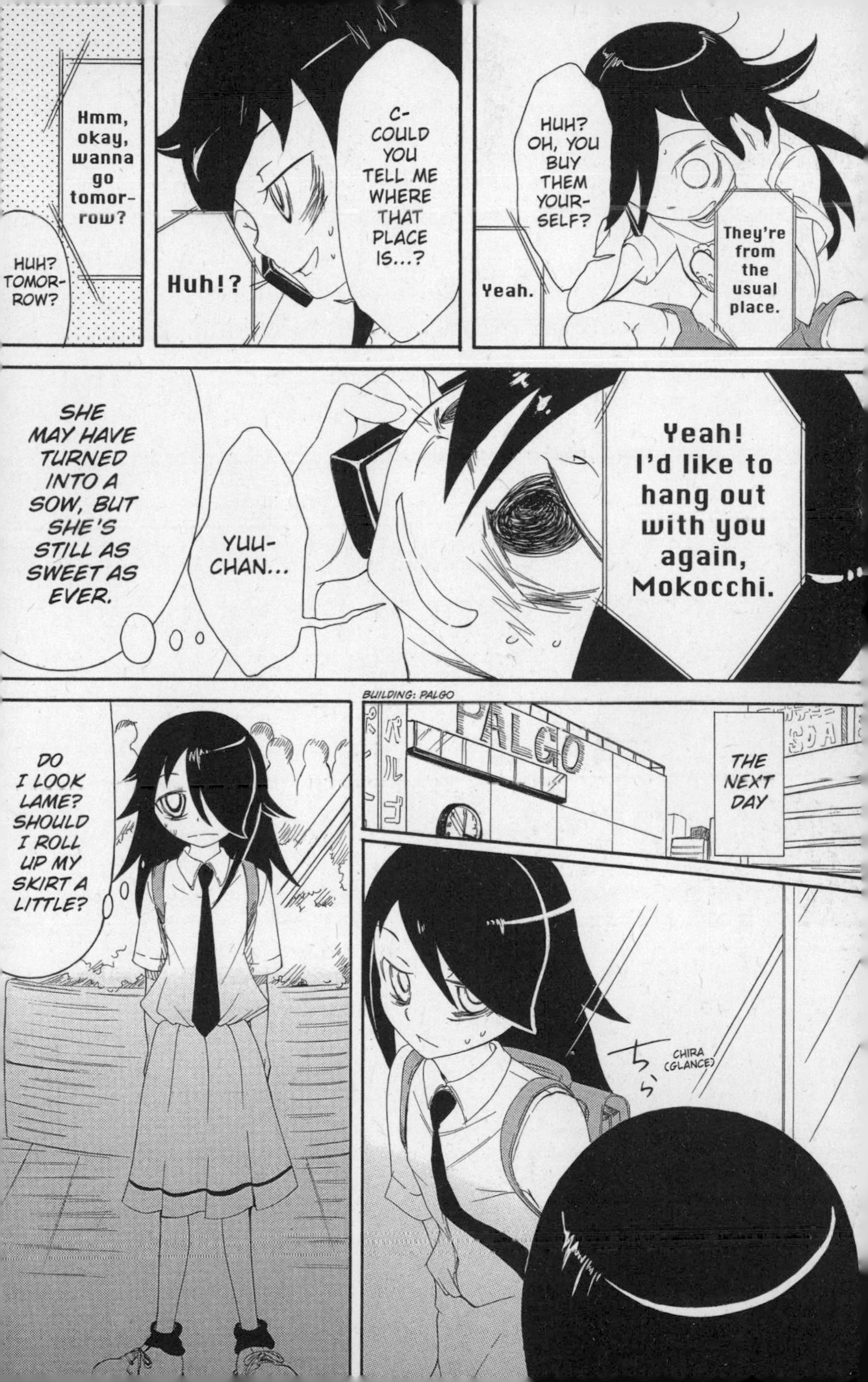
HUH? OH, YOU BUY THEM YOURSELF?
They're from the usual place.
Yeah.
C-COULD YOU TELL ME WHERE THAT PLACE IS...?
Huh!?
Hmm, okay, wanna go tomorrow?
HUH? TOMORROW?
Yeah! I'd like to hang out with you again, Mokocchi.
YUU-CHAN...
SHE MAY HAVE TURNED INTO A SOW, BUT SHE'S STILL AS SWEET AS EVER.
BUILDING: PALGO
PALGO
THE NEXT DAY
ちら
CHIRA (GLANCE)
DO I LOOK LAME? SHOULD I ROLL UP MY SKIRT A LITTLE?

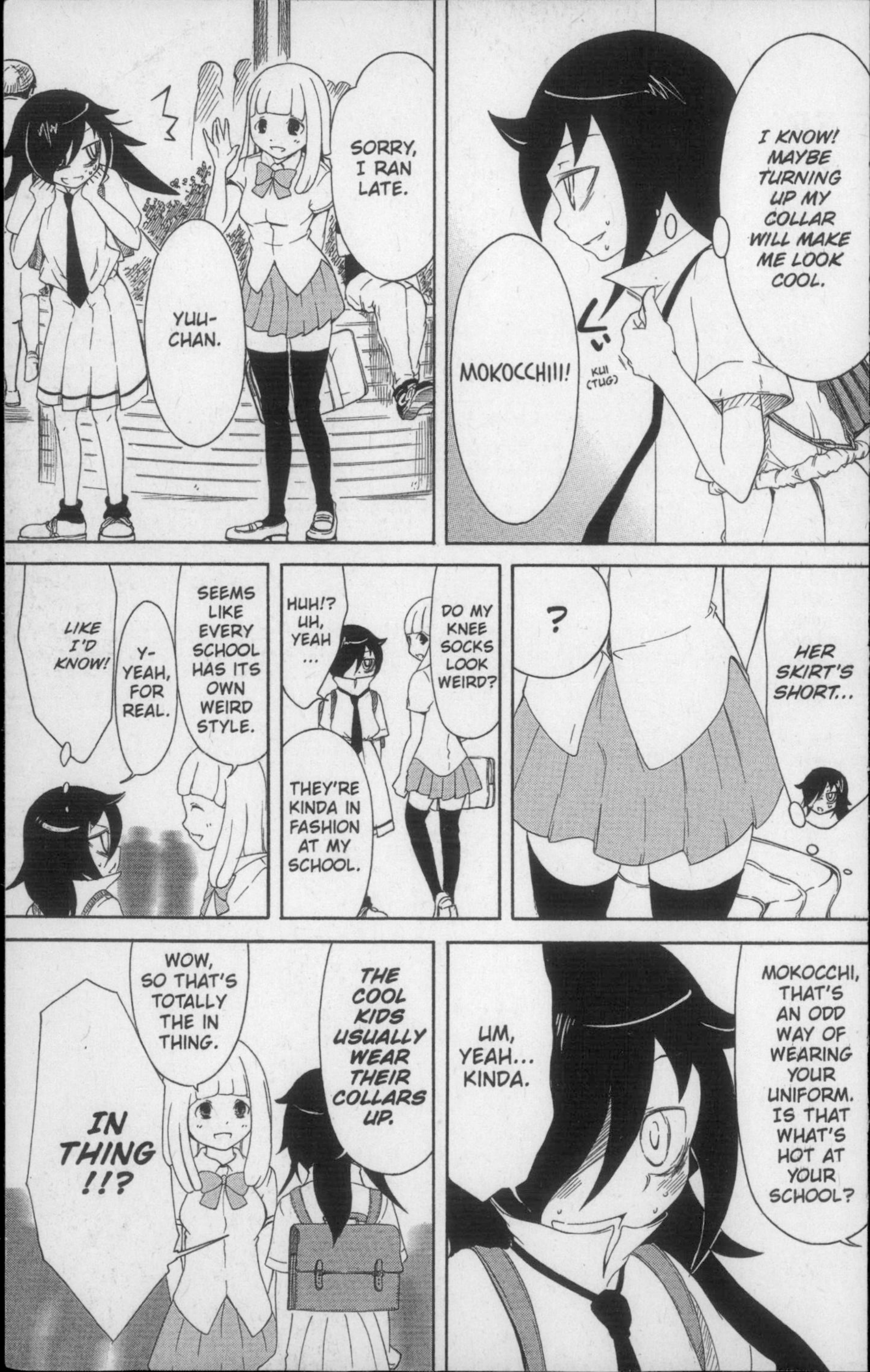
I KNOW! MAYBE TURNING UP MY COLLAR WILL MAKE ME LOOK COOL.
MOKOCCHIII!
KUI (TUG)
SORRY, I RAN LATE.
YUU-CHAN.
HER SKIRT'S SHORT...
?
DO MY KNEE SOCKS LOOK WEIRD?
HUH!? UH, YEAH ...
THEY'RE KINDA IN FASHION AT MY SCHOOL.
SEEMS LIKE EVERY SCHOOL HAS ITS OWN WEIRD STYLE.
Y-YEAH, FOR REAL.
LIKE I'D KNOW!
MOKOCCHI, THAT'S AN ODD WAY OF WEARING YOUR UNIFORM. IS THAT WHAT'S HOT AT YOUR SCHOOL?
UM, YEAH... KINDA.
THE COOL KIDS USUALLY WEAR THEIR COLLARS UP.
WOW, SO THAT'S TOTALLY THE IN THING.
IN THING!!?

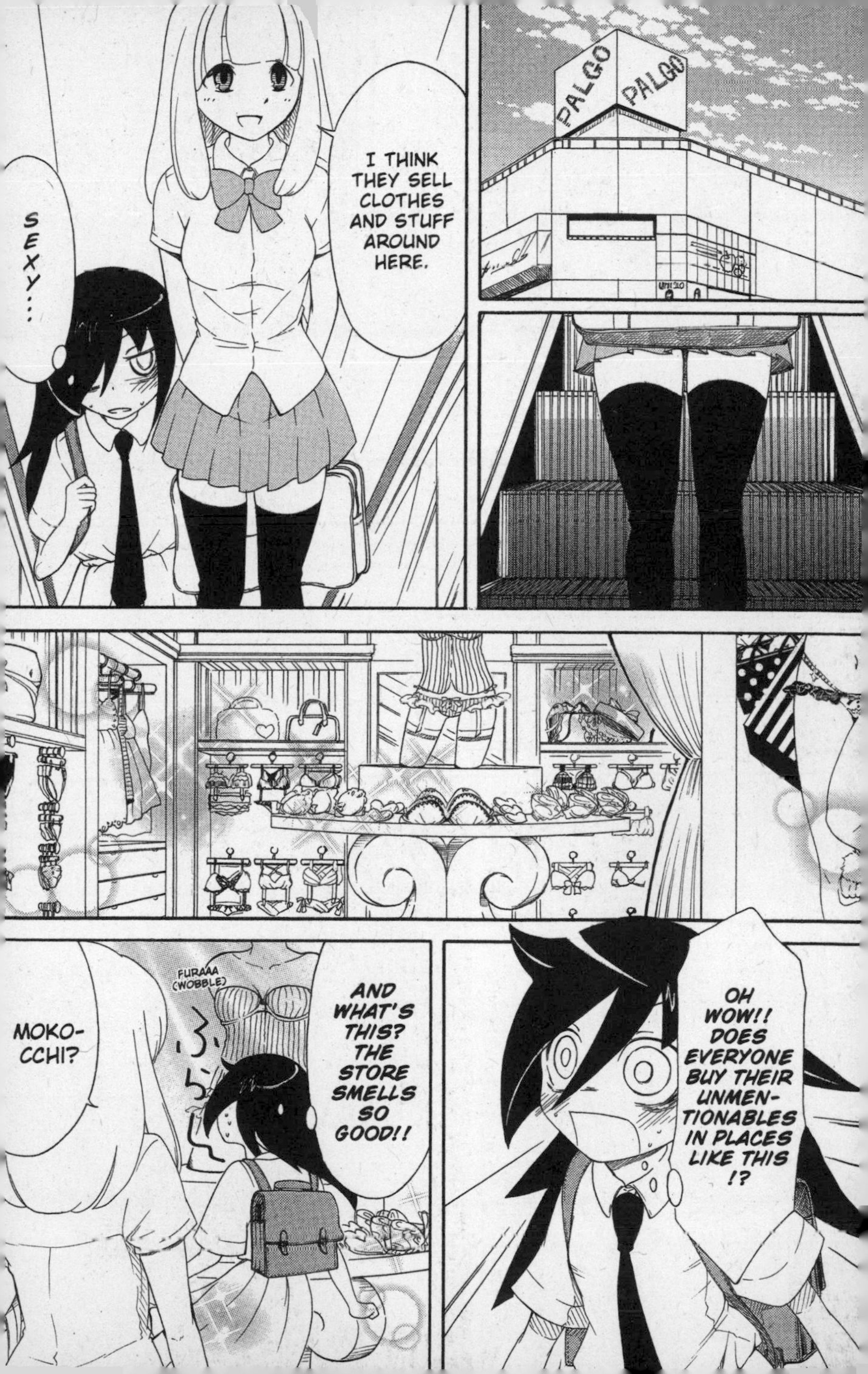
PALGO
PALGO
I THINK THEY SELL CLOTHES AND STUFF AROUND HERE.
SEXY...
OH WOW!! DOES EVERYONE BUY THEIR UNMENTIONABLES IN PLACES LIKE THIS !?
AND WHAT'S THIS? THE STORE SMELLS SO GOOD!!
FURAAA (WOBBLE)
MOKO-CCHI?

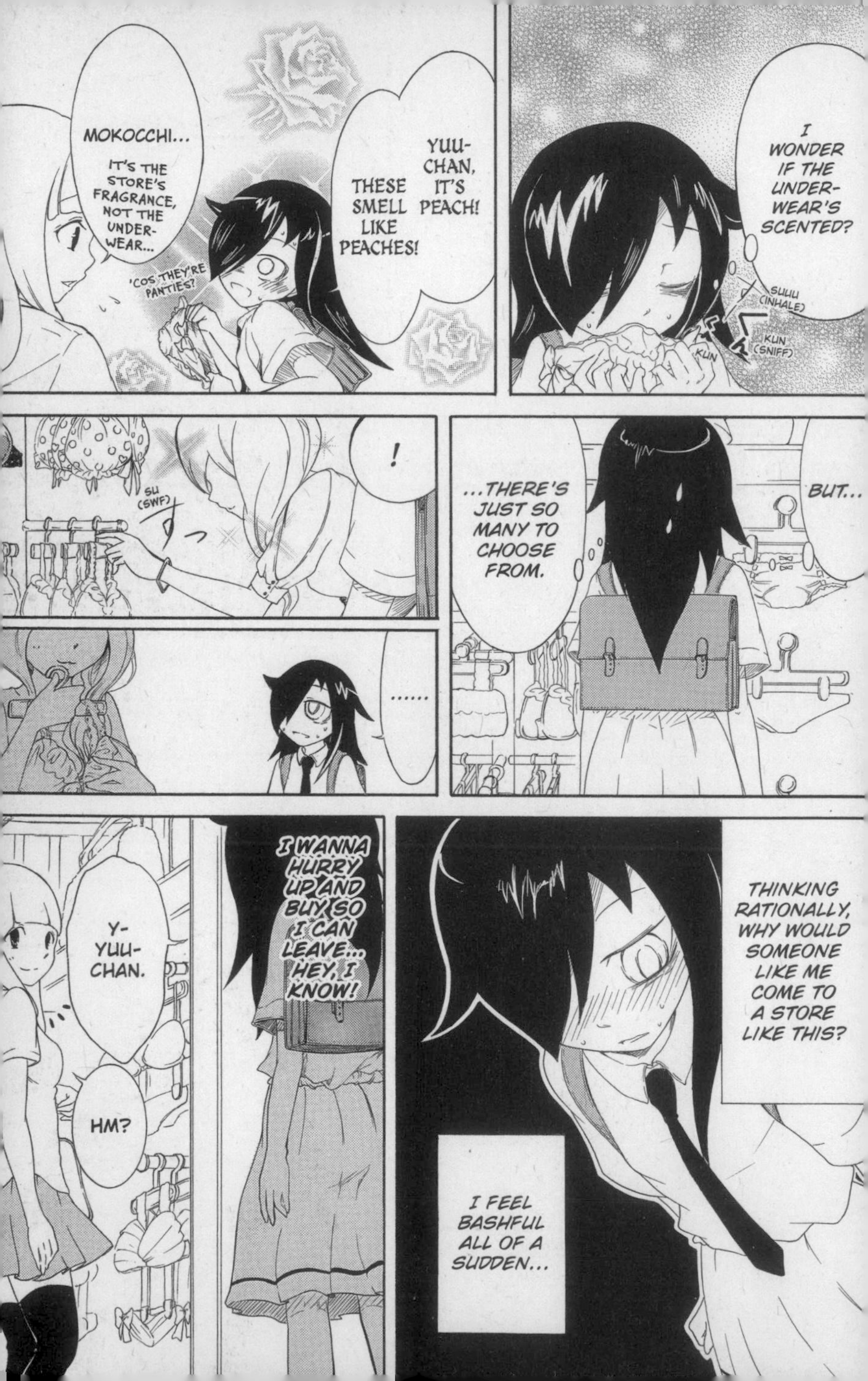
I WONDER IF THE UNDER-WEAR'S SCENTED?
SUUU (INHALE)
KUN (SNIFF)
KUN
YUU-CHAN, IT'S PEACH!
THESE SMELL LIKE PEACHES!
MOKOCCHI...
IT'S THE STORE'S FRAGRANCE, NOT THE UNDER-WEAR...
'COS THEY'RE PANTIES?
BUT...
...THERE'S JUST SO MANY TO CHOOSE FROM.
!
SU (SWF)
......
THINKING RATIONALLY, WHY WOULD SOMEONE LIKE ME COME TO A STORE LIKE THIS?
I FEEL BASHFUL ALL OF A SUDDEN...
I WANNA HURRY UP AND BUY SO I CAN LEAVE... HEY, I KNOW!
Y-YUU-CHAN.
HM?

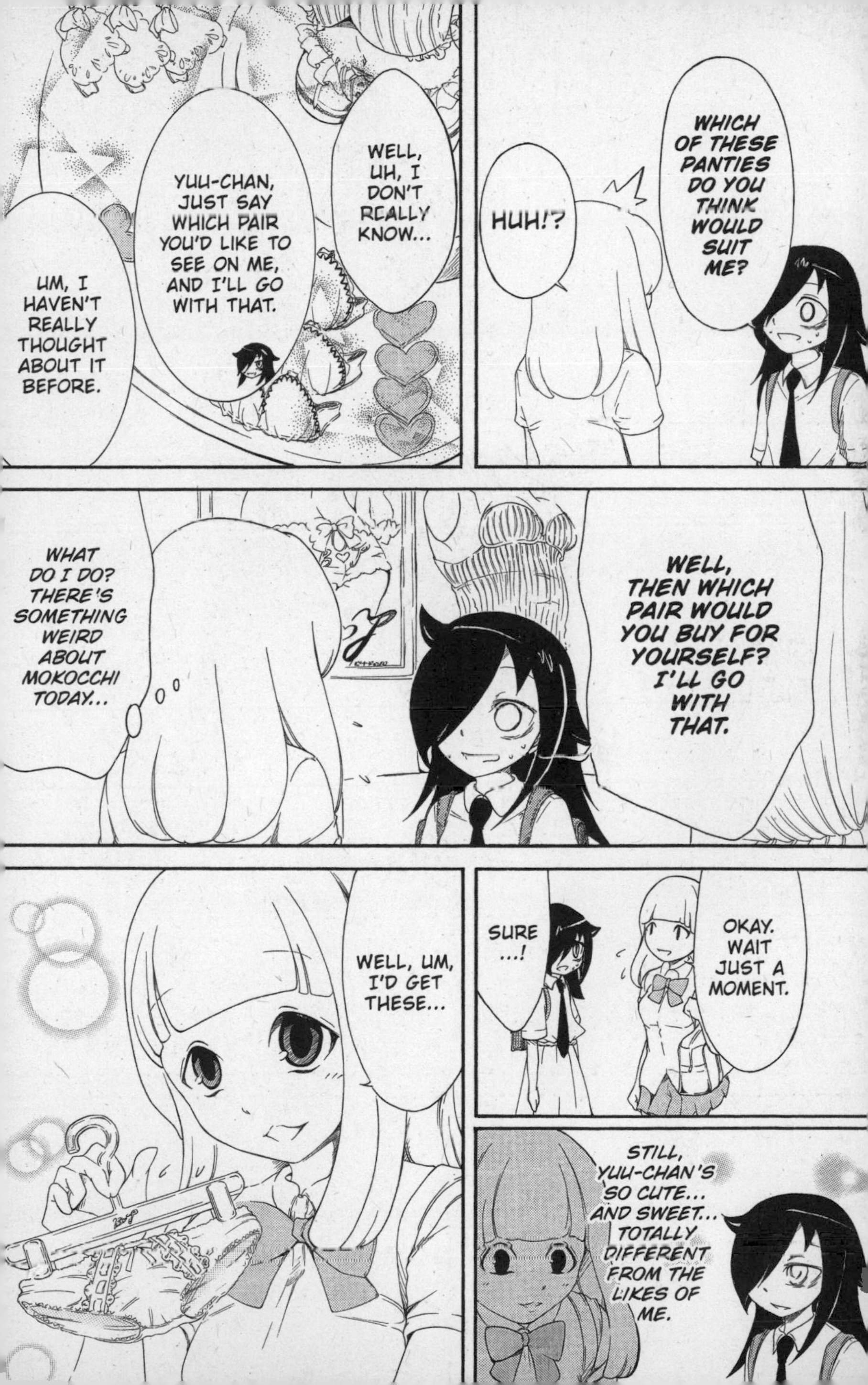
WHICH OF THESE PANTIES DO YOU THINK WOULD SUIT ME?
HUH!?
WELL, UH, I DON'T REALLY KNOW...
YUU-CHAN, JUST SAY WHICH PAIR YOU'D LIKE TO SEE ON ME, AND I'LL GO WITH THAT.
UM, I HAVEN'T REALLY THOUGHT ABOUT IT BEFORE.
WELL, THEN WHICH PAIR WOULD YOU BUY FOR YOURSELF? I'LL GO WITH THAT.
WHAT DO I DO? THERE'S SOMETHING WEIRD ABOUT MOKOCCHI TODAY...
OKAY. WAIT JUST A MOMENT.
SURE ...!
STILL, YUU-CHAN'S SO CUTE... AND SWEET... TOTALLY DIFFERENT FROM THE LIKES OF ME.
WELL, UM, I'D GET THESE...

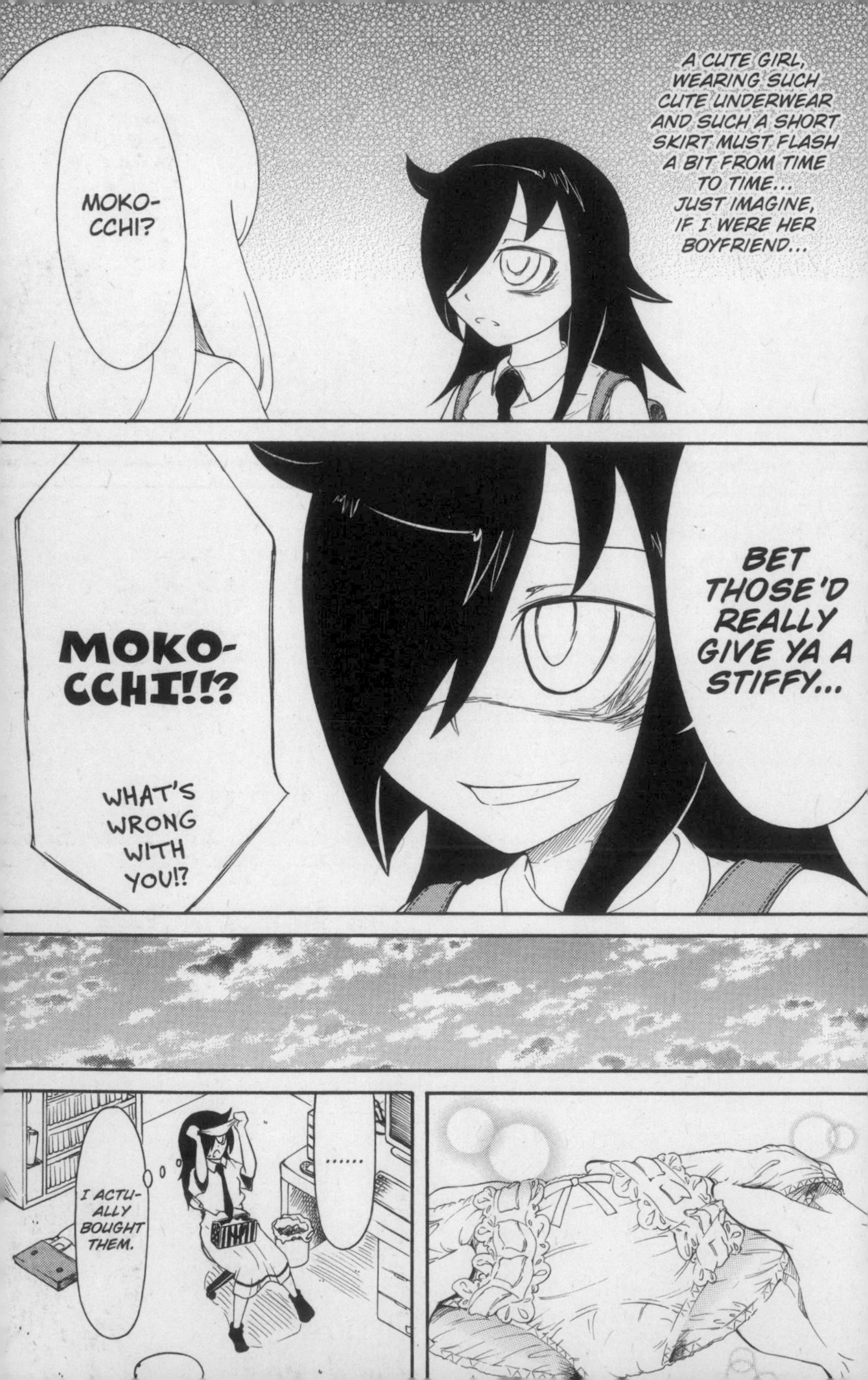
A CUTE GIRL, WEARING SUCH CUTE UNDERWEAR AND SUCH A SHORT SKIRT MUST FLASH A BIT FROM TIME TO TIME... JUST IMAGINE, IF I WERE HER BOYFRIEND...
MOKO-CCHI?
BET THOSE'D REALLY GIVE YA A STIFFY...
MOKO-CCHI!!?
WHAT'S WRONG WITH YOU!?
......
I ACTU-ALLY BOUGHT THEM.

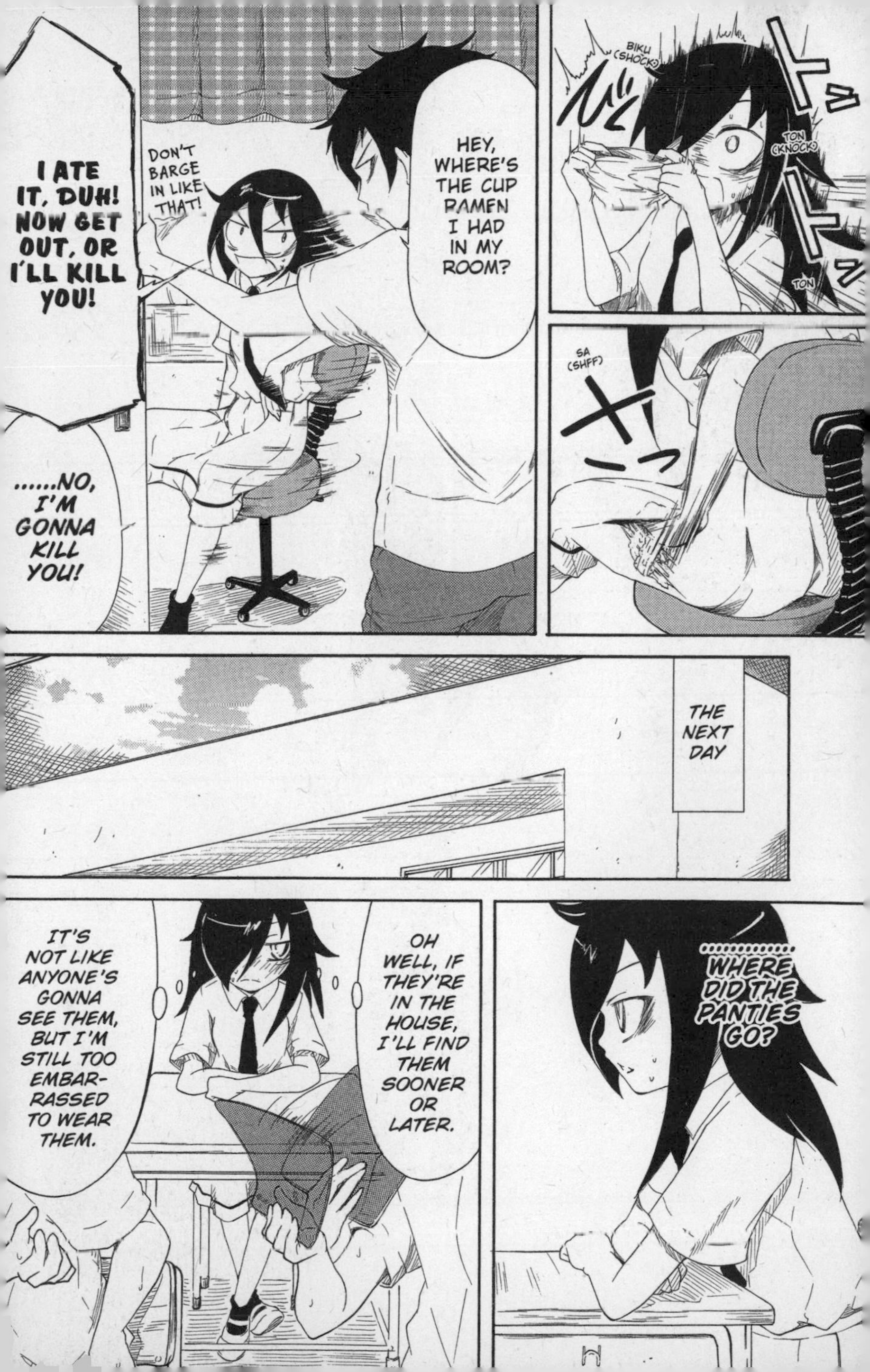
BIKU (SHOCK)
TON (KNOCK)
TON
SA (SHFF)
HEY, WHERE'S THE CUP RAMEN I HAD IN MY ROOM?
DON'T BARGE IN LIKE THAT!
I ATE IT, DUH! NOW GET OUT, OR I'LL KILL YOU!
......NO, I'M GONNA KILL YOU!
THE NEXT DAY
..........WHERE DID THE PANTIES GO?
OH WELL, IF THEY'RE IN THE HOUSE, I'LL FIND THEM SOONER OR LATER.
IT'S NOT LIKE ANYONE'S GONNA SEE THEM, BUT I'M STILL TOO EMBAR-RASSED TO WEAR THEM.

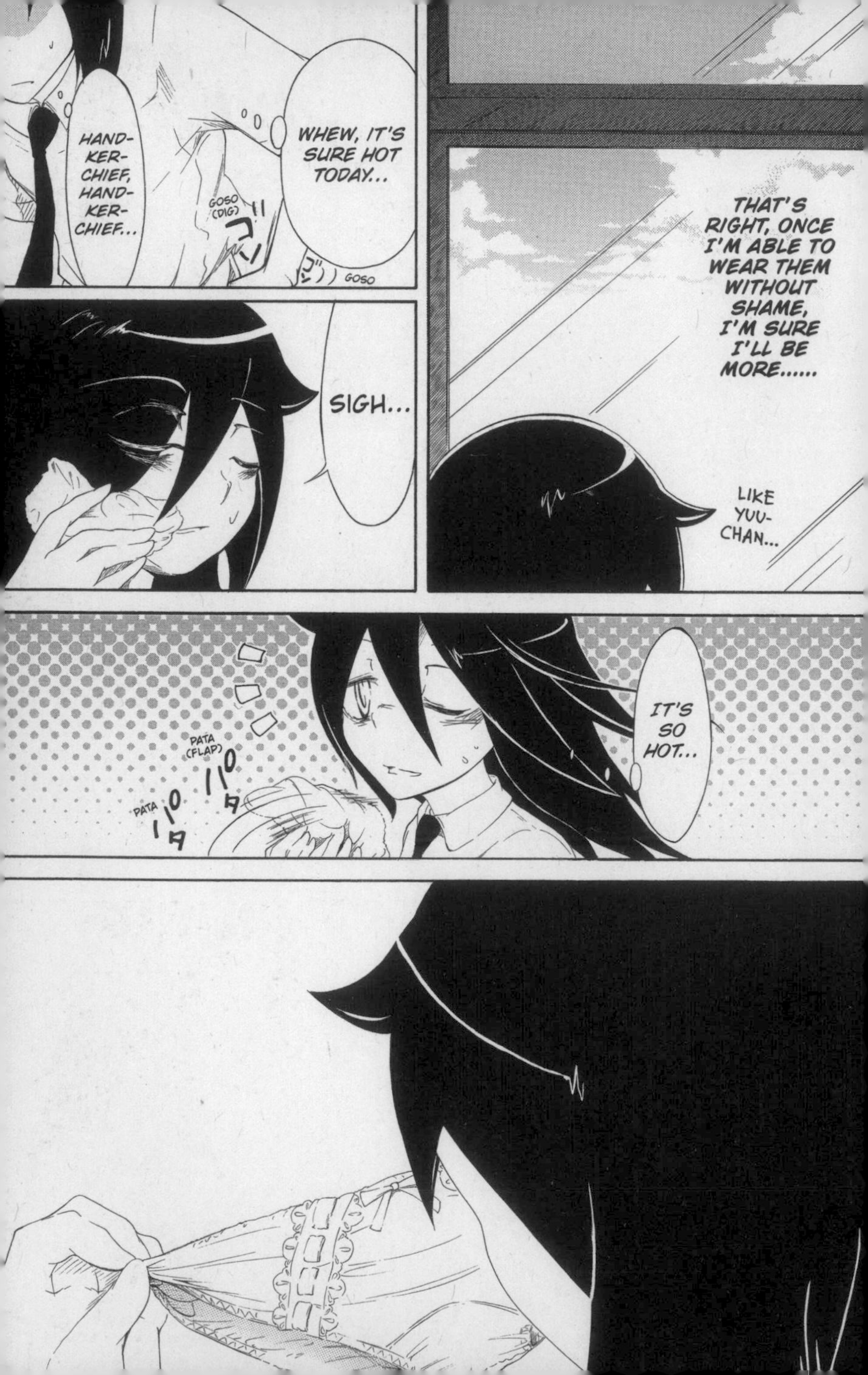
THAT'S RIGHT, ONCE I'M ABLE TO WEAR THEM WITHOUT SHAME, I'M SURE I'LL BE MORE......
LIKE YUU-CHAN...
WHEW, IT'S SURE HOT TODAY...
GOSO (DIG)
HAND-KER-CHIEF, HAND-KER-CHIEF...
GOSO
SIGH...
IT'S SO HOT...
PATA (FLAP)
PATA

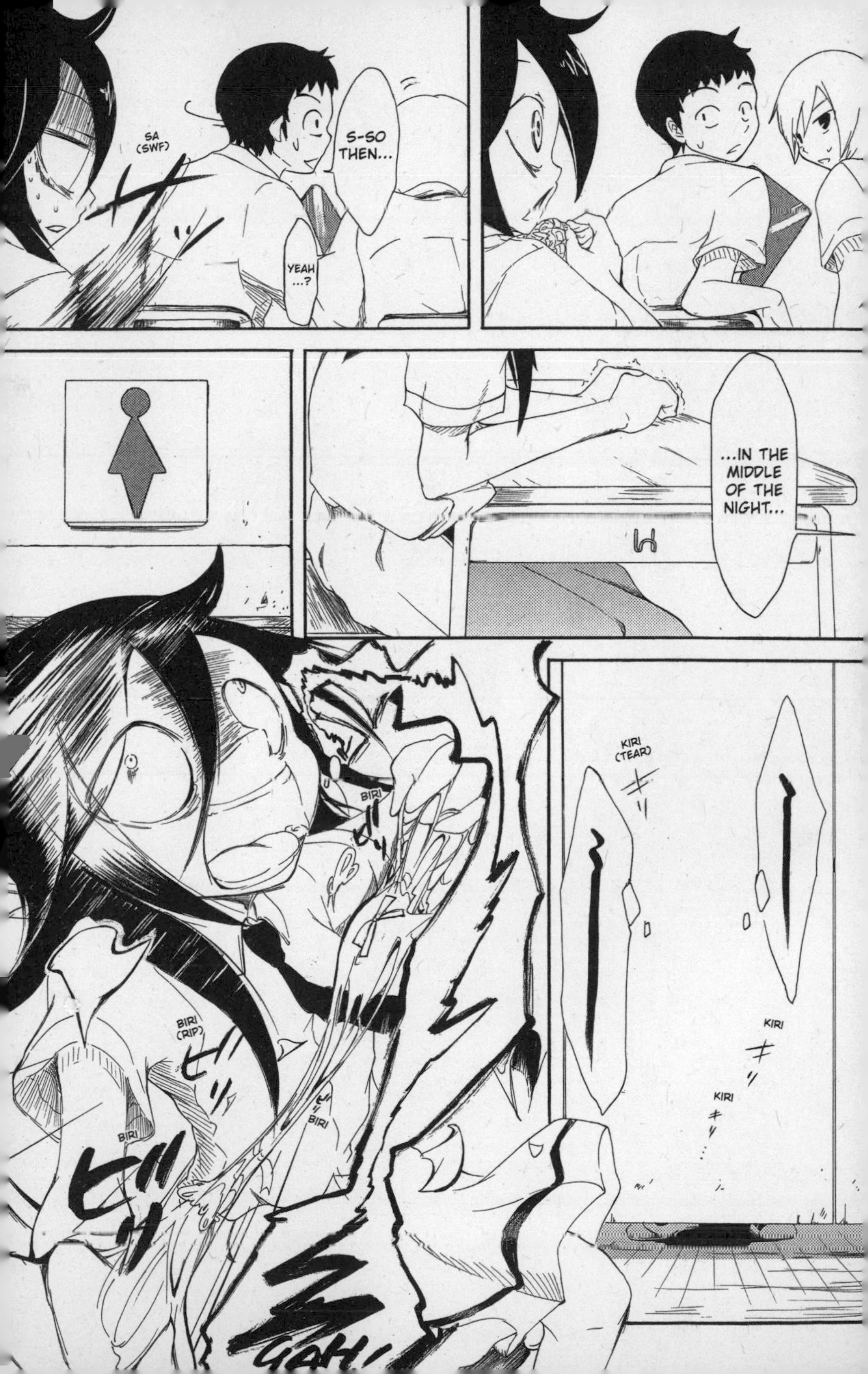
S-SO THEN...
SA (SWF)
YEAH ...?
...IN THE MIDDLE OF THE NIGHT...
KIRI (TEAR)
KIRI
KIRI
BIRI
BIRI (RIP)
BIRI
BIRI
GAH!

No Matter How I Look at It, It's You Guys' Fault I'm Not Popular!

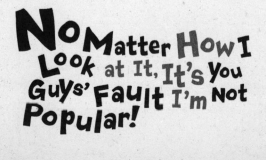

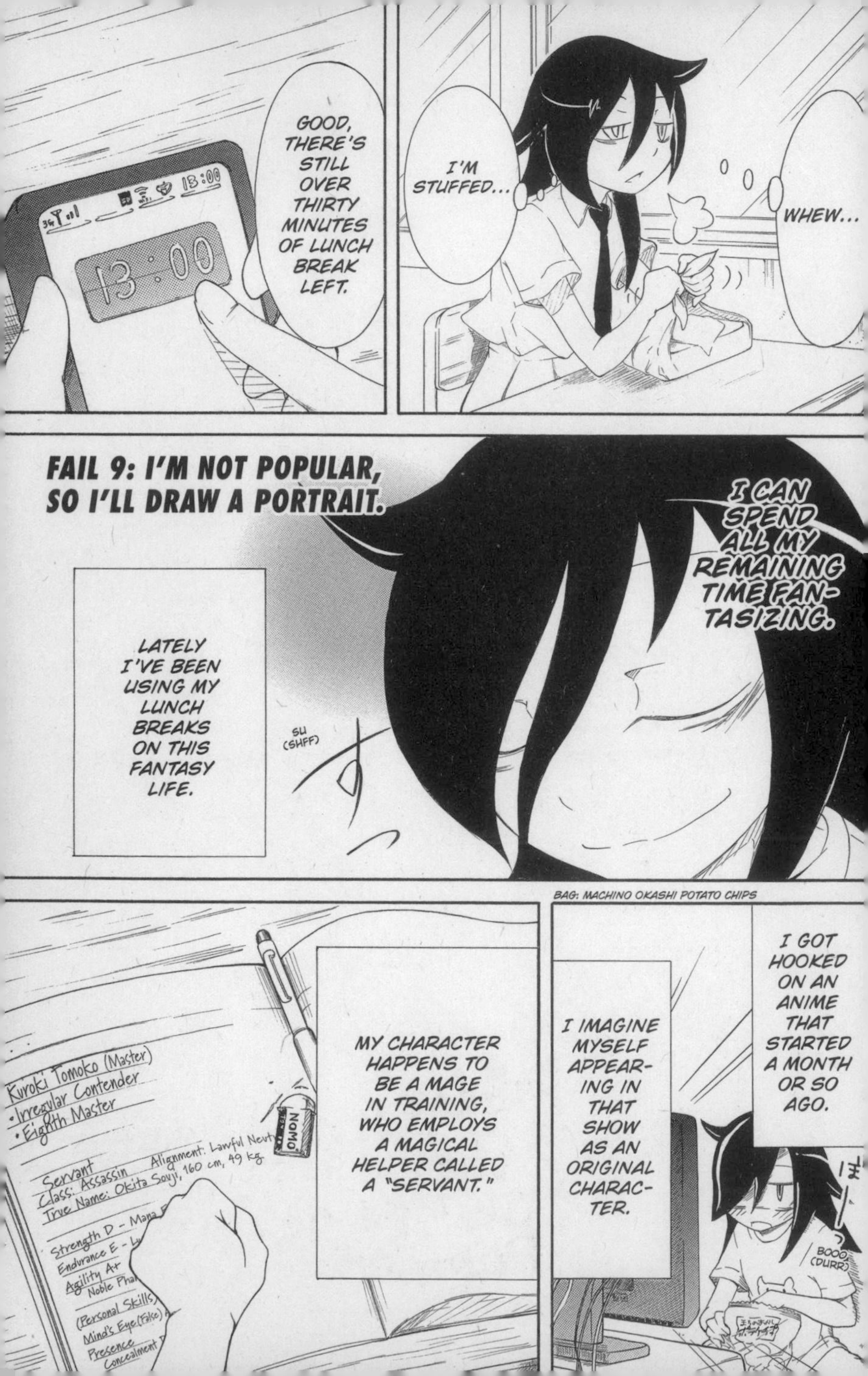
WHEW...
I'M STUFFED...
13:00
GOOD, THERE'S STILL OVER THIRTY MINUTES OF LUNCH BREAK LEFT.
FAIL 9: I'M NOT POPULAR, SO I'LL DRAW A PORTRAIT.
I CAN SPEND ALL MY REMAINING TIME FAN-TASIZING.
SU (SHFF)
LATELY I'VE BEEN USING MY LUNCH BREAKS ON THIS FANTASY LIFE.
BAG: MACHINO OKASHI POTATO CHIPS
I GOT HOOKED ON AN ANIME THAT STARTED A MONTH OR SO AGO.
BOOO (DURR)
I IMAGINE MYSELF APPEAR-ING IN THAT SHOW AS AN ORIGINAL CHARAC-TER.
MY CHARACTER HAPPENS TO BE A MAGE IN TRAINING, WHO EMPLOYS A MAGICAL HELPER CALLED A "SERVANT."
Kuroki Tomoko (Master)
•Irregular Contender
•Eighth Master
Servant Alignment: Lawful Neut
Class: Assassin
True Name: Okita Souji, 160 cm, 49 kg.
Strength D - Mana
Endurance E
Agility A+
(Personal Skills)
Mind's Eye (False)
Presence Concealment
NOMO

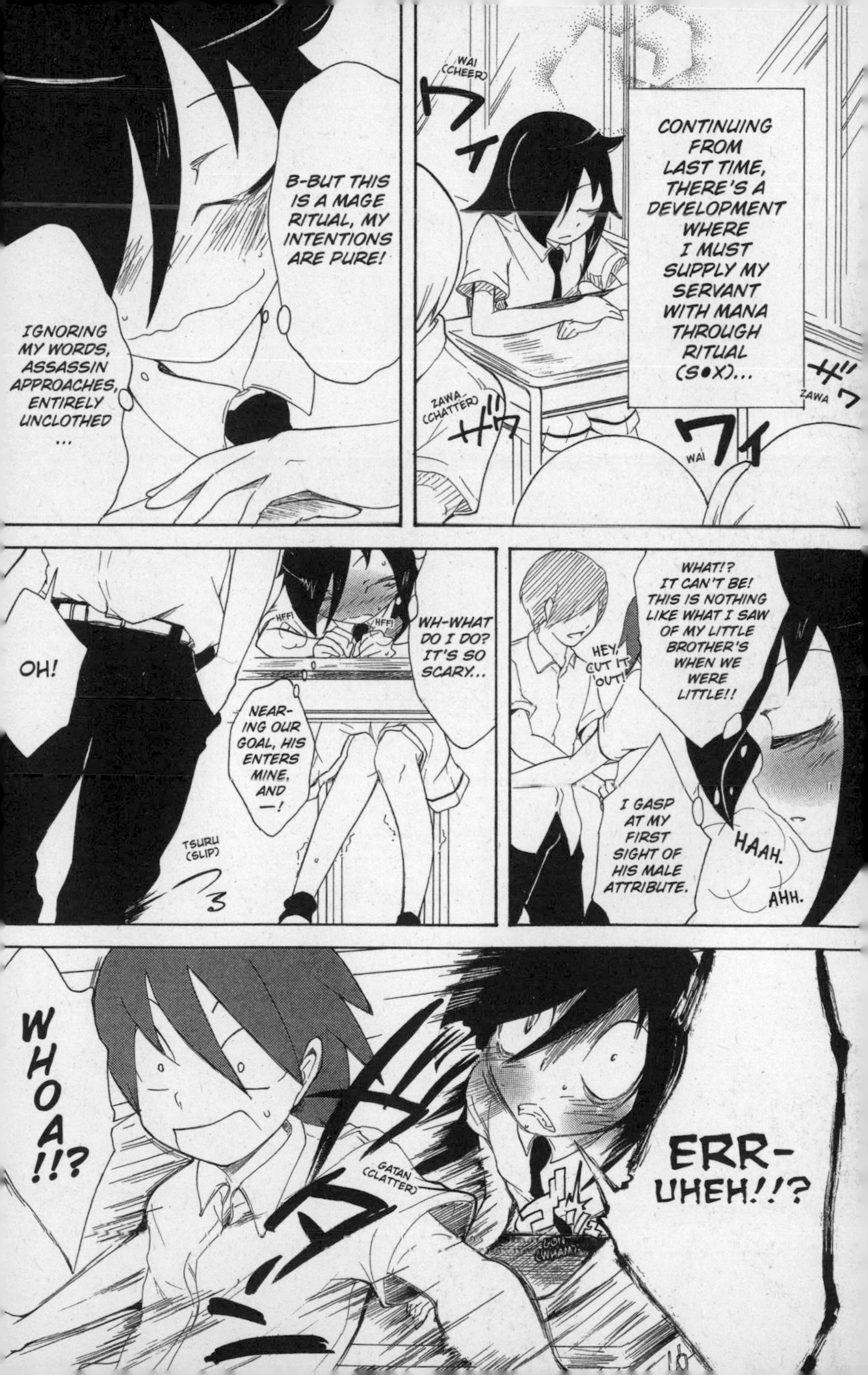
WAI (CHEER)
CONTINUING FROM LAST TIME, THERE'S A DEVELOPMENT WHERE I MUST SUPPLY MY SERVANT WITH MANA THROUGH RITUAL (S●X)...
ZAWA
WAI
ZAWA- (CHATTER)
B-BUT THIS IS A MAGE RITUAL, MY INTENTIONS ARE PURE!
IGNORING MY WORDS, ASSASSIN APPROACHES, ENTIRELY UNCLOTHED ...
WHAT!? IT CAN'T BE! THIS IS NOTHING LIKE WHAT I SAW OF MY LITTLE BROTHER'S WHEN WE WERE LITTLE!!
HEY, CUT IT OUT!
I GASP AT MY FIRST SIGHT OF HIS MALE ATTRIBUTE.
HAAH.
AHH.
HFF! HFF!
WH-WHAT DO I DO? IT'S SO SCARY...
NEARING OUR GOAL, HIS ENTERS MINE, AND—!
TSURU (SLIP)
OH!
ERR-UHEH!!?
GATAN (CLATTER)
WHOA!!?

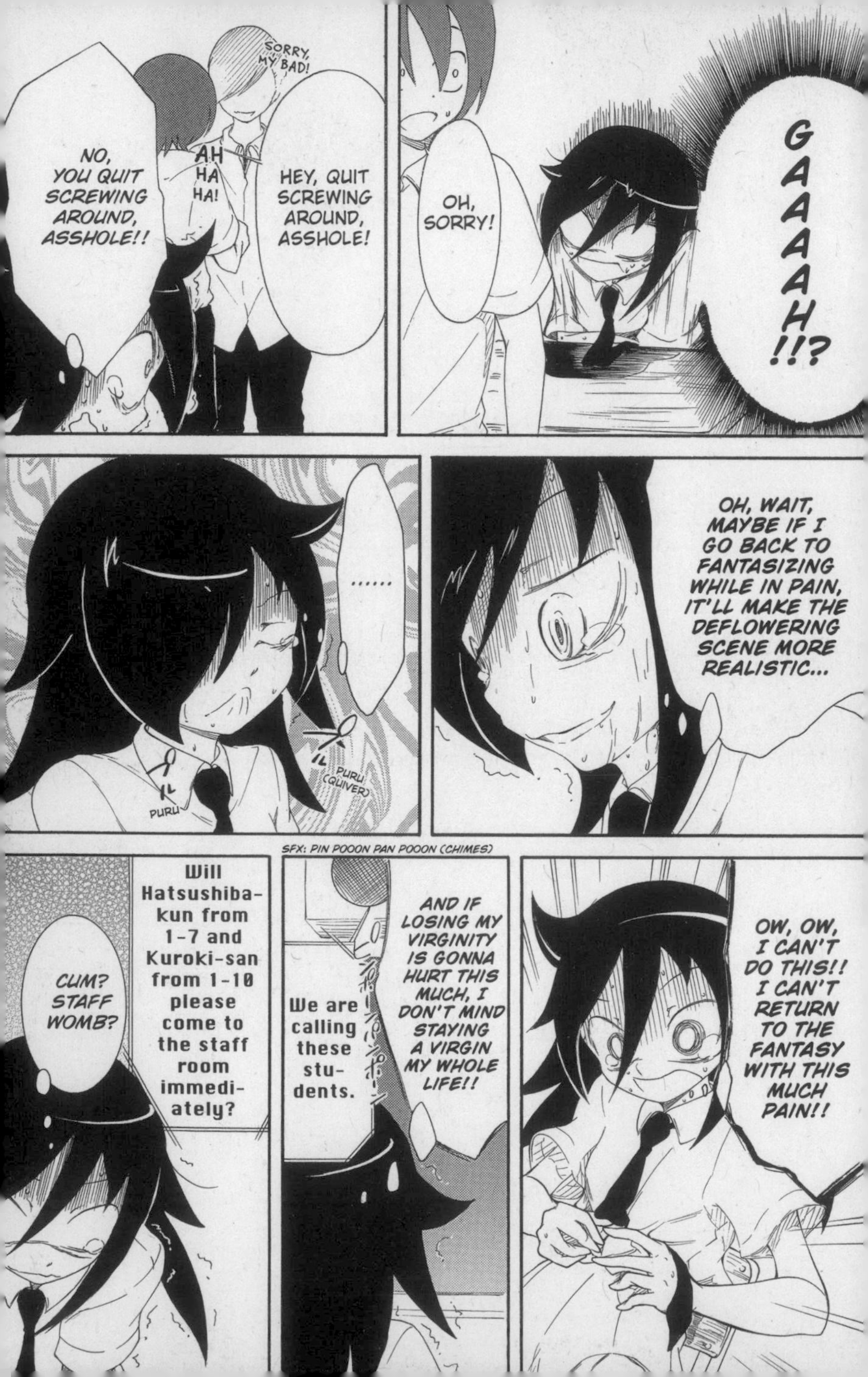
GAAAAAH!!?
OH, SORRY!
SORRY, MY BAD!
HEY, QUIT SCREWING AROUND, ASSHOLE!
AH HA HA!
NO, YOU QUIT SCREWING AROUND, ASSHOLE!!
OH, WAIT, MAYBE IF I GO BACK TO FANTASIZING WHILE IN PAIN, IT'LL MAKE THE DEFLOWERING SCENE MORE REALISTIC...
......
PURU (QUIVER)
PURU
SFX: PIN POOON PAN POOON (CHIMES)
OW, OW, I CAN'T DO THIS!! I CAN'T RETURN TO THE FANTASY WITH THIS MUCH PAIN!!
AND IF LOSING MY VIRGINITY IS GONNA HURT THIS MUCH, I DON'T MIND STAYING A VIRGIN MY WHOLE LIFE!!
We are calling these stu-dents.
Will Hatsushiba-kun from 1-7 and Kuroki-san from 1-10 please come to the staff room immedi-ately?
CUM? STAFF WOMB?

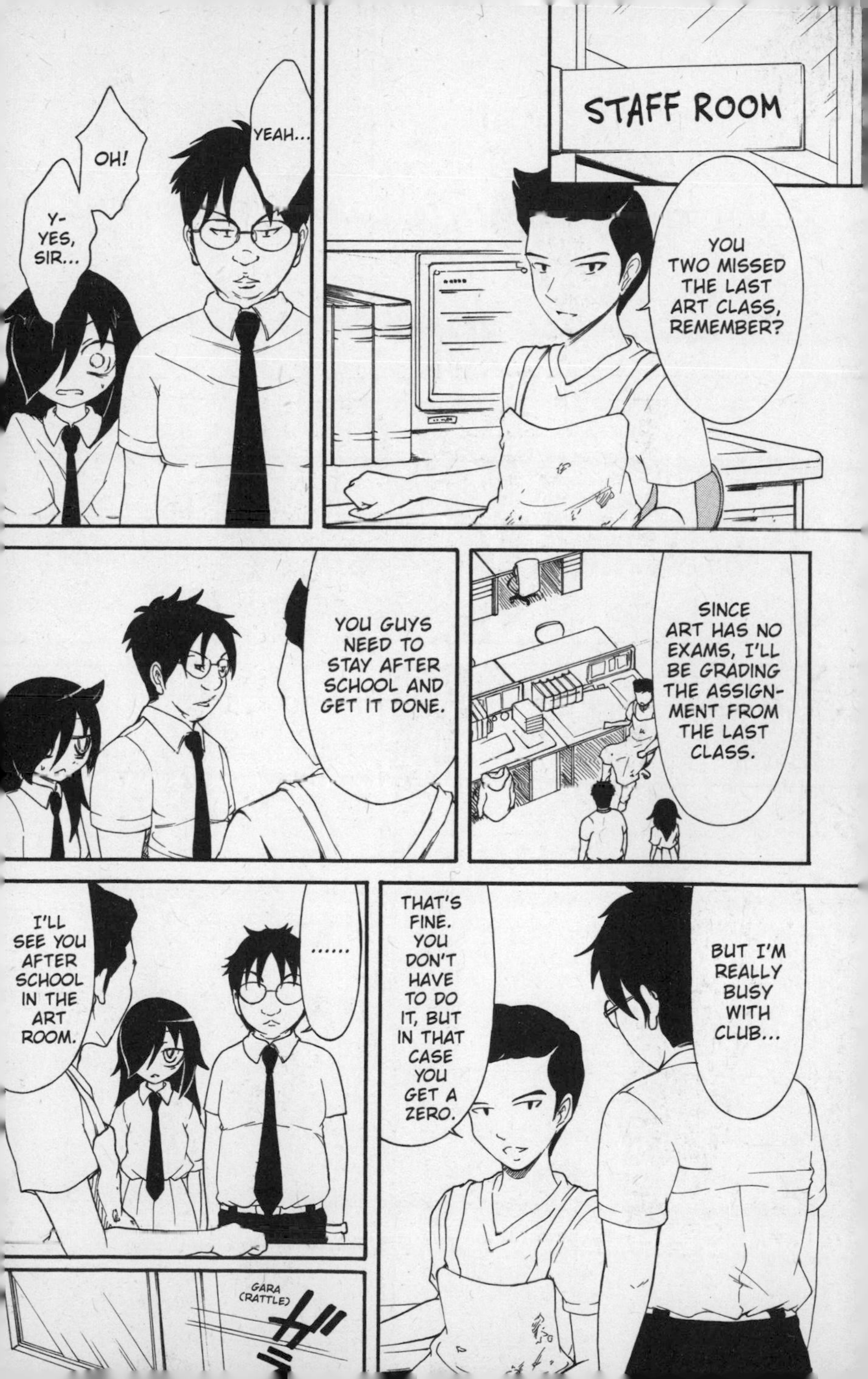
STAFF ROOM
YOU TWO MISSED THE LAST ART CLASS, REMEMBER?
YEAH...
OH!
Y-YES, SIR...
SINCE ART HAS NO EXAMS, I'LL BE GRADING THE ASSIGN-MENT FROM THE LAST CLASS.
YOU GUYS NEED TO STAY AFTER SCHOOL AND GET IT DONE.
BUT I'M REALLY BUSY WITH CLUB...
THAT'S FINE. YOU DON'T HAVE TO DO IT, BUT IN THAT CASE YOU GET A ZERO.
......
I'LL SEE YOU AFTER SCHOOL IN THE ART ROOM.
GARA (RATTLE)

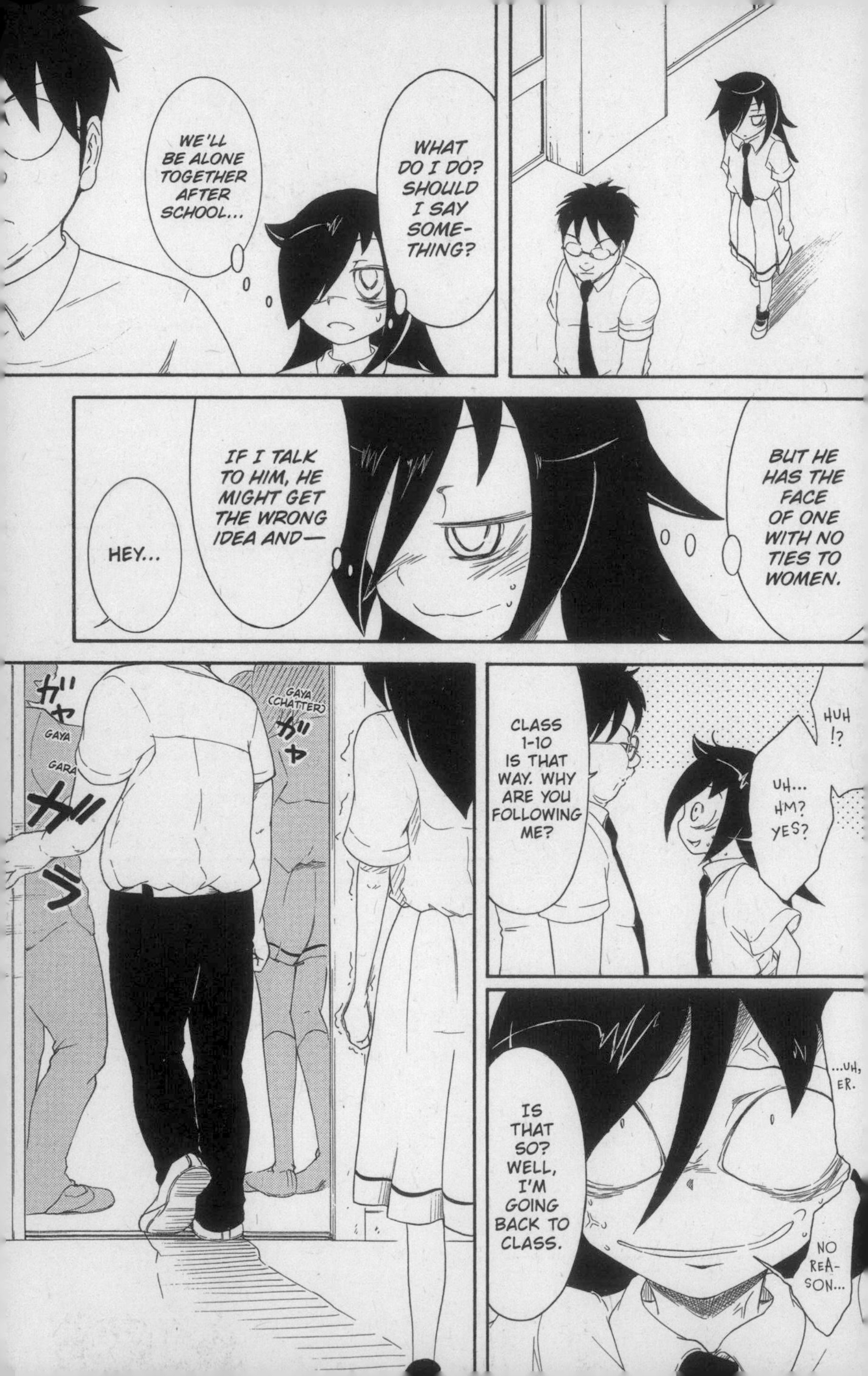
WHAT DO I DO? SHOULD I SAY SOME-THING?
WE'LL BE ALONE TOGETHER AFTER SCHOOL...
BUT HE HAS THE FACE OF ONE WITH NO TIES TO WOMEN.
IF I TALK TO HIM, HE MIGHT GET THE WRONG IDEA AND—
HEY...
HUH !?
CLASS 1-10 IS THAT WAY. WHY ARE YOU FOLLOWING ME?
UH... HM? YES?
...UH, ER.
NO REA-SON...
IS THAT SO? WELL, I'M GOING BACK TO CLASS.
ガヤ
GAYA (CHATTER)
ガヤ
GAYA
GARA
ガラ

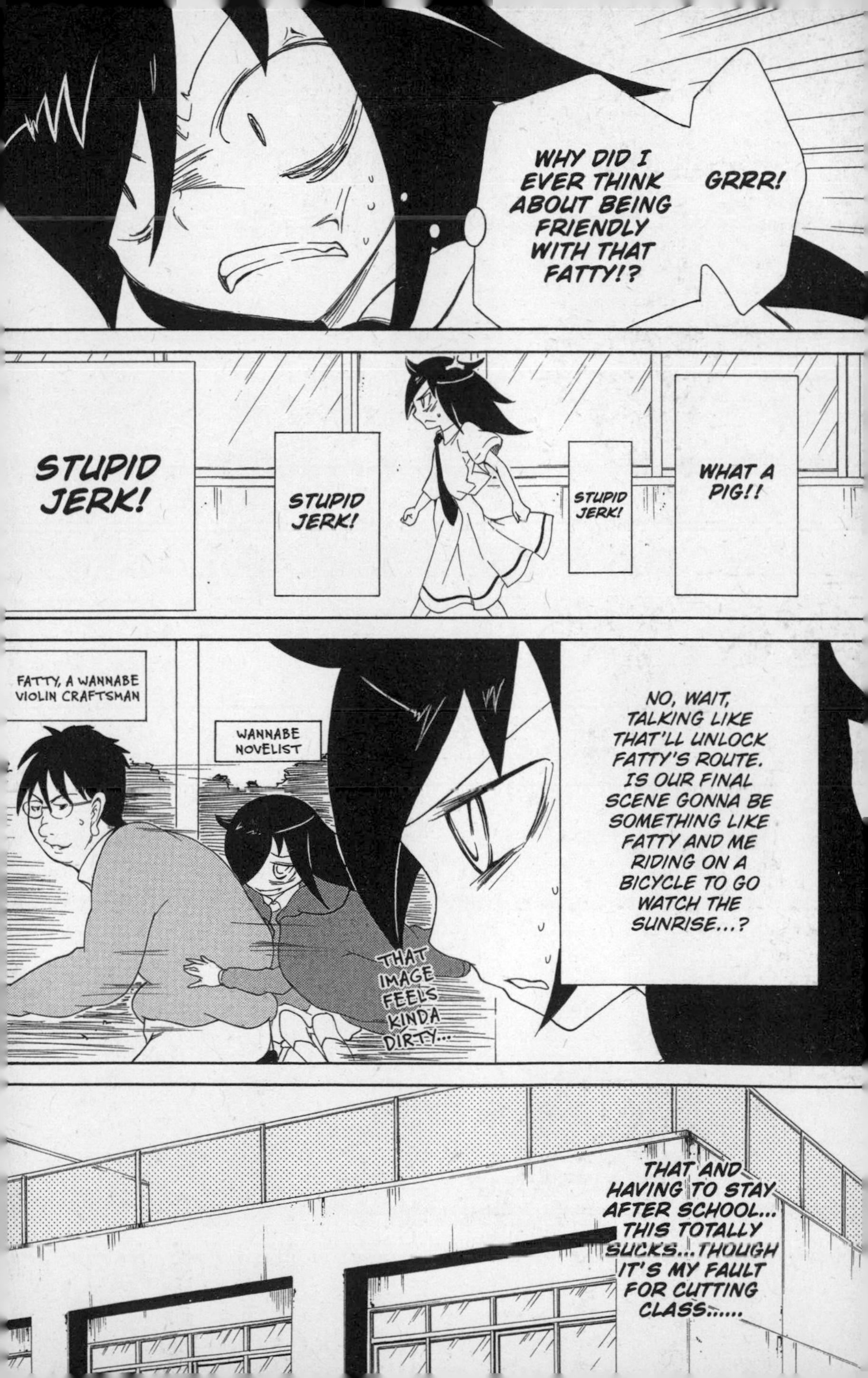
GRRR!
WHY DID I EVER THINK ABOUT BEING FRIENDLY WITH THAT FATTY!?
WHAT A PIG!!
STUPID JERK!
STUPID JERK!
STUPID JERK!
NO, WAIT, TALKING LIKE THAT'LL UNLOCK FATTY'S ROUTE. IS OUR FINAL SCENE GONNA BE SOMETHING LIKE FATTY AND ME RIDING ON A BICYCLE TO GO WATCH THE SUNRISE...?
THAT IMAGE FEELS KINDA DIRTY...
WANNABE NOVELIST
FATTY, A WANNABE VIOLIN CRAFTSMAN
THAT AND HAVING TO STAY AFTER SCHOOL... THIS TOTALLY SUCKS...THOUGH IT'S MY FAULT FOR CUTTING CLASS......

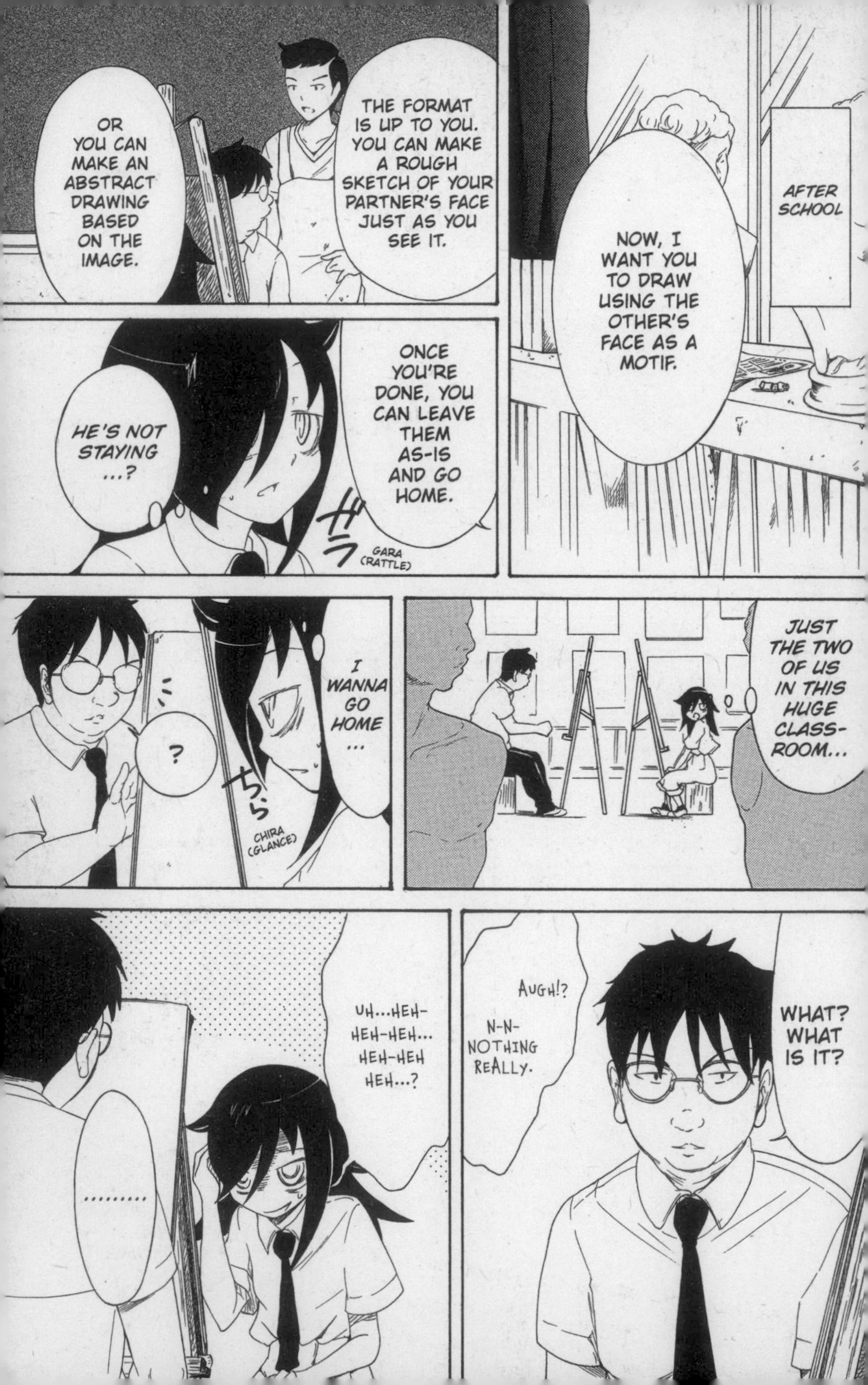
AFTER SCHOOL
NOW, I WANT YOU TO DRAW USING THE OTHER'S FACE AS A MOTIF.
THE FORMAT IS UP TO YOU. YOU CAN MAKE A ROUGH SKETCH OF YOUR PARTNER'S FACE JUST AS YOU SEE IT.
OR YOU CAN MAKE AN ABSTRACT DRAWING BASED ON THE IMAGE.
ONCE YOU'RE DONE, YOU CAN LEAVE THEM AS-IS AND GO HOME.
ガラ
GARA (RATTLE)
HE'S NOT STAYING ...?
JUST THE TWO OF US IN THIS HUGE CLASS-ROOM...
I WANNA GO HOME ...
ちら
CHIRA (GLANCE)
?
WHAT? WHAT IS IT?
AUGH!?
N-N-NOTHING REALLY.
UH...HEH-HEH-HEH... HEH-HEH HEH...?
....

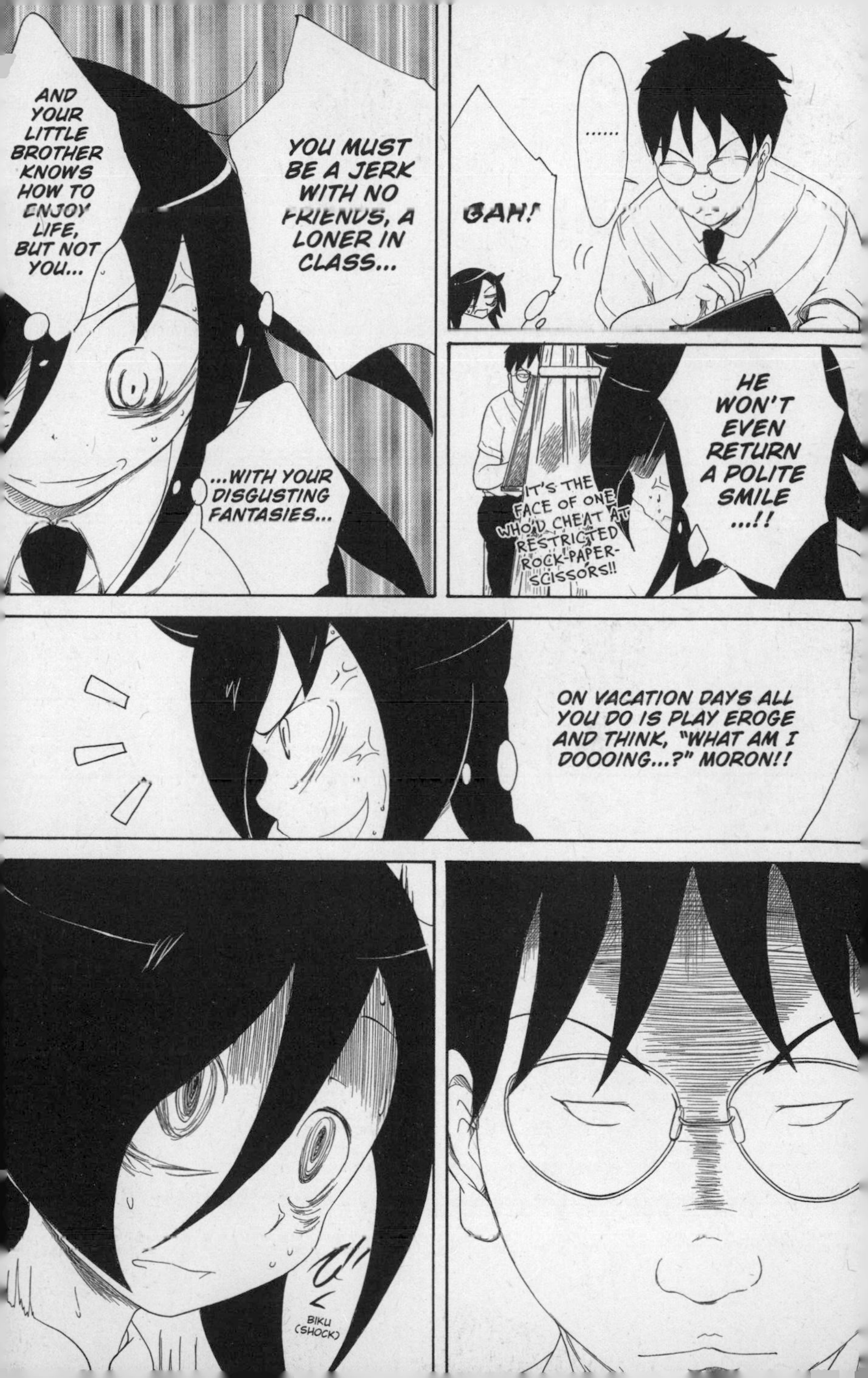
......
GAH!
HE WON'T EVEN RETURN A POLITE SMILE ...!!
IT'S THE FACE OF ONE WHO'D CHEAT AT RESTRICTED ROCK-PAPER-SCISSORS!!
YOU MUST BE A JERK WITH NO FRIENDS, A LONER IN CLASS...
AND YOUR LITTLE BROTHER KNOWS HOW TO ENJOY LIFE, BUT NOT YOU...
...WITH YOUR DISGUSTING FANTASIES...
ON VACATION DAYS ALL YOU DO IS PLAY EROGE AND THINK, "WHAT AM I DOOOING...?" MORON!!
BIKU (SHOCK)

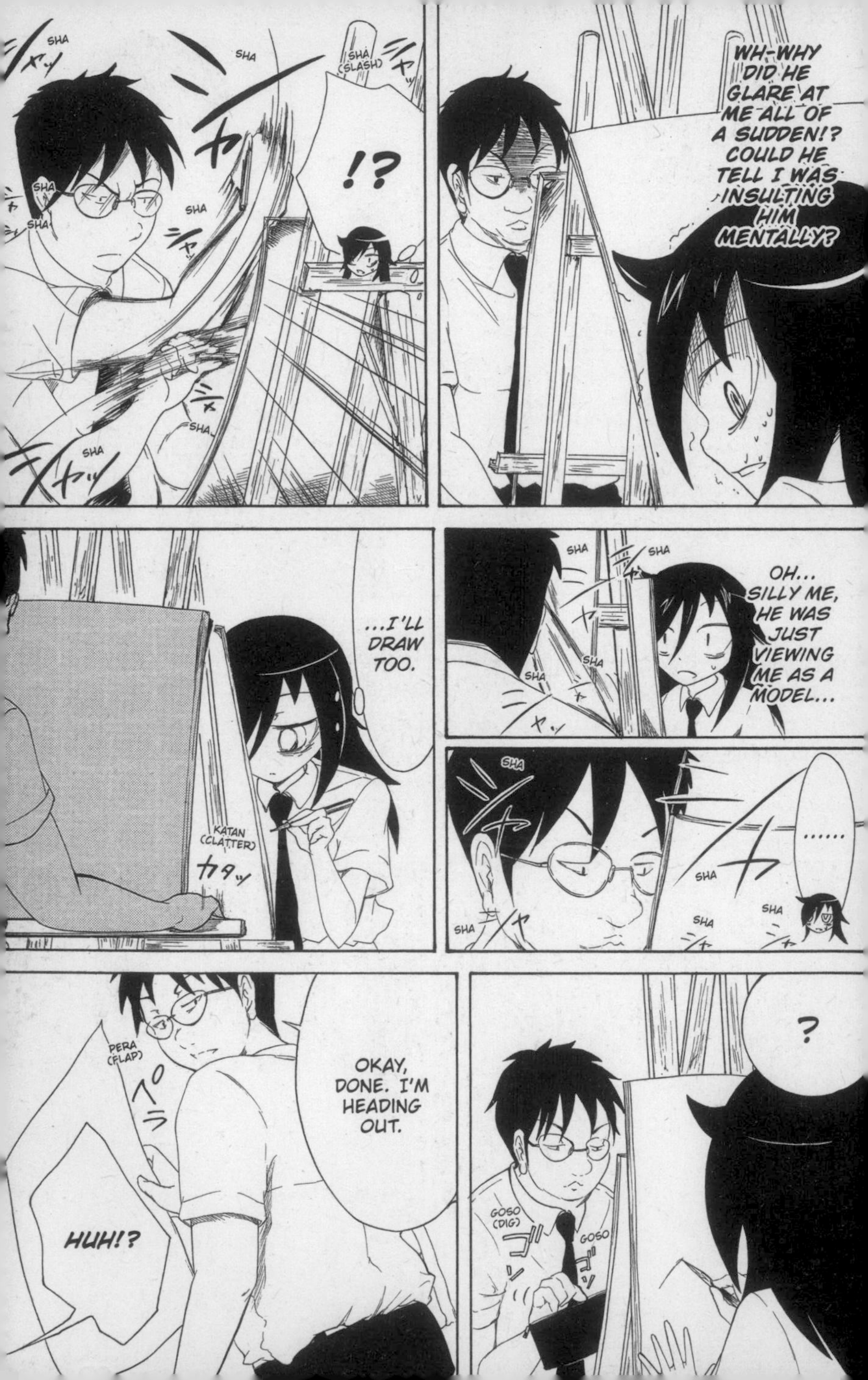
WH-WHY DID HE GLARE AT ME ALL OF A SUDDEN!? COULD HE TELL I WAS INSULTING HIM MENTALLY?
SHA
SHA
SHA (SLASH)
SHA
SHA
SHA
SHA
SHA
!?
SHA
SHA
OH... SILLY ME, HE WAS JUST VIEWING ME AS A MODEL...
SHA
SHA
SHA
......
SHA
SHA
SHA
SHA
...I'LL DRAW TOO.
KATAN (CLATTER)
?
GOSO (DIG)
GOSO
OKAY, DONE. I'M HEADING OUT.
PERA (FLAP)
HUH!?

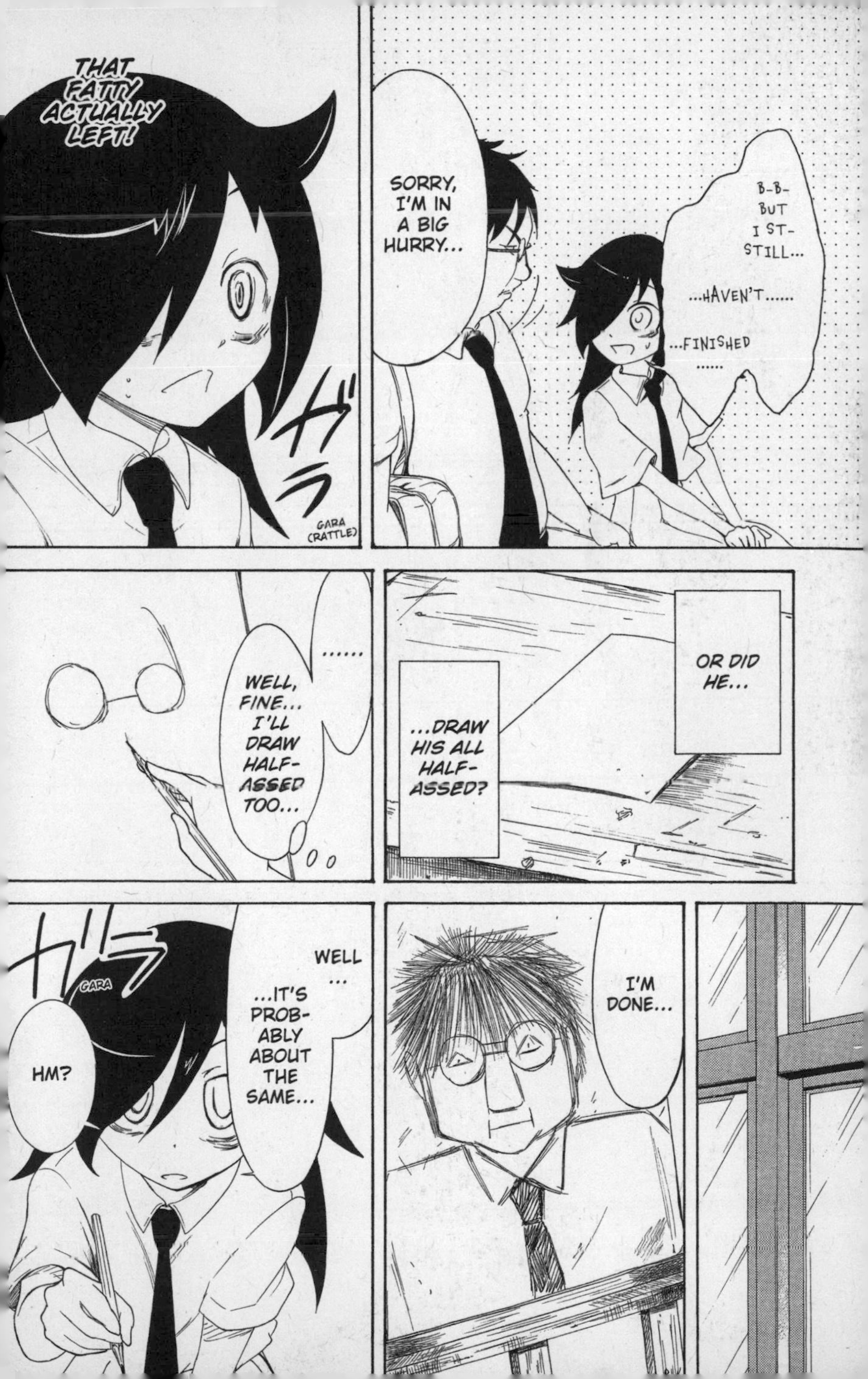
B-B-BUT I ST-STILL...
...HAVEN'T......
...FINISHED ......
SORRY, I'M IN A BIG HURRY...
THAT FATTY ACTUALLY LEFT!
GARA (RATTLE)
OR DID HE...
...DRAW HIS ALL HALF-ASSED?
......
WELL, FINE... I'LL DRAW HALF-ASSED TOO...
I'M DONE...
WELL ...
...IT'S PROBABLY ABOUT THE SAME...
GARA
HM?

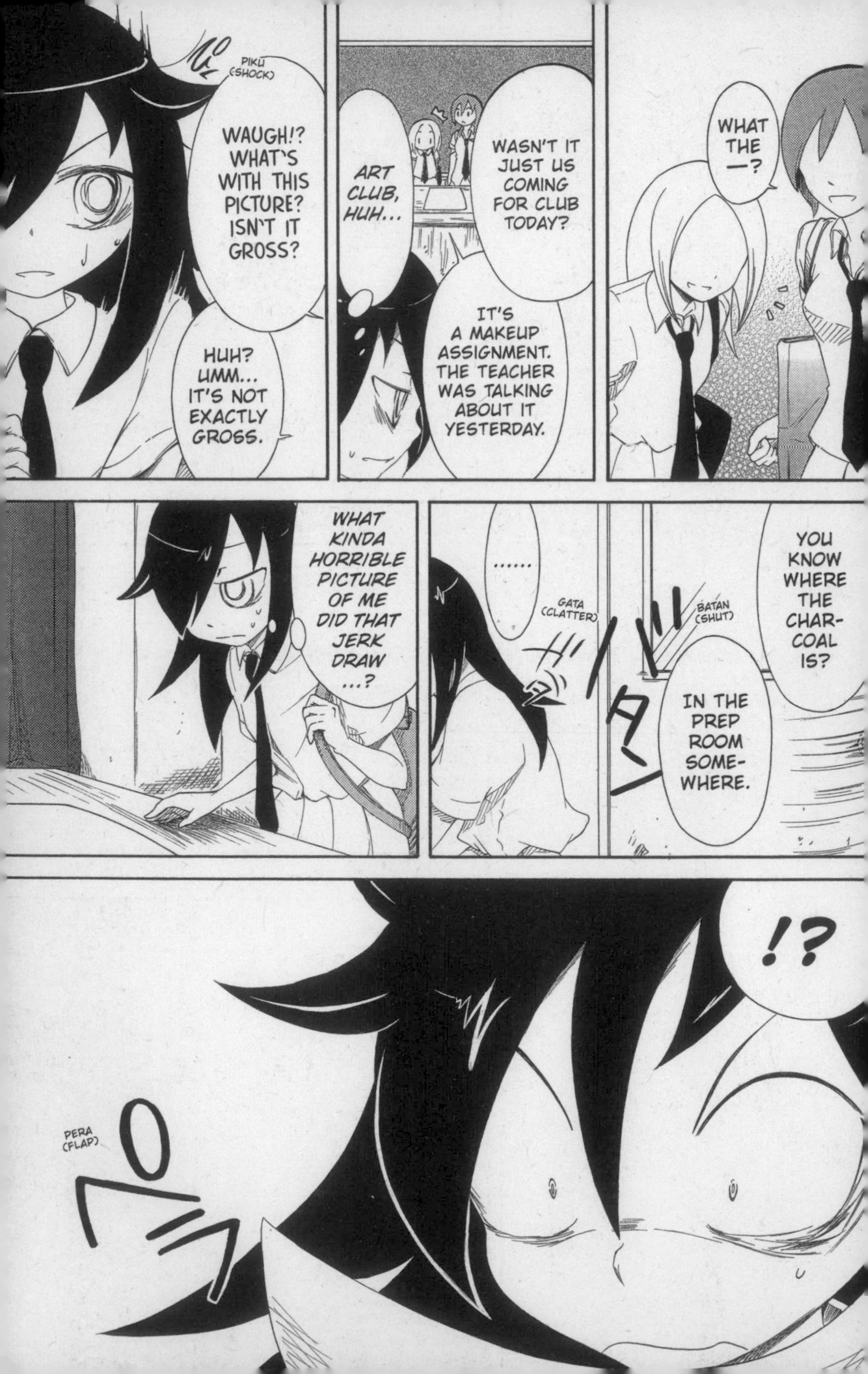
WHAT THE —?
WASN'T IT JUST US COMING FOR CLUB TODAY?
ART CLUB, HUH...
IT'S A MAKEUP ASSIGNMENT. THE TEACHER WAS TALKING ABOUT IT YESTERDAY.
PIKU (SHOCK)
WAUGH!? WHAT'S WITH THIS PICTURE? ISN'T IT GROSS?
HUH? UMM... IT'S NOT EXACTLY GROSS.
YOU KNOW WHERE THE CHAR-COAL IS?
IN THE PREP ROOM SOME-WHERE.
BATAN (SHUT)
GATA (CLATTER)
......
WHAT KINDA HORRIBLE PICTURE OF ME DID THAT JERK DRAW ...?
!?
PERA (FLAP)

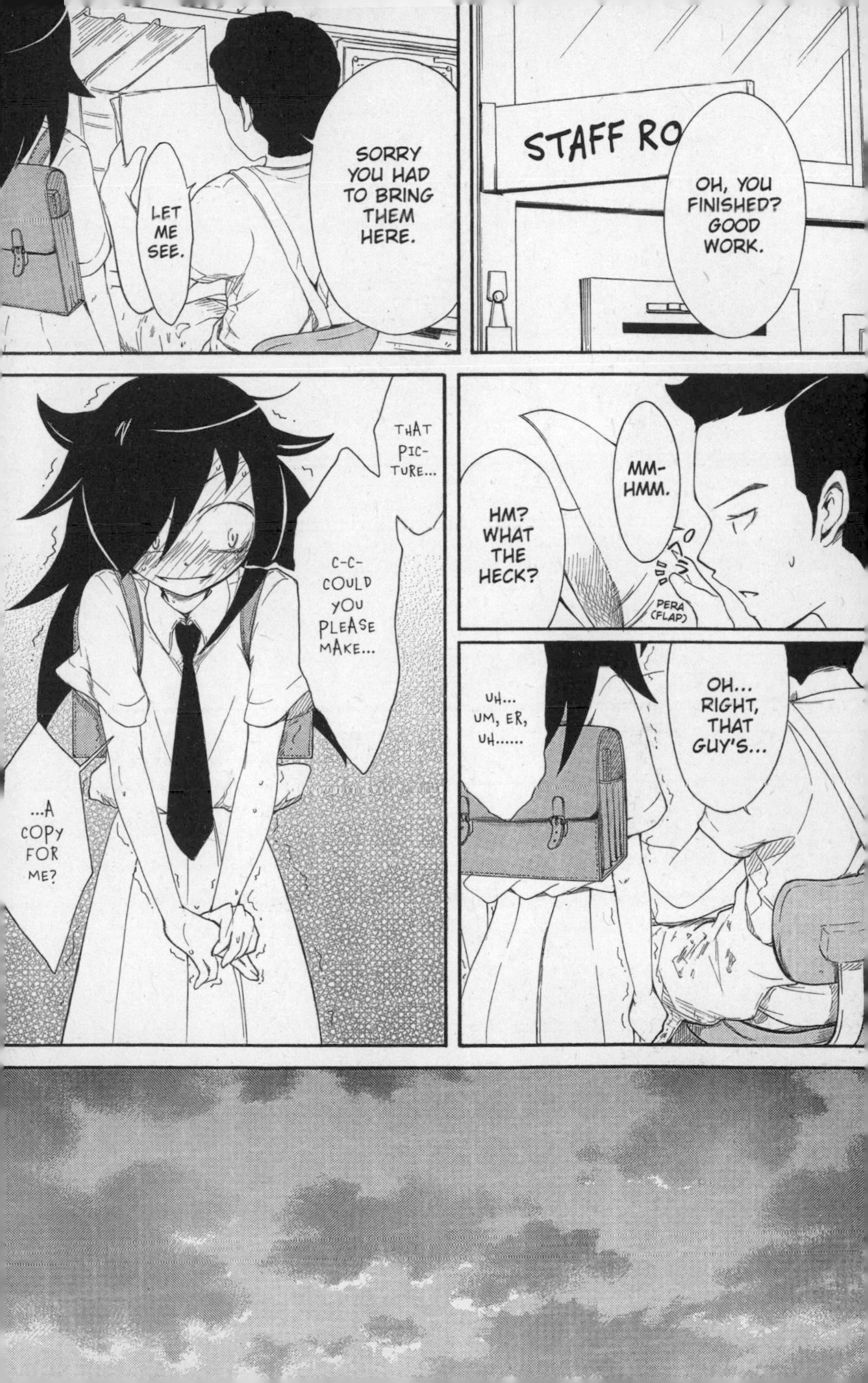
STAFF RO
OH, YOU FINISHED? GOOD WORK.
SORRY YOU HAD TO BRING THEM HERE.
LET ME SEE.
MM-HMM.
PERA (FLAP)
HM? WHAT THE HECK?
OH... RIGHT, THAT GUY'S...
UH... UM, ER, UH......
THAT PIC-TURE...
C-C-COULD YOU PLEASE MAKE...
...A COPY FOR ME?

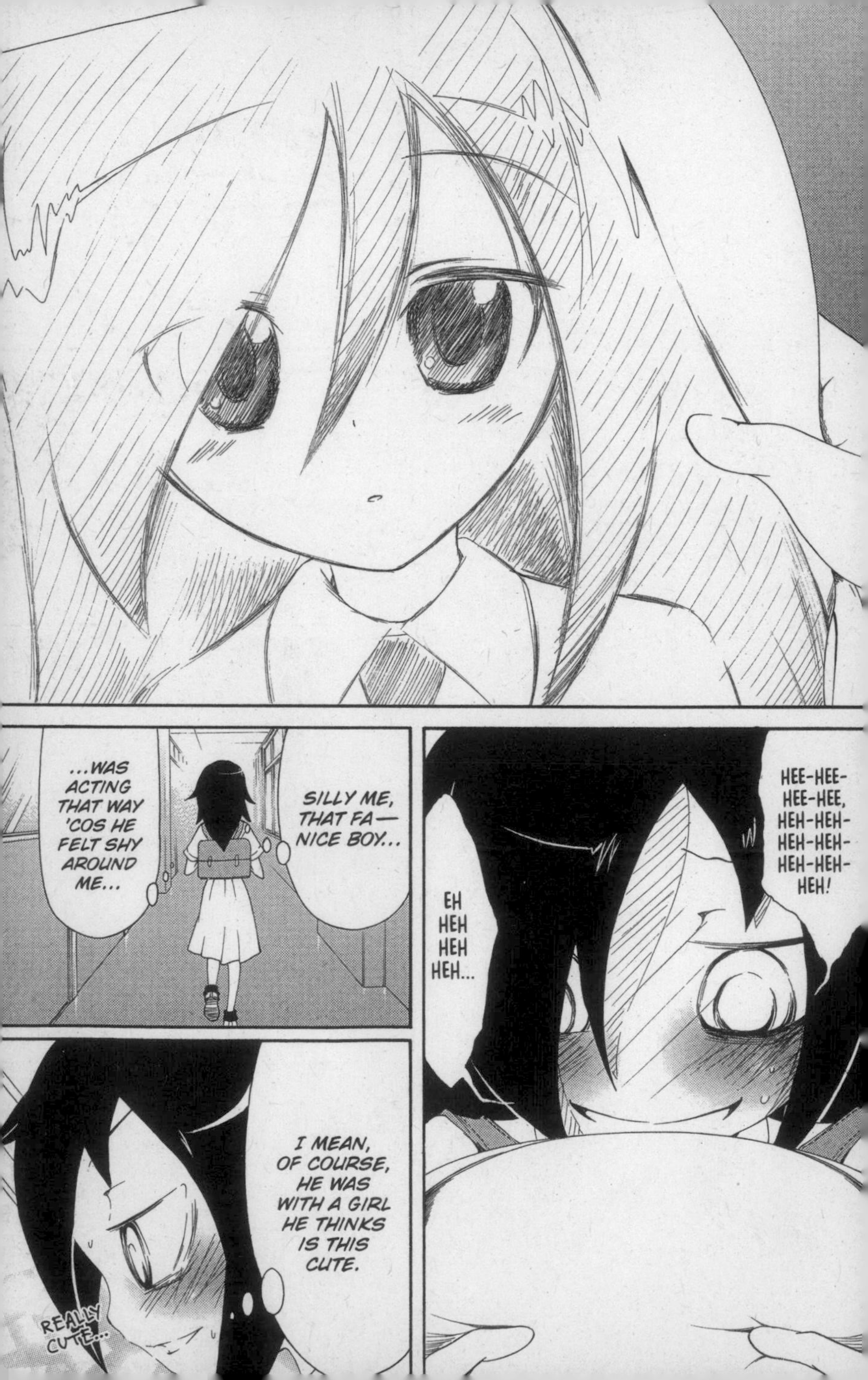
HEE-HEE-HEE-HEE, HEH-HEH-HEH-HEH-HEH-HEH-HEH!
EH HEH HEH HEH...
SILLY ME, THAT FA— NICE BOY...
...WAS ACTING THAT WAY 'COS HE FELT SHY AROUND ME...
I MEAN, OF COURSE, HE WAS WITH A GIRL HE THINKS IS THIS CUTE.
REALLY CUTE...

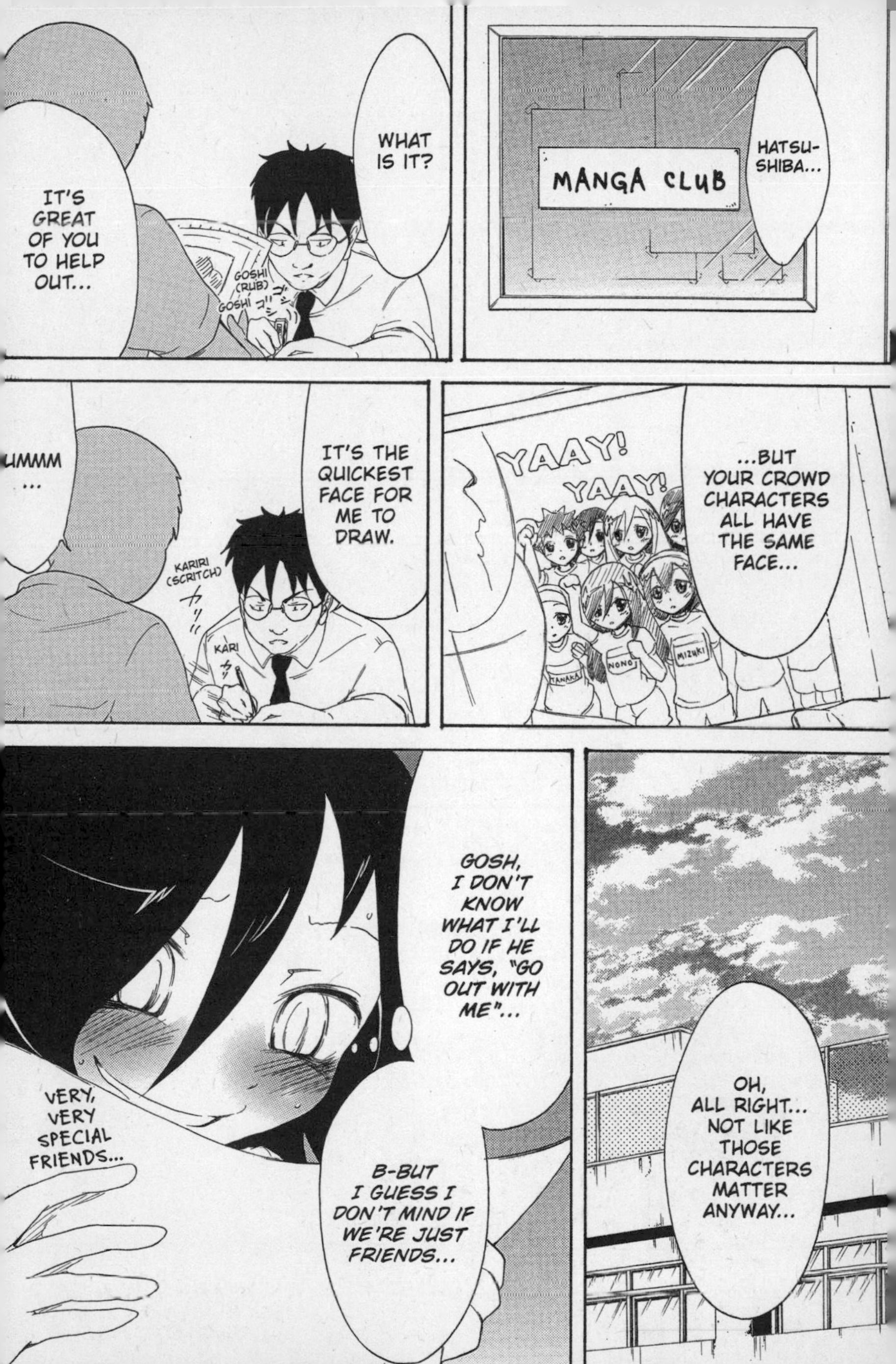
HATSU-SHIBA...
MANGA CLUB
WHAT IS IT?
IT'S GREAT OF YOU TO HELP OUT...
GOSHI (RUB)
GOSHI
...BUT YOUR CROWD CHARACTERS ALL HAVE THE SAME FACE...
YAAY!
YAAY!
MIZUKI
NONO
TANAKA
IT'S THE QUICKEST FACE FOR ME TO DRAW.
UMMMM ...
KARIRI (SCRITCH)
KARI
OH, ALL RIGHT... NOT LIKE THOSE CHARACTERS MATTER ANYWAY...
GOSH, I DON'T KNOW WHAT I'LL DO IF HE SAYS, "GO OUT WITH ME"...
B-BUT I GUESS I DON'T MIND IF WE'RE JUST FRIENDS...
VERY, VERY SPECIAL FRIENDS...

TO BE CONTINUED IN NO MATTER HOW I LOOK AT IT, IT'S YOU GUYS' FAULT I'M NOT POPULAR ②!

No Matter How I Look at It, It's You Guys' Fault I'm Not Popular!

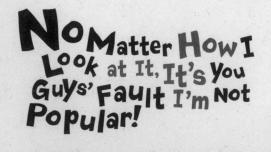

WITH SPECIAL THANKS TO
YUUJI ASAKURA-SAN FOR
HELPING WITH CHAPTER 9

BONUS

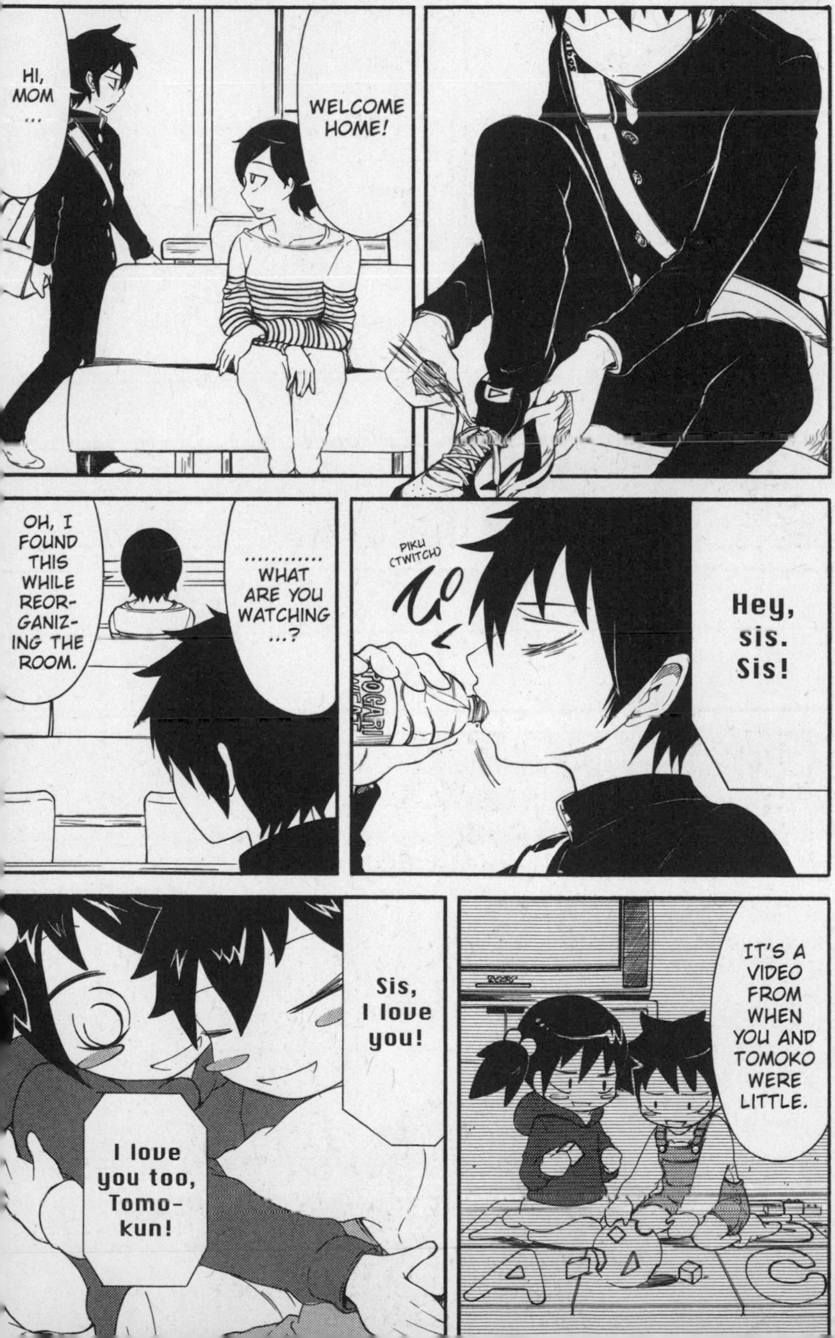
WELCOME HOME!
HI, MOM ...
Hey, sis. Sis!
PIKU (TWITCH)
.... WHAT ARE YOU WATCHING ...?
OH, I FOUND THIS WHILE REOR-GANIZ-ING THE ROOM.
IT'S A VIDEO FROM WHEN YOU AND TOMOKO WERE LITTLE.
Sis, I love you!
I love you too, Tomo-kun!

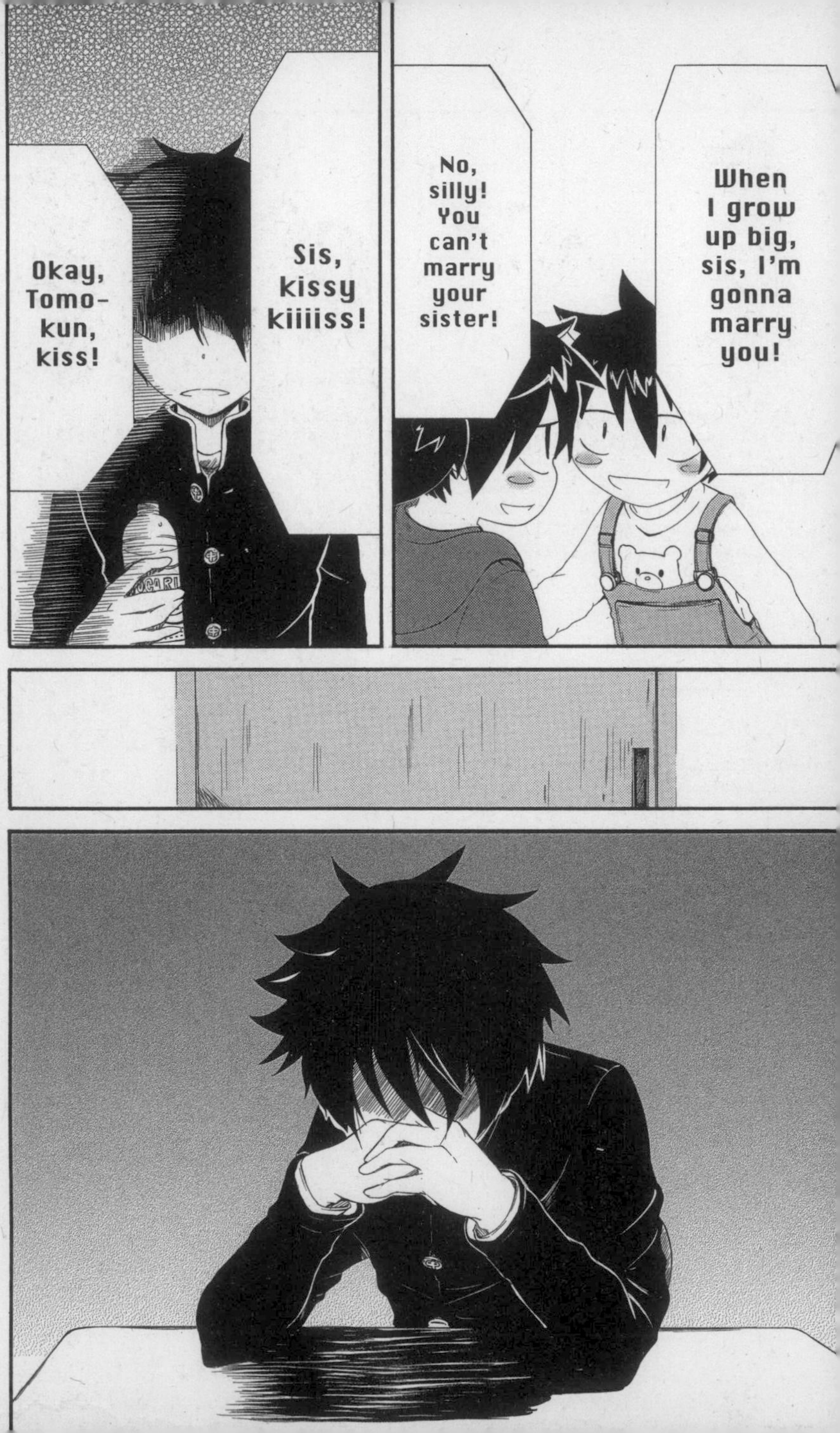
When I grow up big, sis, I'm gonna marry you!
No, silly! You can't marry your sister!
Sis, kissy kiiiiss!
Okay, Tomo-kun, kiss!

COVER BONUS

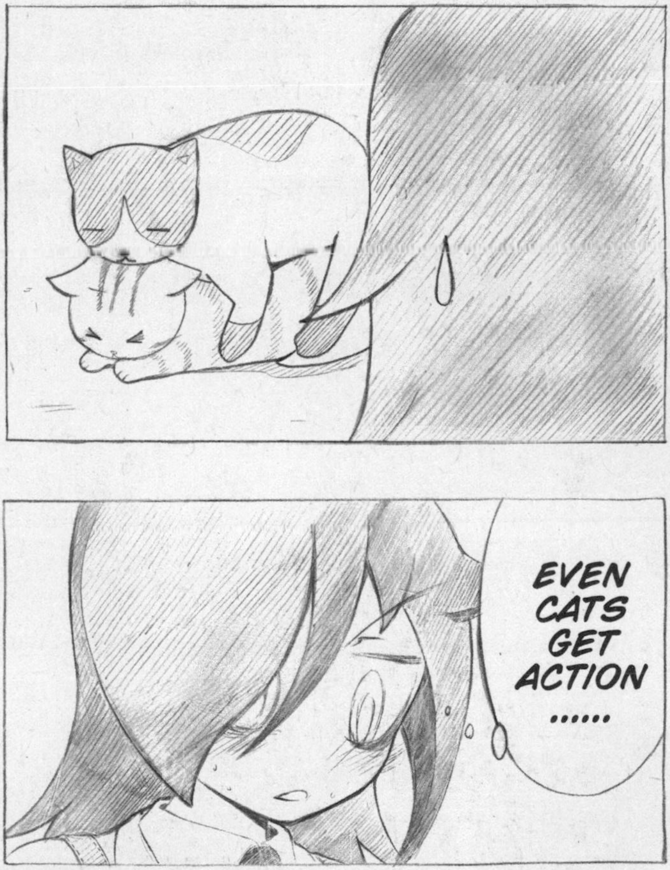
EVEN CATS GET ACTION ......

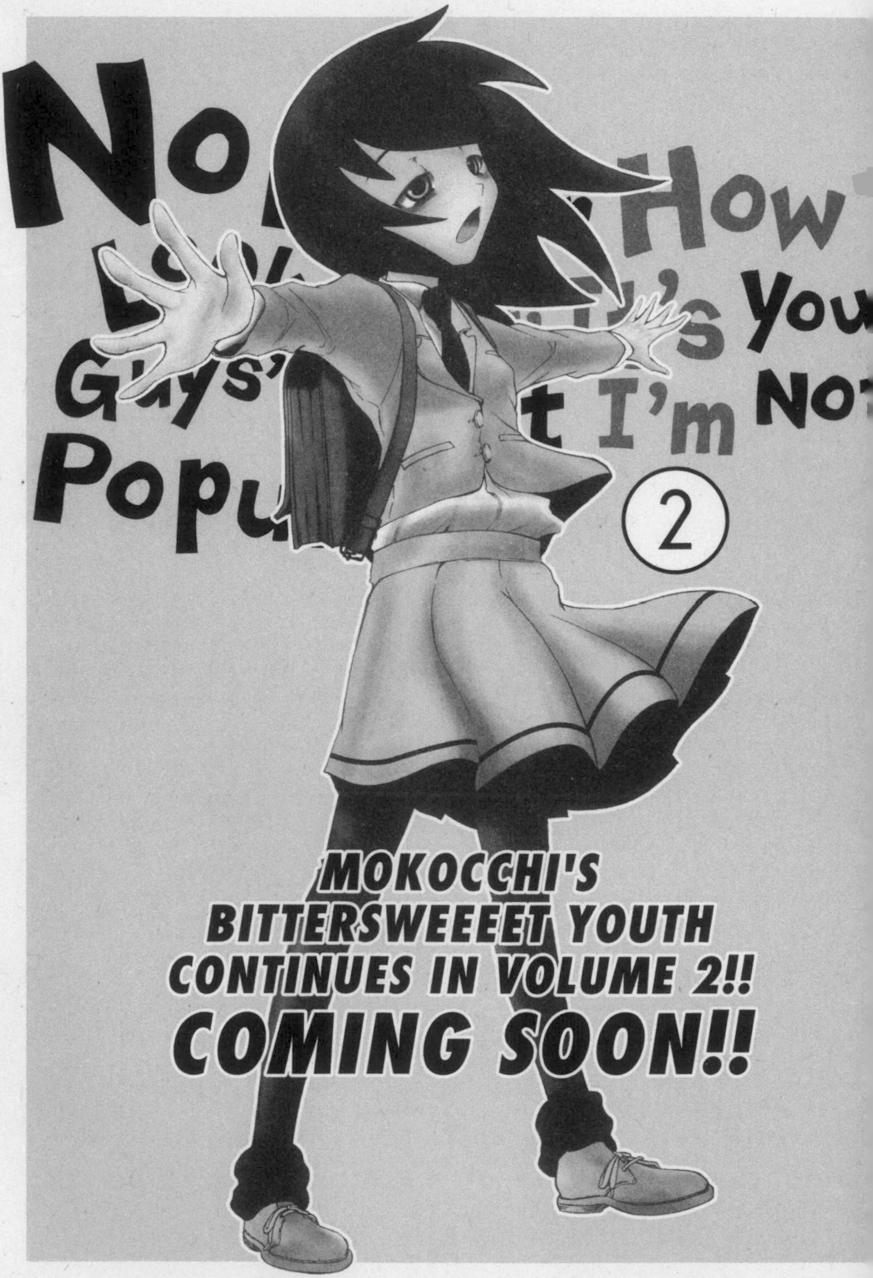
2
MOKOCCHI'S
BITTERSWEEEET YOUTH
CONTINUES IN VOLUME 2!!
COMING SOON!!

PAGE 5
Otome games are dating simulation games with a female protagonist that are targeted at a female audience.

PAGE 14
Loli is a term for prepubescent girls, derived from the controversial novel *Lolita*.

PAGE 14
This babe's so hot, the boys keep coming back for more, am I right!!? In the original, Mokocchi uses *shimei hairu* to describe her level of hotness. The phrase is commonly associated with hostess clubs and escort services to describe the most popular girls, who are designated by name by clients.

PAGE 16
Rakuden is a reference to the popular Japanese Rakuten website and online payment service.

PAGE 16
Kuroki is written with the kanji for "black" and "tree."

PAGE 22
"Tiny aliens from *Ga•tz*" is a reference to the manga and anime series *Gantz*, where the recently dead are revived and forced to kill invading aliens in order to stay alive.

PAGE 22
Paras•te is a reference to the alien invasion manga *Kiseijuu* by Hitoshi Iwaaki, which was released in North America under the title *Parasyte*. Partway through the series, a parasite transfers to the protagonist's school as a student named Hideo Shimada; his parasite cells go out of control after getting sulfuric acid thrown on him while attacking another student.

PAGE 24
Twice-cooked pork is a Szechuan dish named *hui guo rou*.

PAGE 27
Win•lev is short for *Winning Eleven*, a Konami soccer video game series released under the name *World Soccer: Winning Eleven* in Japan and South Korea and *Pro Evolution Soccer* in other countries.

PAGE 30
The **magazine cover** is a reference to *Shounen Magazine*, a manga anthology for boys, while **AKB** refers to the popular girl group AKB48.

PAGE 35
KARI-KARI Kun is a reference to a Japanese popsicle brand called Gari-Gari Kun, which is famous for being very cheap. These popsicles are also famous for their sticks, which sometimes have *atari* ("winner") printed on them; these can be traded in for a free popsicle.

PAGE 36
Pan Webou is a reference to a baked goods supplier named Pan Ebou.

PAGE 39
Yandere is a term referring to characters who start out being very affectionate, but their devotion later turns obsessive and destructive, often resulting in violent behavior.

PAGE 40
Hato Boyfriend is a nod to an actual indie otome game parody called *Hatoful Boyfriend*, where the female protagonist interacts with and romances male pigeons of different breeds. The title is a pun on the English word *heartful* with the Japanese word for pigeon (*hato*) substituted in.

PAGE 41
The train station where the girls meet, **Kaihin-Makuhari**, may be familiar to many anime and manga fans for the nearby Makuhari Messe convention center, which used to host Comiket (a large *doujinshi*, or self-published comics, fair) and still hosts lots of *doujinshi-* and *otaku*-centric events.

PAGE 42
High School Debut is a fifteen-volume *shoujo* manga series by Kazune Kawahara that ran from 2003 to 2008.

PAGE 44
Moe-blob shows is derogatory phrase for anime series that feature adorably cute girls and tend not to have much in the way of plot (or male characters).

PAGE 44
Slice-of-life anime series focus on mundane, episodic daily-life events rather than serious story lines.

PAGE 45
The **arcade game** Yuu wants Tomoko to play is a reference to *Pop'N Music*, an arcade rhythm game by Konami.

PAGE 47
The **quiz game** appears to be *Quiz Magic Academy VIII*, a Konami arcade quiz game released in 2011. The game series also inspired an anime.